EARTHEN VESSEL

Other works by the author

Some of Us are Black (Family Publications) 1993
Worker Apostles (Catholic Truth Society) 1994

For Mary and Rob

CHARLES WALKER

*from your friendly and
appreciative neighbour
Charles Walker*

Earthen Vessel *30 5.09*

The Story of a Reluctant Priest

ST PAULS

IN APPRECIATION

The author is deeply indebted to Teresa de Bertodano who edited this text and to Paddy Padgham who saw that it was transferred to the right sort of floppy disc for publication.

ST PAULS Publishing
187 Battersea Bridge Road, London SW11 3AS, UK
www.stpauls.ie

ISBN 085439 649 7

Set by TuKan DTP, Fareham, Hampshire, UK
Printed by Interprint Ltd, Marsa, Malta

ST PAULS is an activity of the priests and brothers
of the Society of St Paul who proclaim the Gospel
through the media of social communication

Contents

Introduction 7

Preface by Lord Harris of High Cross 9

Foreword by Monsignor Anthony Philpot 13

1. Childhood at Rotherhithe 17

2. The war 38

3. Cambridge 58

4. Wells and Woolwich 80

5. Peterhouse 99

6. Rome 123

7. Brixton 143

8. Abbey Wood 160

9. Young Christian Workers 177

10. Caribbean Chaplaincy 200

11. Brixton again 220

12. Clapham and Rye 238

Introduction

But we have this treasure in earthen vessels.
(2 Corinthians 4:7, Authorised (King James) Version)

We are only the earthenware jars that hold his treasure.
(2 Corinthians 4:7, Jerusalem Bible)

In these words, St Paul indicates the contrast between the splendour of the priesthood and the inadequacies of its human practitioners. According to the teaching of the Roman Catholic Church, ordinary human priests partake of the perfect priesthood of the living Christ. It is inevitable that such priests have their human weaknesses. Nevertheless, the perfect priesthood of Christ is still to be discerned in the priest of common human clay. It is remarkably refracted through the gifts and qualities of individual priests and can be recognised despite their human frailties.

This is the story of one such earthen vessel. It describes his background, his nurture and education, his journey of faith, his ten years of Anglican ministry and his change to the Roman Catholic priesthood. It is a human story; it is also a 'graceful' story. There have been periods of great perplexity, some of darkness and distress, but predominantly the story is one of great happiness. And perhaps the most abiding benefit of all – at no time has it been a life without meaning.

Preface

In a lifetime spent on the fringes of academia, journalism and politics, I have been fortunate in getting to know well many I privately came to refer to as 'heroes', a few of whom, like Keith Joseph, Friedrich Hayek and Milton Friedman, might stand as truly worthy of hero-worship. Charles Walker would be embarrassed to be included among such exemplars. But then so would the others: modesty is a necessary qualification for my private pantheon. Even more important are probity, common decency and above all – less common – unflinching devotion to advancing a worthy conception of human well-being.

As my oldest friend for over half a century – since our first meeting as gauche but hopeful London grammar school lads at Queens' College Cambridge in 1945 – Charles from the start revealed these essential qualities. What I think first brought us together was a shared, almost cockney, sense of fun combined with an intensely serious interest in the great political issues of the day. Though younger than many ex-service students, he stood out as a mature, sympathetic personality who early attracted a diverse range of admirers from opposite poles of the political spectrum. In unending arguments, we all sought a hint of his approval and, when it was not forthcoming, submitted to his impartial (though by my standards somewhat left-wing) mediation.

The immediate impression on first encounter was that he was handicapped by the absence of a right arm which had been amputated in infancy following a road accident. Yet it swiftly became clear that no concessions were called for, whether in making sandwiches for visitors, opening a bottle of wine, playing as captain of college football, driving his car or – later – administering Holy Communion. As he writes here completely without bravado: 'I don't ever remember having a right arm and therefore I have never missed it.'

Though he can now be seen as predestined for the ministry, the reader of these pages will learn that he read English and History at Cambridge. His writing is always lucid and spare and without the least showiness. It is allied to a discriminating eye for observation and a good sense of atmosphere, as in the vivid glimpse of the London Blitz, 'intoxicating days' in post-war Cambridge both as an undergraduate at Queens' and later as Chaplain of Peterhouse, training for the Anglican ministry at Wells in Somerset ('pure Trollope'!) and subsequently studying for conversion to the Roman Catholic priesthood at the Beda College in Rome. From Peterhouse, he offers glimpses of the Master, Herbert Butterfield, 'non-drinking, puckish, iconoclast, chain-smoker'; of Denis Brogan, who 'used to complain he could never forget anything'; and of Mervyn Stockwood, 'flamboyant, imaginative, amusing and very kind'.

As one to whom his multitude of friends have continued through life to turn for advice and sympathy with personal tragedies, he never seemed to have problems of his own. Yet here he lifts the curtain just sufficiently to reveal his full share of family trials, romantic disappointments, a second 'attack of matrimonial longing', periods of uncertainty and turmoil culminating in a 'dark night of the soul' before converting to Catholicism in 1960. No doubt these troubles sharpened his awareness of human frailty – his own no less than others' – and enriched his ministry as Fr Charles in Brixton and later as Canon Charles of the Catholic archdiocese of Southwark.

He became as much at home in prison chaplaincy as in setting up youth clubs and a boys' hostel and in organising a credit union, a steel band and a housing association. At

Abbey Wood there was a smart parish club where some of the customers seemed to believe that by drinking Catholic beer they could fulfil the law of Christ! Hard lessons were learned from projects that did not flourish. The above-mentioned boys' hostel project failed because of an unwise choice of warden.

Along with presiding over marriages, baptisms and funerals and all the other commitments of parish life, he enters fully into the fun of accompanying his folks on trips to the hopfields in Kent and outings to the seaside. Nor did he complain when a teetotal parish priest topped up the local MP's tea with whisky to help him think straight on their anti-abortion campaign.

The most dramatic of all the varied experiences he recounts followed the Brixton eruption in the spring of 1981. Charles emerged as the popular choice as chairman of the Community/Police Consultative Group for Lambeth which had been proposed by Lord Scarman in his famous report on the Brixton disorders. Gradually under his chairmanship the Group moved from outright hostility to the police to a sense of common responsibility for law and order in the borough.

This absorbing story is throughout lit up by a natural personal warmth allied to keen observation. In part he provides a perceptive travelogue, displaying hearty enthusiasm for the West Indies, Italy, Ireland, Norfolk and the USA, seen from a Greyhound bus. In the matter of multi-racial development, he contrasts the melting pot of the United States with the 'mosaic' of Canada. Among dozens of cameos, my favourite is the haunting story of Don Lorenzo Milani, a remarkable Italian priest falsely accused of being a *prete rosso*, who despite being terminally ill with leukæmia ran a marvellous unconventional school at Barbiana in the Tuscan hills north of Florence.

As Catholic Chaplain to the Caribbean community of south London he has made a number of trips to the West Indies to 'educate himself'. It is clear that the islands have had him in thrall and he gives delightful pictures of the people and their culture.

He finally had to retire in 1998 after four years as parish priest of St Vincent's, Clapham Common. During this time he used to take some pride in being the Catholic parish priest of the busiest railway station in Britain (and probably in Europe), Clapham Junction. Now resident in East Sussex, he looks after the small congregation at St Teresa's, Northiam. He declares that he never expected to become a country parson in his old age.

Lord Harris of High Cross

Foreword

Three worlds intermesh here, the industrial, the inter-racial and the religious. Uniting them in his own person is Charles Walker, an unusual man by any standard. He is a distinguished and genial figure, managing to be wise and welcoming at the same time, and has been one of the major figures of the Catholic Church in his part of London for thirty years at least. Indeed, he has lived the vast majority of his life in London south of the river. In this book he tells us his own history, but this is also an evocative view of the twentieth century in war and peace, and especially of London in that century.

I have known Charles for twenty years. Our meeting came about through our shared membership of the Jesus Caritas Fraternity of Priests, for which he was, for some time, responsible in England. Jesus Caritas is more than a support group for clergy. It is really a pattern for living the gospel – or trying to do so – taking as an example the eccentric but saintly Charles de Foucauld, the French officer who became a hermit in the Sahara. It involves a closeness to the poorest people in society, it involves a willingness to pray contemplatively, it involves an anti-careerist mentality and the promotion of brotherhood and mutual encourage-ment among priests. You might think to be national leader of such a movement would be sufficient enthusiasm for a lifetime.

Then I got to know Charles Walker better and realised that he had two other enthusiasms. They were equally massive. His feeling for young people in the secular world of industry was enormously deep. His national role in the Young Christian Workers was his way of expressing this. It was, in fact, the best way of transforming youngsters at work into apostles in their milieu, firing them to translate the Christian gospel into their own idiom, to make sense of it for folk the clerical Church would never reach. In England the YCW was never a huge organisation. In Belgium and France it has shaped the Church for half a century. Charles, quintessentially English, was well aware of the dynamic potential of this movement. Equally impressive was his sympathy with the Afro-Caribbean people of south London. To watch him at work with his West Indian flock was an education in itself. He moved among them with a genial calm and gentle humour, and their esteem for him was something you could reach out and touch. He expressed this sympathy in difficult but concrete ways, chairing committees in the 1980s which did much to defuse racial tension and effect reconciliation, blazing a trail in painstaking, laborious, step-by-step healing of wounds. His sheer delight in the company of families from Trinidad, from Jamaica, from St Lucia, was never feigned. He was at home with broad-ranging issues of policy and was prepared to sit on committees and advisory bodies, but this was balanced by time spent with families and individuals at home, in hospital and in prison. I never discovered where Charles found the time and energy to do all that he did, and to do it so thoroughly and professionally, and to do it with so much love.

And now, reading this book, I realise the additional gift he has always had of work collaboratively done and properly planned. In its simplest form this comes down to reading the papers before a meeting (priests are not famous for this), and of being prepared to argue your case intelligently and persuasively: with Charles the case is always a reasonable and moderate one, but this does not mean that he's not passionate about it, and tenacious. So often pastoral clergy are impatient with committee work, finding it tedious and insufficiently prophetic: Charles has been deeply and patiently involved with it in every area of his professional life, and has made it work for the gospel.

The core of this story is not a tale of movements, but one of a personal journey of discovery. From a butcher's shop in Rotherhithe through grammar school to Queens' College, Cambridge. From a fruitful ministry in the Church of England to Catholicism, and training for the priesthood in Rome during the years of the Second Vatican Council. From being in love, and almost married, to a celibate decision which was to be a lifetime's commitment. It is remarkable that in none of these transitions has Charles found it necessary to turn his back on what went before. His affection for his roots, for the person who in other circumstances might have been his wife, and for the Church which nurtured him, are still in place.

Readers will find a lot in these pages which reminds them of their own experience of the twentieth century – 'the way we were'. To write a foreword to an autobiography which is also a history of the very best sort, not just theoretical but lived, is a privilege.

Monsignor Anthony Philpot

1
Childhood at Rotherhithe

My birthplace was Rotherhithe in south-east London. The date was 15 June 1924. Rotherhithe in those days was part of the borough of Bermondsey and was almost completely working class. Tucked along the south bank of the Thames facing Wapping and the Isle of Dogs, it had had a long maritime history. The *Mayflower* which took the Pilgrim Fathers to New England was a Rotherhithe ship. The handsome early eighteenth-century parish church of St Mary near the riverside, hemmed in by wharves and cranes, is a repository of these maritime memories. There is a splendid monumental ship of the early seventeenth century which would have been a likeness of the *Mayflower*. Christopher Jones, master and part owner of the *Mayflower*, is buried in the churchyard. In the eighteenth century another Rotherhithe mariner, Captain Henry Wilson of the *Antelope*, was wrecked off an island in the East Indies. 'The barbarous people showed us no little kindness,' the captain gravely reported, and in gratitude he brought their chieftain's son, Prince Lee Boo, to England to be educated. Sadly the prince fell victim to smallpox while living at the home of Captain Wilson in Rotherhithe and a tablet in the church records his death.

In the 1920s and 1930s, the life of Rotherhithe was still dominated by the riverside and maritime activity. Small ships used to anchor off Church Hole Stairs by St Mary's, and Ted Dedman the boatman, always known as 'Tacho', would row out from the Spreadeagle, a quaint old riverside pub, very much a spit and sawdust place in those days, to bring the crew ashore and otherwise minister to their needs. In the post Second World War years, the 'the Spread' was smartened up and renamed the Mayflower to capitalise on its Anglo-American associations and so qualify for the London tourist track.

The waterfront at Rotherhithe was richly Dickensian both in its buildings and in its people. Rotherhithe Street follows the line of the river for nearly two miles. During my boyhood, it was a narrow thoroughfare with tall Victorian warehouses on either side, and on working days it was choked with commercial traffic, a lot of it still horse-drawn. One of my classmates at school was the son of a haulage contractor supplying such horse and cart transport, and I remember vividly the firm's depot in a side street near Tower Bridge – splendid horses, decorated carts, tough car-men and the all-pervading smell of the stables. The 'guvnor', my friend's father, round in shape, rosy cheeked, always hoarse in voice as he shouted instructions to his chaps but always cheerful too, could have stepped straight out of the pages of *The Pickwick Papers*. He used to call me 'young Walker'.

During the nineteenth century, the Surrey Docks were constructed out of the marshy hinterland of the Rotherhithe waterfront. These were vast interconnected basins with access to the river by lock gates at two points. The largest of these basins, Greenland Dock, used to accommodate large ships, including 10,000-ton Cunarders plying between London and Nova Scotia. These brought grain from Canada for the most part but they also carried deck cargoes. I remember one leaving for Canada with a train on board – could it have been the *Flying Scotsman*? – for some sort of goodwill tour. The main business of the Surrey Docks, however, was timber. This used to come in from Canada, Scandinavia, Russia and the Baltic, and a large part of it was man-handled. In my mind's eye I can still see the deal porters with three or four large planks of timber on their heads, following each other up and down narrow gangways with the plank ends vibrating from the effort.

Most Rotherhithe men were some sort of docker. Deal porters handled timber; corn porters carried sacks of grain in and out of riverside warehouses. There were men called stevedores who worked in the holds of ships and others who worked on the quayside. I learned about 'tally clerks' who checked the cargo in and out of the ships. This was a sort of white-collar job among dockers, sometimes given to an elderly or disabled docker to spare him physical exertion. Dockers were very close-knit communities and the younger men would invariably take on the heavy work for those of their number who could no longer manage it. They would also see that their less able brothers drew full pay.

All this local lore came home to me gradually during my schooldays and especially during the years of the Second World War when I used to hear men yarning about their work while on Civil Defence duty. Another source of Port of London knowledge was some of my father's friends. I remember hearing about a pilot's job, which was something very special. These men used to navigate ocean-going ships up and down the intricacies of London River and they needed a detailed knowledge of every bend and current and every trick of the tide. Lightermen were also among the river's elite, at least in earlier days. A classic lighterman would row a huge 'lighter' or barge with a single oar, using the tide and currents for his motive power. Later, tugs took over the movement of barges and the lighterman's job was reduced to tying up and letting go. Busy little tugs with a string of four or more barges behind them were among the most familiar sights of the river. A less frequent but more romantic sight were the Thames sailing barges, which used to tack up the river from their havens in Essex and Suffolk laden with every conceivable type of cargo for the capital, much of it market garden produce. These were the 'red sails in the sunset' of Gracie Fields' song. They were rugged, lumbering craft, generally a family home as well as a family business, but they were an endearing feature of the river.

As I must relate later, in the 1930s I belonged to a youth club which had a small riverside former warehouse as its headquarters. We boys used to watch the myriad activities of the river from its windows. There was always a kaleidoscope to look at: a large ship would come up to go through Tower Bridge and dock in the Pool of London; always there would be barges strung out behind tugs hurrying somewhere up- or down-river; police launches would cruise officiously in and out of their Wapping headquarters just opposite us; all along the banks there would be nodding cranes, including a big one on the roof of Free Trade Wharf across the river; *London Mammoth* might appear – a huge floating crane that could lift a fully laden barge out of the water; at the end of Cherry Garden Pier just a little up-river from us there might be some boys swimming in the river with careless rapture (the water was like brown soup); finally, just as dusk was falling, the *Golden Eagle* or one of her sister ships would paddle backwards towards her berth by the Tower of London, her lights ablaze and with music reverberating towards both river banks. This was the end of her day trip to Southend. In 1940, *Golden Eagle* would come to a heroine's end while assisting in the Dunkirk evacuation.

There is more, much more, to be said about Rotherhithe and its people. This much, I hope, gives a little flavour of my 'home village' as I grew up. I was, of course, too young to appreciate either the place or the people at this stage of my life. It was the war years that opened my eyes. But the reader will understand that I was a thorough little Londoner by birth and upbringing, and that Rotherhithe was my cradle.

The Walker parents

We had a shop – a butcher's shop – so I suppose we were petite bourgeoisie. I had no idea of this sociology until I was arguing during an election with a school friend who lived in the same street. This lad was fiercely Labour and I murmured to him that my father voted Conservative. He said, 'Of course he does – he's got a shop!' This seemed an entire irrelevance to me at the time. It was a long time afterwards that I learned about the economic basis of ideology.

My father was a very popular local figure, universally known as Frank Walker. He was particularly a man's man. I remember one of his associates saying, 'I'd do anything for your dad.' As a young man he had been a keen Methodist, a member of the choir at the Lower Road Church where a notable minister, Dr Scott Lidgett, had presided. The cares of this world had taken the edge off his religion in all the years that I can remember; perhaps Freemasonry had taken its place, for he was a very dutiful member of his Lodge. I can remember him studying his little black book of masonic ritual during slack moments in the shop.

He was a natural sportsman, and this was part of his appeal with other men. He had been a good cricketer in his youth but in his middle years he became a county bowls player. The bowling green in nearby Southwark Park occupied many of his summer evenings, and I would sometimes keep awake for his return from a county match to find out if he and Surrey had won. He would spend a lot of winter evenings in the Dock Club by the main gate of Surrey Docks. I appreciated these jaunts because he would collect cigarette cards from his drinking pals for me. In the mornings I would search the ticket pocket of his jacket for the previous evening's donations. He was a pipe smoker himself.

Occasionally my father would take me to Smithfield meat market where he would do his buying for the shop. Always he got a cheerful welcome from the salesmen. On the phone afterwards, he would tell Kent the Carrier, or one of the other delivery firms he patronised, where to pick up his purchases: 'Armour top shop' might come into the story, or 'Swift's under the clock', 'Oliver Borthwick's' or somewhere in the Poultry Market. There is a bar on one of the platforms of Liverpool Street underground station where my father would always pop in for a drink on our way home; I would have to wait outside with a fizzy grapefruit.

Mother was originally a country girl from Herefordshire. She had gone into service in Manchester but had left to join the Salvation Army and came to London to train as a nurse. She remembered vividly the great Albert Hall rallies when the old General, William Booth, would preach himself to a standstill and then hand over to his brother Bramwell to pray for those whose hearts were touched to the penitent form – 'Bring them up, Bramwell, bring them up.' Mother was a talented mimic and in later years she could recapture the flavour of those meetings marvellously. As a Salvation Army midwife before the First World War, Mother experienced the abject poverty of the people of Hoxton, one of the direst of the London slums. She used to speak of the 'submerged tenth', what we would now call our 'underclass'. Such human beings lived in a degradation that was almost complete. Mother would deliver babies in hovels and wrap them in newspapers because the people had nothing else.

The SA moved Mother to Bermondsey and it was there that she met my father. My aunt – his sister – used to say that he fell in love with her Salvation Army bonnet. To marry outside the SA was a considerable fall from grace: Mother lost her Captain's status but she remained in close touch with the SA for a large part of our childhood. Various officers would come and visit her and there would be long godly colloquies in the front room. We all knew that if we were around at the time of the officers' departure we would have to join in the closing prayers so we tried to make ourselves scarce. The Rotherhithe Citadel was at the top of our street. I don't ever remember Mother being an habituée during my schooldays, but she must have been known as a kindred spirit because a simple-minded young man who used to attend the Wednesday evening meetings would call by the shop the following morning and shout in to Mother the spiritual fruits of the previous evening's meeting – 'Two souls last night, Mrs Walker, two souls!' This was the number of those who had come up to the penitent form at the meeting. Mother would always manifest great delight at the tally.

By stages, however, Mother thought her way out of non-conformist Christianity. For a brief time she and my father would shop around various chapels. I remember being taken to the City Temple in Holborn one Sunday evening to hear Dr Norton preach. I seem to remember him saying, 'Mussolini has said that he will keep the peace of Europe with a million bayonets – what a peace!' but maybe I read this rather than heard it. There was also a brief flirtation on Mother's part with spiritualism. I believe she was under considerable stress at the time and consulted a medium. Later she had a spiritual experience which led her to great peace and serenity. This was a vision of Christ himself. She was quite sure that she had seen the Lord and afterwards no ordinary stress or heartache could affect her happiness. She went around with a perpetual song in her heart.

Perhaps as a result of this experience, Mother read deep spiritual books like *The Ascent of Mount Carmel*, of St John of the Cross and *The Mystic Bride*, a study of St Catherine of Siena. These actual volumes are now in my possession. I doubt if it occurred to Mother that these were Roman Catholic books. They must have seemed to her simply aids in her search for God.

Another of her spiritual authors was Evelyn Underhill. As I remember, Evelyn Underhill used to lace her writings with quotations from the Latin Church Fathers. I would sometimes come home from school to find Mother absorbed in Evelyn Underhill's book and she would give me the job of trying to construe one of these quotations. I was a faltering Latin scholar even at the *amo, amas, amat* level. The Church Fathers were way beyond me. But to satisfy Mother I had to make an effort, and my translations would always be very approximate and sometimes sheer guesswork. I don't think she was deceived.

In spite of her and our father's non-conformist affiliations, Mother had all her progeny except me baptised and confirmed at our Anglican parish church, St Mary's, which was quite 'high church'. I was baptised in our local hospital, St Olave's, when I might not have survived a street accident (of which more later). I was nearly three years old by then and I have no idea why I was so lately made a Christian and might have missed being made one at all. I, like my brothers before me, was a choirboy at St Mary's, but the rector suspended me for misbehaviour and subsequently I joined a scout troop which paraded at the neighbouring Anglican church which was somewhat 'lower' than St Mary's. There I was duly confirmed in my scout uniform, and I still remember the text of the Bishop of Kingston's sermon. Perhaps I wasn't altogether a villainous child.

One day I came home from school to discover that Mother had been confirmed that afternoon into the Church of England at Southwark Cathedral. Our rector, Canon A.P. Daniels, had quietly been preparing her. She remained a devout Anglican all her remaining days.

My brothers and sisters

We were seven children in the family, and I was number six. The family was really in two parts. The first five, two boys and three girls, were all in the process of leaving home in the years before the war, while I and my younger brother Ian were still working our way through school. All of us boys went, one after the other but with lengthy overlaps, to St Olave's Grammar School at Tower Bridge. The girls all went to the sister school, St Saviour's, near that fabled intersection in south London, the Elephant and Castle.

My eldest brother and sister were twins. He was always

known in the family as James, though he was christened Frank Ewart in honour of our father and Mr Gladstone. My eldest sister was called by us 'Girlie', but her proper name was Irene.

None of us except our youngest brother were academic high-flyers. James probably collected some O levels, known in those days as General Schools Examinations, and left St Olave's in the Great Depression of the early 1930s. Mother had seen to it that he did a Pitman's secretarial course and he eventually fell on his feet by becoming secretary to Alexander Korda, the head man of London Film Productions at Elstree. He worked at the studios in different administrative jobs while Korda was making all his most notable films – 'The Private Life of Henry VIII', 'The Shape of Things to Come' and others. Mother, who had hitherto regarded the cinema as one of the devil's most insidious works, now became an avid film fan.

Girlie, in contrast to my two other sisters, was a 'goodie' at school. She was a monitor and brought home prizes for good behaviour. She left home to train as a nurse, and by the time the war broke out she had collected a string of nursing qualifications, including one as a health visitor. She was also signed up with the QAs – Queen Alexandra's Royal Army Nursing Service – in case war should break out. When it did, she promptly married her fiancé, Bert Quirk, and produced twin boys at the height of the Blitz.

By contrast, my sister Nellie (her real name) was a young lady of misrule at St Saviour's. Poor Mother was summoned to see the headmistress several times to save her school career. It seemed that whenever there was trouble among the girls, Nellie was always at the centre of it. I doubt if she left school with anything but sighs of relief from the management. My earliest memories of her subsequent career are that she became a model at Harrods. I have some pictures of her showing off skiing gear. She was by this time quite glamorous.

Sister Betty, the next one down, also had a turbulent

school career but she was less an authoress of trouble than Nellie. She was the one who discovered the silent button in the shop's till, but she was really a sweet-natured innocent. She learned to be a hairdresser after she left school. I can just remember her working at a place called Perfect Perms in Oxford Street. For many years afterwards she did the hair of well-to-do clients at the Dorchester Hotel. Neither Nellie nor Betty were ever short of suitors.

My elder brother David was also a modest achiever at school, so much so that my father began to doubt whether even the small fees he paid for our education were worth it. The senior one of us was invariably late on the first day of term because of Father's reluctance to sign the cheque for the term's fees. For a short time, David worked in the shop after leaving school, but he decided to join the RAF when Kingsley Wood as air minister began to expand the service as the Second World War began to loom. Mother shed some tears as her boy went off with his little suitcase to report at the recruit centre at Uxbridge. He came back on leave with peaked cap, button-up-at-the-neck jacket, winged trousers and puttees, and we were all very proud of him.

David had an excellent thirty-six-year career in the RAF. He was due to go to France shortly after the declaration of war in 1939, but somebody at the Air Ministry turned up the information that he had previously volunteered to join the Empire Air Training Scheme as an armament instructor. So instead of going to the war in France, he went away from it to Canada. He eventually finished the war in Austria with a fighter squadron, having reached there by way of North Africa and Italy. In the post-war years he was commissioned, and he eventually retired from the RAF as a squadron leader.

At the beginning of the war, brother James joined the army, enlisting in the REME, the Royal Electrical and Mechanical Engineers. He caught meningitis during the first winter and we were fearful that he might die. We all assaulted the gates of heaven for his recovery. Mercifully, he survived that crisis and came through the war. He too took part in the Italian campaign, and he and David managed a meeting in Naples.

Ian and I, ten and fifteen respectively in 1939, were evacuated with our school, first to Uckfield in Sussex and then to Torquay in Devon. I left school and returned to London in time for the Blitz. Ian continued his school career in Devon and laid the foundation for great academic and sporting success in the post-war years. At the same time, it is possible that wartime separation from the family helped to induce the mental distress that blighted his student days and early working life. From the days we were in Torquay together, I can never remember a time when I wasn't worried about him. After the war, he won an Exhibition in Classics to St John's College, Oxford, where he took a good degree in Greats and collected an athletics Blue in his first term. At this time, he regularly represented Great Britain in the long and the triple jumps, and he was likely to have been chosen for the Helsinki Olympics until he wrecked his right knee in a training accident. He was the first of us to die. This was in 1972 at the age of forty-three. In spite of many tribulations, he had developed into a brilliant teacher.

Myself

I have said something about myself as a small boy. Before I was three, an accident occurred which was far more distressing to other people than to me. Outside the shop, I was struck by a passing lorry and my right arm was severely injured. I half remember that I had seen my sister Girlie hailing a bus by putting up her arm. Perhaps I thought I could stop the lorry by the same means. At our local hospital, another St Olave's, the doctors decided that they had to amputate. Of course, this was a heartbreak for all my family but, curiously, no great trauma for me. I don't ever remember having a right arm and therefore I have never missed it. I grew up almost entirely habituated to managing with my left arm alone and I scarcely ever thought about it. Not to be able to go into the forces during the war was a great grief to me but otherwise I have felt a minimum of external restraints. My family were always completely confidence-inspiring. I was never allowed to think that anything was impossible. Indeed, as I think of my childhood, I marvel at the freedom I was allowed. There was no attempt to protect me from the outside world – indeed, I think I was allowed to play in the streets more freely than any of my brothers and sisters did. As a small boy, I can remember playing all the traditional street games with the local children – famous games like hopscotch, tippy-cat, and tin-can-copper. Later, as a boy scout I used to revel in knock-abouts like British bulldog and Jimmie, Jimmie Knacker, and I turned out to be quite a good footballer and a fair cricketer.

In the depths of her distress over my accident, Mother received what she later described as her 'message from heaven'. That message could have been an alternative title of this story: 'It shall be well with the child.' She also told me that some time after the accident, one of our customers, presumably an Irish Catholic lady, came into the shop in tears and wrapped a rosary round my neck. I have a dim and doubtful memory of this incident but I still have what I have always understood to be the crucifix of that rosary.

Schooldays

I was sent first of all to Keetons Road School. This was in a slightly smarter district of Bermondsey than the one in which we lived. The alternative was Albion Street School, very near to us, but Mother decided that this was too rough and rudimentary. My younger brother Ian actually went to a private school at Catford for the same reason. I used to taunt him for going to a 'sissy school'.

But like all my brothers I was destined for St Olave's at Tower Bridge. I have a fine collection of form photographs of each of us. I was David's junior for a few years (James had left long before I got there) and then I took charge of Ian's induction. We all followed each other into Sydney House. Drake, Raleigh, Howard, Burghley and Grenville were the others – the school was very conscious of its Elizabethan roots.

St Olave's was an amalgamation of two Elizabethan charity schools in old Southwark and Bermondsey at the southern end of London Bridge. One taught Latin and a little Greek, the other began as a 'three Rs' institution with lesser pretensions. The original schools – one was St Saviour's, the other St Olave's – took their names from their respective parishes. Both were in the vicinity of the Globe Theatre, and there is a fair chance that William Shakespeare had our Elizabethan predecessors in mind when he described 'the whining schoolboy, with his satchel, and shining morning face, creeping like snail unwillingly to school'.

Both schools were parochial foundations belonging to the emergent Church of England, but in 1586 St Olave's (now also a grammar school) acquired its most notable and turbulent early 'Latin Master' in Robert Browne. Browne was not only a hard-line Puritan but also a dangerous 'separatist' who gave his name to the 'Brownist' sect, a forerunner of the Congregationalists, who were militantly non-conformist. He ended up in gaol for his pains. It was his spiritual kinsfolk who boarded the *Mayflower* in Holland, where they had assembled from various parts of England, and sailed, via Plymouth in Devon, to found the Plymouth colony in New England.

During a major reorganisation of the school in the post Second World War years, the house names of the Elizabethan celebrities were discarded and those of a group of local worthies involved in the foundation were adopted instead. One of these was Robert Harvard, a 'fleshmonger' in what became Borough High Street, near London Bridge. His son John was probably a pupil at St Saviour's before becoming a graduate of Emmanuel College, Cambridge. John followed the Pilgrim Fathers to New England and left funds for the founding of the university in Cambridge, Massachusetts, which bears his name.

Having had interesting separate histories for over three hundred years, the two schools were amalgamated in 1896 with the combined title of St Olave's and St Saviour's Grammar School for Boys. In 1902 a school for girls was created out of the same foundation with the patronal names the other way round. Over the years, the two boys' schools had moved from place to place in their traditional catchment area, the old St Olave's having once to make way for the building of London Bridge railway station in the middle of the nineteenth century. The building attended by the Walker brothers was that of 1892 – an imposing edifice in Tooley Street, Bermondsey, which was the centre of the dairy produce and wine trade of London. The girls' school, always known as St Saviour's, was where my sisters went.

As we made our way to St Olave's each morning, Tooley Street was alive with lorries, carts and trolleys; the smells of bacon, butter and cheese competed with one another, and not so far away the scent of vinegar and spices also hung in the air. Trams rattled past constantly and there were always horses and carts being manoeuvred by raucous car-men, so our schooling was anything but calm and cloistered. We were a school community of about 450 boys. There was a little prep school department of about forty boys under the age of eleven, but most boys joined at eleven and were allocated to Lower Four A, B or C. We had a considerable number of scholarship boys, bright lads from local elementary schools; the rest of us were fee-payers. If you were a fee-payer, you also had to pay for your books. The fees, however, were very modest.

St Olave's Grammar School – or 'Stogs', as we called it – drew its boys mainly from the south-east quadrant of

London. In the 1930s, there was a large number of boys from old Southwark, Bermondsey and Rotherhithe, mainly on 'junior county' scholarships, but an increasing number were coming from the outlying suburbs by train to London Bridge station. In the post-war years there was a dramatic fall in the number of local candidates; the great majority of the boys were now coming from the Kentish suburbs. This was one of the strong arguments for abandoning Tooley Street for a green-field site at Orpington. The new buildings were opened there in June 1964.

Every year, the school would forward its brightest citizens into higher education, perhaps as many as half a dozen to Oxford or Cambridge. There was a particularly good classical tradition, of which my younger brother Ian was a product. In the 1930s, most other boys seemed to leave at sixteen and a lot went into office jobs in the City of London. St Olave's was a rumbustious place for the early teenage years and one had to learn to survive. It became more civilised the longer one stayed. Apart from the sixth form, reputations depended mostly on sport. Discipline from the staff, however, was tight and the rod was not spared.

I joined the school at the age of eight in the prep department. Boys at this age can be savage to each other, and I seem to remember being at both the giving and receiving end of various forms of persecution. Games were my delight, and despite the loss of my right arm I was a pretty good performer. I was not allowed to do woodwork or metalwork (to my chagrin) but did two lots of art instead. I used to get plaudits for my painting and modelling. At eleven, I was judged to be worthy of the 'A' stream, but most of my pals went into the 'C' and after two years I rejoined them through neglect of my higher opportunities.

I can quite understand how youngsters with considerable talents underachieve in school. Sometimes learning can be among the least of one's preoccupations. There was always something more interesting to do than homework and neither my father nor my mother were inclined to stand over me while I did mine. For at least a year I was on 'daily report'

31

– that is, I had to buy (imagine!) a special little booklet with a page marked up for each schoolday. We had to write in the subject for each period and present it to the teacher for his comment. Anything worse than 'satis' was a disaster because all of us on report had to queue up at the headmaster's desk at the end of the day for his scrutiny. A 'b' for 'bad' meant one thing only: the cane. The head had only to say, 'Upstairs!' and one's fate was sealed. It was generally three strokes on one's behind, with care taken that coat tails did not absorb any of the force.

One of the unusual features of the school year at St Olave's was the school summer camp. This always took place at West Bay in Dorset soon after the end of the summer term. My memory is that a lot of the masters used to take part and the head used always to visit. A number of old boys also came, some of quite ancient vintage. One of these was 'Fuscus' Brown, a rather grizzly old gentleman who used to tell stories to us younger boys during the course of long walks to such places as Golden Cap. One of his tales was a Tolkien-like fable based on the ebb and flow of City office workers across London Bridge every working day. He made a job in a City office sound like a great adventure!

A large proportion of the school used to sign up for the camp; there always seemed to be hundreds of us. We lived in long lines of bell tents and there were large marquees for eating and indoor games. In addition to the usual sporting contests, the whole crowd of us would play 'puddocks', a kind of baseball with everybody fielding. The bigger fellows would hit huge 'skiers' for us smaller ones to try and catch. There was also a regular water-polo match against the West Bay side which used to evoke a keen partisan spirit in us. Another feature of the camps was the homespun concerts at which there were a number of traditional turns, including the senior master, 'Bill' Witton, in his baggy khaki shorts and rough old pullover, singing 'In the North Sea there lived a whale'.

During the two weeks of the camp, St Olave's the day school began to feel like a very relaxed boarding school. There was a tradition that we could call the masters by their nicknames but I don't ever remember risking it. We all used to enjoy the camp enormously, and for me it was the best experience of St Olave's that I remember. Something of the same feeling accompanied the school's evacuation for the six years of the war, at any rate to begin with. Those of us whose parents wanted us out of London as the war approached (about two-thirds of the total) lost a few days of our 1939 summer holidays by having to report daily to school ready to depart. On the Friday afternoon before the declaration of war, we were all marched along Tooley Street to London Bridge station with our rucksacks, gas masks and (for shame!) an identification label tied to the lapels of our jackets. This made some of us feel like refugees. We compensated for this humiliation by playing the board game 'Crown and Anchor' on the train as if we were hard-bitten warriors.

We arrived at Uckfield in Sussex that evening to be hawked round the town by the billeting officer and his helpers. My brother Ian and I were taken in by a sweet old lady who lived in a council cottage with an old-fashioned kitchen range. I remember one of her jokes: 'Why did Hitler join the Co-op? Because he wanted the checks (Czechs)!' The three hundred of us were spread over miles of rural Sussex and for six weeks we virtually ran wild. We used to meet for a little schooling in church and village halls; one class met in a pub and another in a scout hut. This whole episode must have been a nightmare for the staff. Eventually we were all rounded up and put on another train. This one stopped at Torquay in Devon and this was the school's home for the next six years. We shared the buildings of the local grammar school: our shift was an extended morning from 8 a.m. to 1 p.m.; Torquay Grammar School took over at 1.30 p.m. for a long afternoon.

At Torquay, Ian and I were separated according to our

respective classes. I and a classmate, Reg Fairweather, were billeted with a Mrs Walker and her young daughter Sheila. Her husband was working at an aircraft factory in Bristol and came home at weekends. Sadly, Reg died while on active service with the RAF later in the war. Many hundreds of Olavians (to use our dignified style) joined the RAF during the war. Our alumni were typical RAF material. While we were at Torquay we used to encounter a number of recent old boys in an Initial Training Wing based in the town. Many other seaside towns had such ITWs at the time. Our class of 1938/9, before the evacuation thinned us out, lost three others beside Reg during the war, all in the RAF. As a school, we lost nearly a hundred. This was fewer than in the First World War but our proportionate loss was high for the Second World War because of the level of RAF casualties.

I left St Olave's at the end of the 1940 school year having passed a few General Schools exams but not enough to qualify for 'matric', as we called it: that is, I was not deemed to have matriculated for the University of London at that point, had my ambitions gone that way. I was simply eager to get back to London where the action seemed to be. My brother Ian stayed on at Torquay, or rather, he moved to nearby Paignton where a former business associate of my father had made his retirement home. He and his wife looked after Ian for the rest of the war. But Paignton was a mixed blessing for him. He certainly had a stable study base and used it well, but he was also very isolated there and this may have been a factor in the development of the mental distress he suffered later.

Since I had left school at sixteen and achieved very little, St Olave's never left a deep impression on me. The fact that the school forsook its London milieu in the 1960s also diminished my sense of belonging. Nevertheless, I still have some vivid memories of friends there and various escapades, and I continue to remember the boys we lost in the war. I have to respect St Olave's for the education it

offered all of us and for the splendid success it had with
many, including my brother Ian.

Queens' House

An important part of my education and self-realisation took
place outside of school. I must have been about thirteen
when I was persuaded to join the scouts at Queens' House,
an old riverside warehouse at Rotherhithe which was a
mission centre set up by Queens' College, Cambridge.
Bermondsey and Rotherhithe, along with most inner-
London districts, abounded with schools and college
missions at this time. We had the Oxford and Bermondsey
Clubs not very far from us; Cambridge House, the Charter-
house Mission, and Alice Barlow House and Time and
Talents with similar affiliations, were all within the borough
of Bermondsey. Downside, the Catholic boarding school,
also ran a fine youth centre in Bermondsey but I don't
remember ever coming into contact with it. Most of these
missions took root in the latter part of the nineteenth century
or the early part of the twentieth. It was fashionable at one
time to dismiss the mission movement as the condescension
of the 'haves' towards the 'have-nots'. There is no doubt
that the missions were a facet of the class structure of
British society, but they were a very beneficent one.
Privileged people could have stayed in their own milieu
and perhaps satisfied their consciences with an occasional
donation for good works among the poor. But the back-
street missions in such places as Bermondsey and Rotherhithe represented a genuine concern for the human and
spiritual welfare of people locked into the slums of London
and other big cities, and for many products of public schools
and colleges they were a real participation in the life of the
people and the source of new friendships.

Our links with Queens' College were intermittent. I
suppose some money came our way – there were certainly
regular college chapel collections for Queens' House. More

particularly, we had visits by parties of undergraduates and every Whitsun we camped on college land in Cambridge. In the pre-war years we boys were both a scout troop and a boys' club. As scouts, we were the 7th Bermondsey, Queens' College Own, and our scarf was in green and white halves, the college colours. Tuesdays were scout night; on the other evenings of the week we could go to 'club' for games. When I joined, Queens' House was presided over by 'Captain' Bache who was also the assistant Anglican priest at Christ Church in Jamaica Road, where we had our monthly church parades. He was a benign figure but quite elderly, and most of the leadership in both the scout troop and the club came from a group of fine young men who for the most part were members of the rover crew. These were also the backbone of the bugle band that tootled us along the streets for church parade. I was generally one of the colour party. When the buglers took a rest on these occasions with one of the side drummers beating time, we boys would sing *sotto voce*, 'We are some of the Rotherhithe boys', a local patriotic doggerel.

The undergraduates came more into our ken during the Whitsun camps. We would go off in pairs to have breakfast with them in their rooms and they would come to the camp and play games with us. For me these encounters were a foretaste of things to come, for I became a member of the college by a very unlikely route in the post-war years.

I joined the scouts to play in the football team. We used to compete in the five-a-side playground league on Saturday afternoons in local schools. Most other boys' clubs and scout troops were among our opponents. We had some very good players and for at least one year we were the champions. But it wasn't long before I got very keen on scouting too. I was an avid garnerer of badges – I got them for first aid, camping, 'path-finding' and even for interpreting in French, though this was more a token of aspiration than efficiency. My scouting enthusiasm carried over into the early months of the war. During our evacuation, I joined a troop in Uckfield and another in Torquay but I lost interest, sadly, before I reached the blue riband of scouting attainment, that of King's Scout. Years later I resumed scouting but this time as a scout leader. It became one of my responsibilities when I became a curate in the Anglican parish of St Mary's, Woolwich.

But scouting certainly evoked boyhood idealism in me and helped to put me on the path to religion. Scouting religion is anything but sophisticated, but it is not without its effect on boys. At Queens' House, we also had a Sunday afternoon service in our top-floor chapel with the young men of our rover crew taking a prominent part. Such leadership has a great effect on younger boys, especially as these young men were also our leaders in scouting adventures and games. They were also very 'normal' people. Two of them were ardent jazz fans and would swap copies of the *Melody Maker*, the great popular music arbiter at that time. Nearly all of them were in the forces by the early part of the war. Mercifully, they all came back except one: Ron Harding was killed in the desert with the Eighth Army.

The call-up and evacuation killed off Queens' House in its pre-war form. At the end of the war it reopened as a mixed youth club under the auspices of the Time and Talents organisation. Post-war undergraduates resumed the Queens' College link for a while. I, by this time an undergraduate at the college, organised the first visiting party. But the mission movement really belonged to a time and a spirit that was past.

The story of how I graduated from Queens' House in Rotherhithe to Queens' College in Cambridge belongs to a later stage of this story. The war changed the whole map of life for me, as for so many others.

2
The war

I have related how St Olave's went to war, at least that part of it which was evacuated on 1 September 1939. My brother Ian and I were in the parish church at Uckfield for the actual outbreak on Sunday 3 September. We were all ready for Mattins when the vicar stood up before us with the news that Mr Chamberlain had just announced the declaration of war over the radio. Immediately the air-raid sirens began to wail and we all trooped out. None of us believed that Uckfield was about to be obliterated, but the air-raid warning was an eerie persuasion that the war had really begun and there was no going back.

As the world knows, the war in Western Europe was slow to get going and in rural Sussex the agonies of Poland were a long way away. Even so, we boys felt very committed and most of us followed the news bulletins keenly. Despite the seriousnesses of life, the six weeks we spent in Uckfield were a juvenile idyll. With only a few sketchy lessons and very little supervision, we did pretty well as we pleased. I used to spend a lot of time at the scout hut and did various bits of war work, like collecting waste paper and also foxglove leaves, which were supposed to be medicinal. With no air raids on London as yet, the drift back of evacuees began, but our school numbers seemed to hold up very well. Our days of freedom ended with the transfer of the school from Uckfield to Torquay where life became earnest again. We had regular schooling, organised games and discipline. I think we all went home for the first Christmas of the war. By now safety from air raids had become a less important consideration than continuity of education.

The first months of 1940 passed uneventfully, but I remember being very aware of the campaign in Norway and still more the German invasion of Holland and Belgium. The disasters in France and the Dunkirk evacuation dominated our minds. A lot of the lads petitioned the headmaster to let them join the LDVs (Local Defence Volunteers, later renamed the Home Guard) as soon as its formation was announced. Most of them were shortly to see sterner service than that. The full import of the Dunkirk debacle came home to us when ships came into Torquay with rescued soldiers aboard. They were desperately tired and dishevelled, and though they had all the appearance of a beaten army, we all felt that the 'miracle' of Dunkirk outshone the military disaster that led to it. When France capitulated, a lot of us had the feeling that with a large part of the army back home and with the navy controlling the seas, the war had become much simpler. Churchill's 1940 speeches seemed to encourage the idea that we could win on our own. Perhaps the whole country realised that we were now in extreme peril, but it is amazing how euphoric we allowed ourselves to be.

Our General Schools exams that summer seemed a piffling irrelevance. Nevertheless we sat for them and I managed to pass a few. The school summer term petered out some time in July and I thankfully left school and returned to London.

The Blitz

By the time I reached home, the Battle of Britain had begun. At first all the action was over the Channel and along the south coast, but everyone was taking a huge interest in the tally of German aircraft shot down compared with our own losses. For me at this stage, the war was more an adventure than a peril. Soon, the air battles were taking place all over the south of England, and if one was out and about in Kent, Surrey or Sussex there was the daily spectacle of vast vapour trails, the hornet-like sound of fighter engines and the constant thud of anti-aircraft guns and their puffs of smoke in the sky. There was lots of aircraft wreckage on the ground and bits of German aircraft became prized souvenirs.

It was on 7 September 1940 that the German Luftwaffe launched its first major daylight attack on London. Militarily, the decision to raid London in strength has been judged a great German mistake. The Luftwaffe was doing more to win the Battle of Britain by attacking Fighter Command's airfields than by scattering bombs over the vast expanse of London. Moreover, German losses were going to escalate because their bombers were flying beyond the range of their fighter cover. But if these considerations brought satisfaction to the top brass of RAF Fighter Command, we in the streets of the metropolis had a different experience.

The German bombers reached London about 5.30 p.m. on that Saturday afternoon. I remember seeing them coming over in formation before taking cover. We had a little Anderson shelter in the garden of the Norwegian seamen's mission next door to our shop in Rotherhithe. My father, mother and I dived in there as the ground began to shake with falling bombs. In no time there was a fearful screaming of bombs and a series of heavy explosions very near. Shattered glass was everywhere and a great pall of dust. We climbed out of the shelter eventually to find that a stick of bombs had fallen about two hundred yards away at the top of the street. Various of us picked our way through the wreckage to try and pull some of our neighbours out of the remains of their shops and homes. Some were dead, including a young man who always served in a newspaper shop called Pavely's. The whole scene of destruction and death was an appalling shock. We had been used to the fact that such things had happened in Poland and France. But now it had come to the top of our street.

Very soon what we now call the emergency services began to arrive. There were the lorries of the Heavy Rescue squad. These were equipped with a certain amount of moving gear and were manned mainly by building workers. Ambulances came, and fire appliances. At the centre of each rescue effort was the Incident Officer in a white steel helmet. It was his job to co-ordinate the whole operation and to summon up extra help as needed. Later in the war, some women became IOs and did the job very well.

In the remaining hours of daylight, everybody set to, clearing up the mess and securing doors and windows. It was quite apparent that other localities besides ours had been hit. We could see that large fires were raging in the Surrey Docks very near to us. The bells of fire-engines were ringing continuously, and as the evening progressed appliances were coming into London from all over the Home Counties and even from the south coast.

When dusk came, the air-raid sirens wailed again and soon we were having a heavy night raid. Just round the corner from us what came to be known as an oil bomb fell in a block of council flats. It was not a very large device but soon a fire had taken hold of a ground-floor flat and a group of us, including a policeman, did our best to fight it with buckets of water. The situation was getting desperate, with the flames spreading upwards threatening the whole block, when a light fire tender towing a water pump arrived and with this we were able to save the situation.

The ARP – Air Raid Precautions, such was the designation of the air-raid emergency services at the beginning of the war! – was severely tested that Saturday evening and the night that followed but held up remarkably well. There were local failures but the organisation just about held up. By the time we were getting used to nightly raids, the ARP, later dignified with the title Civil Defence, had become reasonably efficient. At the age of sixteen I became an air-raid warden along with my mother; my father already was one. The ARP had its comic side – we really were a Dad's Army kind of outfit in most respects – but it was 'of the people' and it played a very important part in maintaining London's will to fight the war.

There were a few more heavy daylight raids, notably on Sunday 15 September. Bert Quirk, my eldest sister's husband, was at the wheel of his car that day driving through the East End of London. My sister, heavily pregnant with twin boys who were born in November, was in the car, and so were my mother and father and I. We were on our way to view the Quirks' new home at Ilford. The air-raid alert had been on all day. Suddenly, there was a screaming of bombs and the car was straddled by two explosions, both within three hundred yards of us. We actually saw the bombs burst and the road ahead was immediately littered with debris. My brother-in-law drove up on to the pavement. We looked aghast at each other and then he steered the car round the wreckage and headed off to Ilford at top speed. Mercifully, neither my sister nor her twins came to any harm. That day, the RAF claimed around 180 German aircraft shot down. We learned from a post-war check with German records that the true tally was something over fifty. But this was bad enough for the Germans because 15 September proved to be the last big daylight raid on London. It also proved to be the decisive encounter in the Battle of Britain. From then on the Luftwaffe daylight attacks gradually tailed off and all thoughts of a German invasion were finally abandoned. On 15 September every year, Battle of Britain Day, I invariably picture that scene in the East End with those two bombs bursting just ahead of us.

However, night raids continued without intermission nearly until Christmas. Then they resumed shortly after Christmas with a particularly heavy one which destroyed a large part of the City of London and threatened St Paul's Cathedral. Londoners settled down into an air-raid routine. There was a considerable exodus in the afternoon as people made for the deep shelter of tube stations nearer the centre of London. There were other safe havens too. Platform

Wharf, a newish steel and concrete building near the riverside, a tobacco warehouse, gave shelter to hundreds of people. Each block of flats had a shelter in the basement or an adjacent surface shelter. The latter were brick and concrete structures big enough to shelter perhaps fifty people. One night, one of these in the next street suffered a direct hit. The walls were blown in and the reinforced concrete roof collapsed on to the people. Many of the folk inside must have been killed instantly but the cries of those trapped by the roof were heartbreaking. And these were our neighbours. I remember holding the hand of one of those who was trapped. In due course all the rescue teams were on the scene but it wasn't until the next afternoon that a very large crane was deployed to shift that roof. There were not many survivors.

Incendiary bombs did a tremendous amount of damage to houses, churches and unoccupied buildings. These were devices about 18 inches long by 3 inches in diameter made of some sort of magnesium alloy. They used to detonate on impact and at once there was a small pool of intensely hot material. Lodged in roofs, they were often very difficult to get at and difficult to put out. They used to fall in great clusters and there were ghastly white glares from those that fell in the street. We learned to ignore those burning on pavements or roadways and look for the first signs of fire in the roofs of buildings. An additional hazard came when the Germans put an explosive charge into these bombs. This increased the probabilities of fire by scattering the fragments, and it also had an anti-personnel effect. During the raid of 29 December 1940, such an incendiary fell on the flat roof of the Norwegian Church next door to us. A policeman and I ran up the stairs and on to the roof to find a Norwegian lady trying to beat out the fire that had just started. We had just thrust her aside to tackle the bomb ourselves when the wretched thing blew up. The poor policemen got the full force of the fragments and I got a little piece in my leg. He was badly hurt, so I had to leave the fire for others to deal with in order to get him to the casualty station in nearby St Olave's Hospital. It took four of us eventually to carry him the four hundred yards to the hospital on a stretcher. Poor man, he had to be invalided out of the police. My little wound quickly healed.

Long weary nights

These were some of the excitements of life during the Blitz. There were many others during the peak period of the bombing. But there was also the weariness and the drabness of life during the periods of lesser intensity. For me, this stage of the war is acutely evoked by Beethoven's Fifth Symphony – the one with the Morse code 'V' signal opening. Whenever I hear it, the total feeling of those days envelopes me again. I can hear the sound of the bombers and the crash of the guns, I can see again the shelters lined with sleeping forms in bunk-beds and I can smell the disinfectant and the urine. In those days, too, the war was going badly and we had little to cheer us up except Tommy Handley's *ITMA* programme on the radio. No one who lived through those days could forget *ITMA* (*It's That Man Again*). But there is pride too in the recall of heartbreaks and sacrifices bravely borne and a curious but unassailable conviction that we were not going to be beaten.

My mother was a kind of Florence Nightingale during the weary evenings of the blackout and the long ordeal of the night raids. Wearing her tin hat and ARP coat, with her gas mask round her shoulder, she would set off to do a tour of the shelters with our dog Snooky padding along in front of her. If there was a sound of a bomb whistling down, even if it was some distance away, Mother would bend down and grab the dog before taking cover in some doorway. Snooky's nose at the entrance of the shelter announced Mother's arrival. There were complaints to be dealt with, children to be comforted and elderly people to be reassured.

One night, Mother visited a young woman about to give birth in an upstairs flat and found the midwife already with her. The midwife stayed with the mother-to-be all during the air raid and delivered the baby in the early hours. Mother was so impressed by her devotion to duty that she reported it to the town hall, and the midwife was awarded the George Medal.

When things were quiet at 'M' post, our local ARP headquarters behind the Cock and Monkey pub, our gallant band of wardens fell to arguing with each other. There were half a dozen or so full-timers and a much larger number of part-timers. Between them, the full-timers were meant to man the post throughout the day and night; we part-timers reported in the evenings and were available for the actual night raids. We had food rations allocated to us for our spells of duty. The part-timers constantly complained that the full-timers had the lion's share of the rations. I remember one of the 'high-ups' from the town hall coming down to try and sort out this impossible problem. We were a motley collection of young and old, men and women. Some of our number had been well schooled in the Labour movement and the hapless official was battered by forceful arguments from various spokespersons. One of the full-timers, Bill Huggett, was a former bookie's runner and the ARP was probably the first regular job he had ever had in his life. The suspicion of the part-timers fell heavily upon him. Most of us believed that if Bill hadn't eaten the stuff himself, he had probably sold it. The word of power in the dispute was 'entitled' – if entitlement could be proved then that finished the argument. It was manifest that we part-timers had not received what we were entitled to. I think the matter was resolved by the town hall allocating us more rations. Bill was still on full-time service in the ARP at the end of the war.

The night raids became intermittent and eventually stopped when Hitler and the Luftwaffe became embroiled in Russia. We did have a very bad raid on the night of 10

May 1941. when I collected another small injury – a broken finger while searching a house for an incendiary bomb. This was the raid that is forever remembered by the sight of St Paul's Cathedral silhouetted against the flames that engulfed the City of London. It was also the worst raid of all in terms of damage and casualties, but it was the last until the 'Mini-Blitz' of February 1944, and then the V1s and V2s at the end of the war. London was free of air raids for nearly three years. During this time the RAF's strategic bombing of Germany gathered strength and we Londoners took a grim satisfaction in the fact that the Germans were getting back their own medicine. In fact, the Germans received it back at least a hundred-fold. In 1944 and 1945, Berlin received fearsome punishment and no British city suffered a fraction of the devastation that fell upon Hamburg, Cologne and Dresden. But the Germans took a terrible toll of the bombers we sent. Over 50,000 RAF aircrew were lost over Germany in the five years of the war in Europe. Many of our St Olave's losses would have been among them.

The year 1945 brought the V1s and V2s, which were very nasty while they lasted. The V1 was a precursor of the cruise missile – a rocket-propelled unmanned device with a time mechanism designed to cut out the engine over the target and cause it to dive and explode on impact. I remember seeing the first V1 that came over at night. It was low; we could hear its novel engine note and see the flames coming from its tail. We cheered, thinking it was a German aircraft that was being shot down. We heard the explosion as it fell in the East End. It didn't take us long to realise that these things were a very evil new trick that the Germans were playing on us. For some months, the V1 flying bombs or 'doodlebugs' became a daily and nightly feature of life. We all became adept at listening for the engine note. When it cut out it was time to dive for cover – urgently. They came down in a dive and blew up immediately on impact. They did an immense amount of lateral damage. One doodlebug could easily wreck a whole street. A lot of them fell in south-east London but I don't remember them causing a lot of casualties.

The V2s were a different story. These were a foreshadowing of the inter-continental ballistic missile. They fell vertically without any warning and made huge craters. Two fell in Bermondsey on the first night they were used. One collapsed a large railway bridge leading into London Bridge station, and the other fell by the presbytery of the Roman Catholic church at Dockhead. Three of the four priests were killed, together with the housekeeper. The survivor, Fr Edmund Arbuthnott, became a very dear friend of mine many years afterwards. South London suffered one of the worst incidents of all when a V2 fell in a shopping centre at New Cross one Saturday morning. There were hundreds of casualties.

The resilience of Londoners under air attack became a great propaganda point as the war intensified and as we acquired new allies. The Americans were impressed and our government were anxious to persuade the Russians that there were heroes and heroines in Britain too. 'Bermondsey can take it!' became a national slogan of defiance. My mother used to chuckle over a ludicrous example of our local pride. The lady mayor of Bermondsey, Mrs Louise Brown (always known as Aunt Lou), called a meeting of women to welcome a Russian girl sniper to the borough. This girl was supposed to have shot over a hundred Germans. In her Red Army uniform buttoned up at the shoulder she looked more like a soldier's sweetheart than a mass killer. But the very thought of all those dead Germans sent Mrs Brown into a fervour of Anglo-Russian solidarity. 'Bermondsey can take it!' she cried, and all the assembled womenfolk were meant to take up the chorus. Mother found the whole event acutely embarrassing. 'Fancy parading that poor girl for shooting all those Germans!'

My jobs

Although the Blitz was the major preoccupation of life during the winter of 1940/1, I also had to launch myself on the labour market at the same time. There was a department of the Ministry of Labour called the Headmasters' Bureau. The task of this department was to place early leavers from the grammar schools into office jobs. I was one who qualified for its assistance and as a result had several gruesome interviews. I eventually took a job as a junior clerk with the Strand Electrical Company in Vincent Square, near Victoria. For a fortnight I had the stultifying task of checking endless invoices. It was November 1940. I used to finish around 5.30 p.m. and the night air raid would begin as I was on my way home. One night, I got all the way to Wapping on the East End branch line of the underground and could get no further. The stretch of line between Wapping and Rotherhithe went under the river and it was always sealed off during air raids in case an unlucky bomb should pierce the tunnel and cause flooding. I had to return all the way to central London and then walk most of the way back to Rotherhithe. The raid was going nicely by then, and my parents were worried to death when I was missing for hours. I didn't need much persuading to give that job up.

My next job was with the Social Welfare Department of the old London County Council at its Tooley Street office, not far from my old school which by this time was an emergency fire station. This job was only a little less dreary than the previous one but I stayed in it almost a year. Some of the people were more interesting, including my first girlfriend, Kathleen, who was an Ink Spots fan and for some reason called me Sam. At one stage, I was occupied with the administration of the small maintenance charges parents were expected to pay for their evacuated children. We junior staff seemed to have the discretion of cancelling quite large debts incurred by reluctant payers. I remember one of the girl clerks being heartbroken by the story of one debt-ridden parent and writing off over £100, a small fortune in those days. Another task that came my way was to accompany a wages officer on a weekly round of rest centres. These were schools and mission centres which were used to house families that were bombed out. Our task was to pay the rest centre staff for their services. We went round in a car with the wages packets and receipt books and it was during these tours that I first came into contact with the Roman Catholics. One of our rest centres was a Catholic school behind Guy's Hospital. The priest was the rest centre officer and cheerfully collected his wages; his lady assistant was a nun who swept in to sign for her packet and was gone in a moment. She was in full habit and always struck me as being very mysterious and beautiful. Years later and in quite different circumstances, that priest, Fr Charlie Jones, became a very good friend of mine, but he could never tell me what happened to the nun.

Journalism

I left the Social Welfare office to make a serious bid for the job I really wanted to do – journalism. My father was ready to support me without a job and I helped him in the shop a little. He still had Harry Hannah with him at this time, but soon Harry was to die and Father and Mother would be running the family business together. I began a correspondence course in journalism with a body called the London School of Journalism. I used to do exercises in reporting, sub-editing, headline-writing, summarising and so on, and seemed to be making a success of the course. My tutor wrote to tell me that there was a junior reporter's job going on the *Mid-Sussex Times* at Haywards Heath – was I interested? Indeed I was. I passed the interview with old Mr Haydon, the editor, who told me that the tradition in the newspaper business was that journalistic aspirants paid a premium to learn the job but I could join the *Mid-Sussex* for a wage of 25 shillings a week. My district would be Burgess Hill and the surrounding villages, and there was a lodging available in Burgess Hill vacated by my predecessor, a girl, who had moved on to the *Daily Mail* in London. Already my dreams of 'The Street' were coming into focus.

By 1942, we were into the middle period of the war with no air raids. Great things were happening, though, in Russia, the Middle East and over Germany, and before long the Japanese war would break out and the Americans would begin to arrive in England. When I started on the paper, our part of Sussex was filled with Canadian troops. They used to play softball on the recreation green in Burgess Hill, but all the locals were convinced that it was baseball. Burgess Hill was a small town rather than a village even in those days. It had two Anglican churches, one of which was 'high' and was presided over by Mr Gerald, a very popular clergyman; there was a Roman Catholic church, two Baptist chapels, including a strict one at which 'the gospel will be preached, God willing, every Sunday at 11 a.m. and 6.30 p.m.' There was a flourishing Methodist church whose functions received good coverage in the *Mid-Sussex*, and two Congregationals, the 'top Cong' and the 'St John's Cong'. A lot of the life of Burgess Hill used to centre on these churches and on the Women's Institute, which was a thriving body. Major events at the churches, like anniversary services and harvest festivals, were always worth a column in the paper. Weddings and funerals had to be reported in great detail. At funerals, I used to stand in the church porch and ask each arrival for his or her name. All would be listed in the report, along with the names of those who sent floral tributes. I used to go through all the wreaths when the obsequies were over to get the names. Local papers sell on names, so it is important to get them down accurately. On several occasions I was stopped in the street by persons whose names I had mis-spelt or omitted and who wanted a rectification in the following week's issue.

Funerals, at least the aftermath of them, were always enlivened for me by chats with the grave-digger, 'Tich' Wickens. He used to call me 'mate' and I used to call him respectfully 'Mr Wickens'. He would have some entertaining things to say about the local clergy and often he would pass shrewd comments on the character of the deceased as he filled in the grave.

I developed quite a nose for what were called in the office 'pars'. These were newsy paragraphs. I had several informants dotted around the town who would tell me the local gossip, and quite a lot of it was fit to print. I accomplished two especially notable stories. One was an interview with an ancient gentleman who remembered the old Burgess Hill fair, which had expired about the beginning of the twentieth century. His memory was a bit rocky and I wasn't sure I understood him very well because his Sussex burr was pretty deep. But I duly wrote the story up and it got a good position on the features page. The other important piece was again an interview, this time with the rear-gunner of Wing Commander Guy Gibson's Lancaster on the Dam-Busters raid. The rear-gunner was a Burgess Hill man. That raid, of course, had been one of the RAF's great spectaculars and the town was very proud that one of its sons was a member of the leading crew. I received some plaudits for the story. Sadly, Guy Gibson was lost with all his crew, including our Burgess Hill man, on a subsequent operation.

My routine was to take a train each weekday morning from Burgess Hill to Haywards Heath. On most days, our chief reporter, Mr Church (I don't think I ever knew his first name, I certainly never used it), was on the same train because he too lived in Burgess Hill. He used to call me 'old boy'. At the office, I would write up my stuff in long-hand which he would then sub-edit. My punctuation and paragraphing left much to be desired at first but I improved under his tutelage. He was very competent himself and was really the prop of the paper. The elderly editor, Mr Haydon, would sit in the front office, flanked by his deputy, Mr

Gregory, and seemed to hold court most of the time to a stream of visitors. Most Mondays I was required to help with proof-reading. This was a laborious task – I used to read over the 'copy' while the proof-reader corrected the proofs. One day of this was more than enough for me, but for the proof-reader it was his daily task. When I joined the *Mid-Sussex*, the front page was filled with classified advertisements, as *The Times* used to be. We had our first pictures while I was with the paper, and when Mr Haydon died and Mr Gregory took over the paper became almost glamorous. The front page was revamped, we had pictures everywhere, new features and a new layout, and a variety of type faces. I had my pay doubled to 50 shillings a week so I was entirely in favour of the new regime, though sad to see the departure of the old editor who was really a splendid Victorian survival.

Apart from my trips to and from the office, I used to travel everywhere by bicycle. I enjoyed pedalling around the villages to pick up the news even if the way was often blocked by a line of tanks. I became great friends with my landlady, Mrs Packham, and her husband Ernie and also our neighbours across the 'twitten' (Sussex for a passage-way). These were the Herzig family. Old Mr Herzig was Swiss by birth but had long since settled down in England with his Sussex wife. They had a daughter, Mary, and a son, David, and we often had deep conversations about the meaning of life, the necessity of religion and the progress of the war. There was a lot of fundamental reflection among young people in those days. I suppose the war had blown away the trivialities that so easily occupy young minds. At that stage of the war some of us had certainly started to think about the shape of the post-war world. I went to church often in the line of business but I seem to remember being a little agnostic in those days, though I don't think I was ever very far from faith.

Every month the Burgess Hill Women's Institute used to meet, and the press coverage of this was a priority. There was always a press table and I would be there together with the reporters of the *Sussex Express and County Herald* (the Lewes paper) and the *Sussex Daily News* (the Brighton paper). The *Sussex Express* man was a slightly bizarre person who used to converse at the top of his voice. But he was a very lively reporter and his accounts were always worth reading, especially for a tyro like me. The *Daily News* reporter was a rather elderly sobersides but he was always the soul of courtesy and had a very winning smile. I used to take copious notes of the proceedings; the *Sussex Express* reporter used to write up his stuff while the meeting was still going on and he would generally breeze out before the end.

I used to enjoy the WI. Every meeting included prayers and 'Jerusalem'. Most often there would be a talk, some of them very interesting. I remember good ones on Sussex castles and Sussex industries. At the end there would be prizes for the monthly competition – best cake or best pot of marmalade. Everything had to be faithfully recorded. It used to intrigue me that the ladies used to wear their hats throughout the meetings.

Further studies

After a year, I decided to leave the *Mid-Sussex* to acquire some more education. I had discovered, or so I thought, what I wanted to do in life and people had told me that I was good at it. Mr Gregory, the new editor, was particularly encouraging. So my sights were now firmly on the national press, but I knew that I was too much of an ignoramus to make an immediate bid.

So I returned to London (in time for the V1s and V2s) to study for university entrance. King's College, London, used to run a journalism course before the war and my first thought was to get ready for its restart when the war was over. Accordingly, I did another correspondence course and managed to complete my matric. Then I came to a full stop. I was unemployed and felt it. I was very unsure which way to go and my objectives seemed to be further away than ever before. I remember this as one of the most miserable periods of my life. The experience has given me a lasting sympathy with young people searching for a direction in life. We did not take drugs in those days, but with a little imagination one can appreciate how easy it is to look for the sort of solace they offer.

The situation was rescued by an initiative of my mother. She asked the rector of our parish, Canon Daniels, to give me some advice. He thought the best thing was to go for Cambridge – something I hadn't dreamed of. He wrote to a fellow of his old college, Clare, who thought the college would be predisposed to take me on Canon Daniel's recommendation. At the same time he thought Queens' College would consider me on the same basis. Canon Daniels had mentioned in his letter the link I had with Queens' through Queens' House in Rotherhithe. We decided to apply to Queens'.

Queens' must have been intrigued by my application despite my very basic academic qualifications. I doubt if they had ever had an ex-member of the college mission knocking on the door before. I was invited to Cambridge for an interview and saw the senior tutor, L.J. Potts. My career intentions were still for journalism, so English was the course I was bidding for. Mr Potts gave me a piece of W.B. Yeats' poetry to evaluate. The task was a huge mind-stretch for me but, surprisingly, I must have found some sensible things to say. Mr Potts nodded his head approvingly as he read my exercise and then asked me some questions about the piece. He discovered at once that I didn't know that it was a sonnet. I should really have been sunk without trace, but amazingly I was offered a provisional place for the following academic year, beginning October 1944, as long as I could pass the 'Little-go' in Latin. This hurdle was properly known as the Previous Examination and the

Latin paper or its equivalent was required of all who wished to enter the university, including those offering scientific subjects. The Latin required was of no more than General School Certificate standard.

There were just six weeks to go before my first chance of sitting the exam which, if I passed, could clear the way for my going up to Cambridge in October 1944. I was so elated by being offered even a provisional place that I was determined to tackle the Little-go in Latin at this first opportunity. Canon Daniels agreed to tutor me and I beavered away like a man possessed. Alas, I failed the exam and was bitterly disappointed. However, L.J. Potts allowed me to have another try at the end of that year and this time I was able to pull it off. My place at Queens' was confirmed for October 1945, to read Part I of the English Tripos and perhaps Part II of the History. This confirmation was a singular act of faith on the part of the college and a marvellous testimony to Canon Daniels who had both sponsored me and tutored me. Needless to say, I regard A.P. Daniels as one of the great benefactors of my life. L.J. Potts became my supervisor of studies in English and was my prime educator at Cambridge. He and his family became very good friends all the time I was at Queens' and afterwards.

Spiritual awakening

With everything set for Cambridge that autumn, I was lucky enough to get a teaching job for the remainder of the school year 1944/5. I began in January at the Highwood Preparatory School at Mill Hill in north London. I was simply a general form teacher of boys under twelve, and I blush sometimes when I think of instances of the misinformation I disseminated. One of them was the spelling of 'Westminster', when I had gracefully to accept the headmaster's correction in front of the class. Nevertheless, I seemed to give satisfaction as a teacher and I got on well with the boys. This, my first spell as a teacher, was particularly significant because one of my colleagues was John Bowden, a very committed Roman Catholic. John Bowden and I would always have lunch together and we would talk endlessly about religion. His frame of thinking was entirely different from that of my standard Protestant upbringing. I had the usual list of objections to Roman Catholicism and I don't know that he answered them all. But he did present a reasoned case at all points and I had a great respect for his character as a person.

My interest in Christianity was being rekindled at this time by breezes from several different directions. While I was studying to complete my matric, I had been a frequent member of the crowd at Dr Donald Soper's Wednesday lunchtime meetings on Tower Hill. It thrilled me to hear such a powerful Christian message and I enjoyed all the interplay with the crowd. I wasn't going to church anywhere at that time but I responded readily to every intimation of faith that came my way. I remember, too, being an avid listener to the service of Compline late at night on the radio. This was a fresh note of religion for me – something very austere, very beautiful, very 'Catholic'. Then, of course, my contact with Canon Daniels was most important. I felt greatly indebted to him and was soon attending St Mary's regularly and helping out with the scouts and youth club. He was not at all a folksy person. He was much more a scholar-gentleman, very much a product of the ancient universities. Superficially, he could be thought of as an anachronism in working-class Rotherhithe, but in fact the people recognised his devotion both to them and to God. The congregation at St Mary's was very small but even for the few people scattered round the church he would take great pains over his sermons and all the ceremonies would be carried out meticulously.

My debt to Canon Daniels for my university prospects was one thing; I also owe to him in large measure my return to the faith as a young adult. It amounted to both a new sense of God and a conversion of my mind. A very able curate came to St Mary's at the very end of the war. His name was Gordon Davies; he was a graduate of Oxford and a product of one of the liveliest of Anglican theological colleges, Westcott House at Cambridge. He helped me a lot with my reading, introducing me to the works of C.S. Lewis.

I would go up to Cambridge in October 1945, a convinced Christian, but I had no thoughts at that time of becoming a priest. My sights were still set on journalism at the national level. It is curious that at the very time my Anglican belonging was strengthening, the Roman Catholic faith had insinuated itself into my consciousness through my conversations with John Bowden at Highwood Preparatory School.

The war in Europe was now virtually over. There was still the blackout and very tight rationing, but local lads were beginning to come back from overseas service and the doorways and windows of their homes would be bedecked with 'welcome home' signs. There was great merriment in the pubs and the homecomers themselves were not allowed to buy any drinks. Finally the German surrender came. I was among the sea of people in Whitehall to hear Winston Churchill say, 'God bless you all – this is your victory!' That day we chimed the bells of St Mary's in celebration. The bells hadn't spoken for nearly six years, and we were a little apprehensive about whether the ropes and mountings would still be serviceable. Nevertheless we jangled them merrily. That night, the people made bonfires of the bunk-beds from the shelters, the pubs sold out of beer and the lights of London went up again; we sang our hearts out to the Vera Lynn numbers and danced in the streets to the new strains of Glenn Miller.

3
Cambridge

At Cambridge I felt like stout Cortez staring into the Pacific – silent, upon a peak in Darien! The university for me was an ocean of discovery, a vista of infinite possibilities.

I duly reported at Queens' a few days before term began. I queued up with others to see my tutor and then my supervisor of studies. I was due to launch myself at Part I of the English Tripos. For me, my tutor and supervisor were the same person – L.J. Potts. I had to be acquainted with the details of my first-year course and be advised which were the appropriate lectures to go to. I was allocated a set of rooms – B5 in the Old Court – and against all the norms of undergraduate accommodation, I was allowed to stay there for the whole of my three years. Nearly all my friends spent at least one academic year in college lodgings, some of them a good distance away. I became very fond of my little garret in the Old Court. It was a marvellous thing to have one's own quarters in such a beautiful setting. My delight was compounded when my name was painted over the door and at the foot of the staircase.

My friends

Soon I was sizing up my fellow freshmen. The October 1945 entry was a mixture of former schoolboys aged eighteen or nineteen and a large body of ex-servicemen who had been demobilised on early – 'Class B' – releases, all of whom were well into their twenties. I was twenty-one. To begin with I felt at a certain disadvantage with the ex-servicemen but my early friends came from among them. Peter Withington from Preston in Lancashire, reading history, was one. He had served with the Fourteenth Army in Burma and had been invalided out with a tropical disease that limited his activities all the time he was at Cambridge. Peter was a very true man. He was a member of the Communist Party and became president of the Cambridge University Socialist Club. The CU Socialist Club had to be distinguished from the CU Labour Club, which was far less radical.

The third member of an improbable trio was Ralph Harris from north London. Ralph had been a 'Bevin Boy' – he had signed up for the RAF towards the end of the war but by that time the country needed miners more than aircrew. He was drafted into a pit in the north of England. He was very bright – an easy 'First' in all stages of the Economics Tripos. Even as an undergraduate, he was wedded to the classical principles of economics of which he would later become an international exponent. We were a curious triumvir. I suppose a common factor was that we were all three grammar school boys in contrast to public school boys. Another factor was that we were each a 'conviction' person. I was the religious one; neither Peter nor Ralph made any religious profession at this stage of their lives. We each had other friends and other activities. Ralph, for instance, resurrected the Pentacle Club, the university conjurors, and one of his keen associates was Freddie Mutesa, the Kabaka (or king) of Buganda in Uganda, who was a member of Magdalene College. Another close friend of mine was Charles Parker, who was married and lived in lodgings – he and his wife Phyllis occupied the top-floor flat of the L.J. Potts family home. Potts was his tutor as well as mine. Charles had been a submariner during the war and had brought a U-boat to England from Kiel after the German surrender. His flat at the Potts house was equipped with 'loot' from the German submarine, including the radio and a clock. Charles too was a historian. He was also a very talented thespian. He became a very bright-shiner in both college and university theatricals. He was a member of the Cambridge Footlights and the Marlowe Society and the producer of a famous Queens' College production of Shakespeare's *As You Like It* in the summer of 1948. I was associated with him in some of these enterprises, notably the Queens' *As You Like It*, of which more later. Charles' wife, Phyllis, also became a great friend. She too got involved in Cambridge theatricals.

Peter Withington, Ralph Harris and Charles Parker became life-long friends. In later years, it was a very great pleasure for me to become friends also with the wives and children of each of them. Peter and Ralph were short-course men and took their degrees after two years. Charles and I did the full three-year course and we had a lot to do with each other in our final year. Peter Withington went into teaching from Cambridge. He finished up as headmaster of a big comprehensive school in Scunthorpe before dying prematurely from cancer in his early fifties. He stayed in the Communist Party until the Hungarian uprising and afterwards seemed to become disenchanted with active politics. But he retained a tremendous pride in the north of England and a deep sense of belonging to the working class until the day he died.

After Cambridge, Ralph Harris joined St Andrew's University in Scotland as an economics lecturer and combined the academic life with journalism. He ran as a Conservative candidate for Scottish constituencies in two general elections and for a while worked at Conservative Central Office. He eventually created the Institute of Economic Affairs and became one of the most influential market economists in Britain and beyond. He was ennobled by Margaret Thatcher and became Lord Harris of High Cross in Tottenham. However, he too disassociated himself from party politics and takes his seat on the cross-benches of the House of Lords.

Charles Parker went straight to the BBC and became a radio producer. He remained a pure radio man all his broadcasting days, avoiding the allurements of television. His special creation was the 'radio ballad'. With others he initiated the technique of interweaving taped interviews with folk music which conveyed vividly the life of people in a particular community. *Singing the Fishing*, about the fisher-folk of Grimsby, won an international prize. He also did notable studies of a coal-mining community and of the people of Northern Ireland in the early stages of the troubles. In his middle years, Charles developed into a kind of Christian Socialist. He was very keen on traditional popular culture and led Merry England-type folk dancing at the village wedding of his daughter Sara, who is my god-daughter. He also took up the cause of the travelling people. Sadly, he had a row with the administrators at the BBC and left the Corporation to freelance. Like Peter, he died prematurely in his fifties.

But these subsequent histories take the story too far forward. A lot of undergraduates were keenly interested in politics in the immediate post-war years. Peter and I joined the Union Society, Cambridge's own House of Commons style debating society, and I spoke once. Peter was very busy with the University Socialists and Ralph held some sort of office in the Conservatives. We used to discuss the problems of the world endlessly among ourselves. I was slightly right of centre in those days (this changed) and I remember taking part in a college debate supporting Ralph on some motion involving human freedom. Not surprisingly, Peter upheld the collective ideal on the other side.

In the 1950s, with the appearance of the 'Angry Young Man' literature, the awkwardness and uncertainties of clever boys from the working class in contrast with the poise and confidence of public school products became a national obsession. There was certainly a reality in the contrast and some felt it acutely. And I suppose those of us from working-class backgrounds did adopt, consciously or unconsciously, some middle-class mores. But I don't remember feeling unduly nervous about social graces, still less angry, nor, in my judgement, did Peter, Ralph or Charles. By then we were well into the new criterion of 'merit', but merit signifying not simply brain-power and general 'nous' but inner qualities of life as well. Peter, for instance, never lost his Lancashire accent nor his 'folksy' attitudes but everybody recognised his quality as a person.

College life

I tried the Christian societies in college. The Christian Union turned out to be heavily evangelical and I was more inclined to Anglo-Catholic ways. I never quite figured out what the SCM (Student Christian Movement) was all about, though I went to a meeting or two. I suppose I judged the membership of these societies as 'not my kind of people'. I settled for the college chapel as the focus of my religion. I made friends with the Dean, Henry St J. Hart, and our chaplain, Henry Chadwick. The Dean had open house on Sunday evenings when all callers listened to music and then conversed over tea and buns. I used to enjoy these very relaxed sessions and also the 'D Society' ('D' for Dean, I guess) which was Henry Hart's special contribution to our general education. Distinguished dons from widely differing fields would give a talk, and discussion followed. Tom Henn from St Catherine's College on the poetry of W.B. Yeats was one that sticks in my memory. I seemed in those days to be interested in nearly everything and I delighted in the exercise of the mind, even though mine was very underdeveloped.

Henry Chadwick at Queens' was at the beginning of a phenomenal academic career. In turn, he became Regius Professor of Divinity at both Oxford and Cambridge and at Oxford he was also Dean of Christ Church, which made him the head of the most distinguished college in that university. After retiring from the Regius Professorship at Cambridge he served for six years as Master of Peterhouse. At Queens' just after the war, he was a very good friend to us raw undergraduates and to me a great encouragement in the ways of faith.

Our college chapel at Queens' was a handsome neo-Gothic addition to the mainly mediæval/Tudor style of architecture which prevailed in the rest of the college. Chapel attendance was purely voluntary by this time, but we were quite a chapel-going student body. I was there Sunday by Sunday at Holy Communion in the morning and at Evensong in the early evening. We had a large 'voluntary choir' at Evensong. The Dean appointed me as one of two ushers. It was our job to show people to their seats and to welcome the 'civilian' visitors we always had. My fellow usher was a shy and scholarly BA called John Manners. We became known as 'the church-wardens'.

My link with the pre-war college mission, Queens' House in Rotherhithe, was preserved mainly through my getting to know the former dean of the college, Charles Wood, who was still in residence though by now as rector of nearby St Botolph's in Trumpington Street, a college living. He was a revered figure, always known as 'the Rector' in college. Later, I would see a lot more of him when I returned to the university as Chaplain of Peterhouse.

At the end of my time at Queens', I organised the first post-war party of undergraduates to visit Queens' House at Rotherhithe, which by now was being managed by a social work organisation called Time and Talents. Others took up the interest afterwards, but the college did not resume even the small degree of responsibility it exercised before the war. In the post-war years, that part of the riverside at Rotherhithe was cleared and the site is now part of a promenade with a magnificent view up and down the Thames.

The English Tripos

Reading for Part I of the English Tripos was a marvellous education for me but I was not a natural-born literary critic. I worked quite hard and wrote reasonable essays but I had large educational arrears to make up. I dutifully attended lectures at Mill Lane and remember some of our mentors with great pleasure and appreciation. I certainly valued all my contact with distinguished minds. Some undergraduates were rather cavalier about lectures – they were not compulsory – but I lapped them up. A Dr Roberts of Pembroke used to delight me with his thoughts on Samuel Johnson's world and still more with his renditions of some of the great man's sayings. Mrs Bennett on Shakespeare was also memorable. I can see her now, a diminutive figure with fuzzy grey hair, scarcely visible above the lectern, reading some of the sonnets and rhapsodising about them. Her enthusiasm certainly got through to me. Strange to say, I did not appreciate F.R. Leavis. He was a giant in the English faculty at that time and his irreverence for certain great reputations went down well with most undergraduates. But he didn't grip me. Maybe I was too conformist in my general outlook at this time and didn't approve of too much rocking of the boat.

My own supervisor of studies, L.J. Potts, was a splendid teacher. He seemed to believe in me much more than I believed in myself. I remember his supervisions with great pleasure and I am sure he did more to educate me than any other teacher I encountered. Alas, I didn't do well in English. I made a mess of my Part I at the end of my second year and felt very depressed after the exams. I collected a Third when I had hoped for at least a 2.2. The sun came out for me academically in Part II of the History Tripos at the end of my third year. I was given a 2.1. I am sure I owe the maturing of my mind to L.J. Potts, even though it bore its fruit in another subject.

History studies

Once I had transferred from the English to the History Tripos for my third year, my supervisor of studies was Robin Laffan. He was a former Anglican chaplain of the college who had become a Roman Catholic many years before but who remained a fellow. He was rather a 'swell', very hospitable to his pupils, but not, I think, a very painstaking teacher. We suspected him of being something of a propagandist for Roman Catholicism. He was a great admirer of the former Austro-Hungarian Empire and there was no doubt which side he was on in the religious turmoil of the sixteenth century. Knowing him was a curious cross-current in my religious quest. I liked him but he did not influence me in matters of religion. In Part II of the Tripos, I was studying three major topics: one was European History from 1485; the second was the Theory of the Modern State, a study in political thought; the third was a special subject for which one was expected to work from primary sources and approach the frontiers of knowledge. My special subject was 'The Elizabethan Church Settlement'.

I was at home straight away with history. Lectures mattered less to me than when I was reading English. Nevertheless, I went to some exciting ones by D.W. Brogan and some gracious, olde-worlde ones from F.A. Simpson. Both were historians who also lectured in political thought. In addition, I took in lectures by Dom David Knowles, the great mediævalist who became the Regius Professor of History, though I wasn't engaged in mediæval studies. David Knowles, a former monk from Downside, intrigued us all. It was clear that his was a mind of the greatest distinction – I always felt, listening to him, that I was on the edge of revelation. But we couldn't understand his religious situation. In the late 1950s when I became Chaplain of Peterhouse, I was to share its high table with Denis Brogan and David Knowles. They were both professorial fellows of Peterhouse.

F.A. Simpson was one of Cambridge's most singular eccentrics. He was a fellow of Trinity and an Anglican clergyman, though at that time he had not exercised his orders for many years. We heard that he had written a book about the French Emperor Louis Napoleon but had been so wounded by a review that he had never produced anything else. He used to walk about Cambridge, slightly dishevelled but invariably amiable, and would react very nervously if one greeted him. Although there were young ladies from Girton and Newnham at his lectures, his opening word was always, 'Gentlemen ...' This, perhaps unconscious, discourtesy apart, his lectures had great charm and great erudition. And they were given in beautiful English. His nervousness would disappear as he became absorbed in his subject matter. Years later, when Mervyn Stockwood became vicar of Great St Mary's, the university church, he cultivated the friendship of F.A. Simpson and helped him back into the religious life of the university, so much so that he began to preach again. When Mervyn Stockwood was made Bishop of Southwark, Simpson was the preacher at his episcopal ordination. It was a remarkable sermon about the dignity of the episcopate and Mervyn's fitness for it, but he hadn't quite noticed that another bishop was being consecrated at the same time and he made no mention of him!

Grappling with my special subject, the Elizabethan Church Settlement, I spent many hours in the university library engrossed in such luminous texts as *Parker's Advertisements* and *Grindal's Remains*. My friend Charles Parker was there too, pursuing his researches. We used to take a break together for a coffee and a smoke. The syllabus for the Elizabethan Settlement paper took no account of Catholic affairs and the work and the fate of the undercover Catholic priests. The subject matter was all about the struggle for control of the reformed Church in England – how the Geneva radicals wanted to complete a pure Protestant reform and how Elizabeth, Archbishop Parker and a few others struggled to construct the halfway house between Rome and Geneva that would become the Church of England. I found all this somewhat disillusioning intellectually, though I did see that something distinct and coherent came with such Anglican writings as Richard Hooker's *Laws of Ecclesiastical Polity*. There was also the enigma of John Donne, a fascinating person who also found a home in the new Anglican set-up.

However, the hero of the time, to my mind, was Edmund Campion, whose famous 'Brag' I discovered. 'Campion's Brag' – as his religious enemies called it – was quite the noblest profession of faith I came across. It was a nine-point manifesto addressed to the Privy Council at the beginning of his clandestine ministry in England as a Catholic priest and a Jesuit. He declared that he had come 'to cry alarm spiritual against foul vice and proud ignorance, wherewith many, my dear countrymen, are abused'. He went on to assure their lordships of the Queen's Council that in matters 'of State or Policy ... I do gladly restrain and sequester my thoughts'. Speaking as a Jesuit and on behalf also of the seminary priests training on the Continent for their perilous undercover ministries in their homeland, he promised that they would 'cheerfully carry the cross you lay upon us, and never to despair of your recovery, while we have a man left to enjoy your Tyburn, or be racked with your torments, or consumed in your prisons'. Nevertheless, he prayed that 'we at last be friends in heaven, when all injuries shall be forgotten'. Both as literature and as religion, Campion's manifesto seemed to me a golden affirmation of the age.

Robin Laffan, our supervisor and director of studies, used to preside over the College History Society, of which another friend of mine, Ian Taylor, became secretary. Notable historians from other colleges were invited in but each term one of us reading for Part II would be deputed to give a paper. Another of my friends, Freddie Bryan Brown, was prevailed upon to speak about 'The Influence of Wealth in Sixth-Century Attica', which must have been his special subject. I fell in for 'The Elizabethan Church Settlement' in the Lent term. I spent virtually the whole of the Christmas vacation putting my paper together. I made great play with the analogy between radical politics in the twentieth century and radical religion in the sixteenth and seventeenth. The hard men of Geneva had a similar mentality to the hard men of Moscow, I suggested. Some of my questioners wanted to push the analogy further and make the Roman Catholics the fascists of the day, but I wouldn't have that.

Robin Laffan had a mission to stop us working on Ascension Day for religious reasons. He always organised a trip on the river for all his pupils and he would begin to arm-twist us from the beginning of the May term. Most of us were very happy to join in, but Freddie Bryan Brown resisted. When asked, he would always reply, 'No, sir, I shall not be coming on Ascension Day.' Laffan would come at him again and again but Freddie was always implacable and made the same short polite reply, 'No, sir, I shall not…'

When the Tripos came in May that year, I was furiously busy with arrangements for the Queens' Quincentenary, but my morale was high and my brains seemed to be functioning well. And I had done some work. As I sat the exams, I knew I had done much better than before. I was at Oxford when the results were posted. Ian Taylor rang to tell me that he and I had both got a 2.1 and so had Freddie Bryan Brown. Charles Parker managed a 2.2 and seemed quite content with it.

Social life

My memories of Cambridge are of almost unalloyed happiness, but there were lots of struggles and some disappointments. My poor results in Part I English certainly sent me into a gloom and I was unsure of myself to begin with in the company of women.

Keeping body and soul together was a considerable

preoccupation in the immediate post-war years. Each day we collected a small loaf from the buttery which was supposed to be enough for tea and a late-night snack. There was an old lady in nearby Silver Street who kept a bakery with absolutely nothing on show. Nevertheless, she always had a queue. We would adopt a suppliant air in asking for some buns and she would invariably say, 'You can have four,' and would disappear round the back of the counter to get them. Something to put on one's bread was another problem. My neighbour on B staircase, Dick Castle, discovered that the herbalist in Rose Crescent had peanut butter, only it was no use going unless one had a suitable jar to hand in. Once a week we used to make the pilgrimage to Rose Crescent clutching our empty jars and come away gratefully with another precious pot-full. Late-night brews were an important social occasion. In my last year, a group of us would meet regularly to listen to the dance music on the American Forces Network programme and to converse. It was the era of Glenn Miller and block-busting shows like *Annie Get Your Gun* and *Oklahoma*. For me, the tunes of that time never fail to bring back the flavour of these Cambridge days.

Freddie Bryan Brown was one of the circle, so were John Silverlight and Ian Taylor. Freddie and John were two very senior citizens. Each of them had served for at least five years in the war and were by now in their late twenties. Freddie had finished up an acting 'half-colonel' (as he described it – he meant lieutenant colonel) in the army in India. He had commanded a regiment of Indian gunners. John Silverlight had also been an artilleryman. He had fought in Greece and Crete and was seriously wounded in North Africa. Ian Taylor was younger and an ex-Royal Marine. John was reading English; the rest of us were historians. Most often, we met in Ian's room, chiefly because he had the best radio. The conversation above the music was often on Tripos questions, though light-heartedly so. Freddie had the theory that the best history was anecdotal.

Apart from his Greek special subject, he was also reading American history and he would regale us with some of the slogans and characters that enlivened the history of the Great Republic: 'manifest destiny' was one, the 'know nothings' another. 'Forty-nine fifty or fight' had something to do with the western Canadian border and there was the 'rope of sand' whose significance I cannot now remember. Freddie could string these anecdotes together into an act at least as entertaining as *1066 and All That*.

Queens' people used to regard the Anchor in Silver Street as an annexe to the college. We would often gather there before Hall and sink several convivial pints. Freddie Bryan Brown would generally be found with another friend of his, Peter Blackaby. He always addressed Peter ceremoniously as 'Blackaby', in much the same way as Sherlock Holmes always addressed Dr Watson by his surname. Blackaby was required to 'supply nourishment' – that is, buy some more beer – or if Freddie ever felt that someone hadn't shown him sufficient respect, Blackaby was instructed to 'fill him in' (punch him on the nose).

In the summer of 1947, I went to my first May Ball. Dick Castle was the organiser of the party and the ball was at Caius College. I hadn't got my dancing sorted out at that stage nor did I have any obvious partner. I asked my sister Betty to come and she cheerfully agreed. For me that night was a learning process rather than an occasion to enjoy, but it was a sufficient success to make me look forward to more of the same, only better. That night, however, proved to be very important in my life because it was then that I met Cita Quigly, a student of architecture in London, who was also in our party. There is much more to say about Cita.

It is worth telling a little of the subsequent histories of some of these Queens' luminaries. Freddie Bryan Brown became a teacher and finished up as senior master at Bishop's Stortford College. His son Andrew is my godson. Ian Taylor settled in Australia and presided over the fortunes of the Josiah Wedgwood Company in the eastern hemisphere. His Catherine is another of my godchildren. John Silverlight became a journalist, finishing up as an assistant editor of the *Observer*. He was also the author of a successful history of the Allied intervention in the Russian Civil War of 1918/19. He too honoured me with a god-fatherhood, that of his son Charles. Dick Castle, having served in the East during the war, had a brief spell in Malaya during the twilight of Empire before joining the Stock Exchange in London. His daughter Sarah is yet another of my goddaughters.

The Quincentenary

The Quincentenary of the foundation of Queens' occurred in the summer of 1948 and proved to be a magical conclusion to our undergraduate careers. We all became better informed about the history of the college. One Andrew Dockett, a rector of St Botolph's and principal of an early student hostel called St Bernard's, was the prime mover. In 1448, Margaret of Anjou, Queen of Henry VI, decided to emulate her husband's grand creation, King's College next door, with a Queen's College 'to laud and honneure sexe feminine'. Dockett's foundation got incorporated into the queen's purpose, but Dockett remained in charge. Then with the accession of Edward IV in 1461 and his marriage to Elizabeth Woodville in 1464, Dockett shrewdly solicited the new queen to become another foundress, 'by right of succession'. Thus Queens' acquired the patronage of the new regime and shifted its apostrophe to follow the 's' – two founding queens instead of one. However, nobody argued that the college was brought to birth in any year other than 1448. So 1948 was our undoubted Quincentenary year.

The Old Court where I lived was the original college, built in 1448, and it incorporated all the essential features of a mediæval collegiate building. The large entrance tower with its first-floor muniment room presides overall. The old chapel is on the north side along with the library. The west side contains the old hall (in our time the only one), the early president's lodgings and the kitchens (also now the old ones). The south and east sides were living accommodation for fellows and students. My garret was on the second floor in the north-east corner. A charming addition to the Court in the seventeenth century was the sundial over the entrance to the old chapel and the library. A very talented undergraduate mathematician of our year supervised the restoration and repainting of the dial for the Quincentenary. From the small belfry above the old chapel, the college bell used to chime all the quarters of the hour. Its note is another of those sounds which can bring back a total recall of those days.

Beyond the Old Court is the Cloister Court. This, with its sixteenth-century half-timbered range of the President's Lodge, is one of the most beautiful corners of Cambridge. Tucked behind the cloister is Pump Court containing the staircase (really belonging to the Old Court) in which the eminent scholar Erasmus lived during his time in Cambridge in the early sixteenth century.

The mathematical bridge across the river was originally constructed in the eighteenth century with only pegs to hold it together. All the main beams of the bridge are tangents to an ellipse. This too is one of the most sketched, painted and photographed features of Cambridge. The Walnut Tree Court with its seventeenth-century range and Bodley's new chapel of 1891 are handsome but the rest of Queens' buildings at the time of the Quincentenary were undistinguished. Since then the new Erasmus building occupies part of the former fellows' bowling green. This building, in one of Cambridge's prime locations along the Backs, was designed by Sir Basil Spence. The college took a considerable risk in approving a contemporary design. It is very definitely in the spirit of the 1951 Festival of Britain era of British architecture, but it also manages to echo the mediæval/Tudor buildings around it. Perspicacious lovers of Cambridge deem it to be a success. By contrast, the Cripps complex on the opposite bank, built in the 1970s and 1980s, has few admirers.

The celebrations

Inevitably, the college's governing body had been planning the Quincentenary celebrations for a long time. The centrepiece was to be a summer visit by the Queen, subsequently Queen Elizabeth the Queen Mother. The first initiative that we undergraduates took was to propose an open-air production of Shakespeare's *As You Like It* in the Cloister Court in front of the President's Lodge. We had brought to life again the college dramatic society, known as the Bats, which had already put on a J.B. Priestley play and an intimate review in the Fitzpatrick Hall (the JCR) during the previous year. The idea of *As You Like It* originated with Charles Parker, and I, as vice president of the United Clubs and custodian of the JCR, took up the suggestion enthusiastically. The governing body needed very little persuasion. We began preparations in the Lent term – January onwards in 1948 – and as soon as the weather allowed, we had regular Sunday afternoon rehearsals in the Cloister Court. That summer, these rehearsals became quite a feature of Cambridge life – a lot of people used to drift by and view our efforts from the cloisters.

When the Queen visited the college on 7 June, we laid on a special rehearsal of *As You Like It* for her benefit. Like all the actual performances, the rehearsal was a great success. Rain threatened for the first scheduled performance but did not materialise; bright sunshine prevailed throughout the second. There were heavy showers during the third but by then we would cheerfully have played through a monsoon. There were packed audiences each time. Everyone

73

was thrilled with the setting. The action took place on the grass before the central oriel window of the President's Lodge with the audience on three sides. At the end of each performance, the 'brawle gaie' – a kind of Elizabethan conga – took us off into the cloisters on either side to very flattering applause. One of the London theatre critics who came thought it a 'good prose performance'. Most of us were happy to settle for that.

However, *As You Like It* was only one of the events of that summer. The Queen's visit was the highlight of the celebrations. As the Clubs and JCR man, I was responsible for what was called the 'Marshal Plan'. Under the direction of the tutors we devised a scheme by which undergraduate marshals with white buttonholes would mark the route that the Queen, escorted by our President, Dr J.A. Venn, would take through the college, and make sure that nothing untoward occurred. One of our number, Brian Target, was appointed the President's ADC and was to be in close and constant attendance. As soon as the Queen stepped into the Old Court – her point of arrival – I was to call for 'three cheers for Her Majesty' and the assembled college lining the four sides of the court would respond with loud and loyal applause.

Everything went well and the Queen was received enthusiastically. After a thanksgiving service in chapel at which the Dean preached in his characteristic style, some of us were presented to her and there was a splendid lunch in the Hall. A garden party followed in the afternoon, admirably watched over by the marshals. By the time the Queen left us that day, she had agreed to be the official patroness of the college, so we now had Queen Elizabeth of the House of Windsor as well as Queen Margaret of Anjou and Queen Elizabeth Woodville to grace our name. The Queen was a most delightful guest. She was interested in everything, responsive to all the people she met, and quite tireless in her participation in the whole lengthy programme. At the time of writing, Queen Elizabeth, for many years now the Queen Mother, has achieved her hundred-and-first birthday. The characteristics that have made her so specially loved in her advanced years were very much in evidence that day at Queens' College in June 1948.

With the royal visit over, there was still a lot of celebrating to come. A large marquee had been set up on the bowling green and this was the venue for a formal dinner for all in residence. We were all there in academic dress and bow ties. I had to make a speech so I pecked very nervously at the succulent dishes placed before me. Happily, the speech seemed to go down well. The President congratulated me and so did a number of others. Among other things, I said how much we appreciated the dons and the college servants, so at least I was popular with them.

Then in the same marquee we had the Quincentenary Ball on 15 June – my birthday, as it happened. Brian Target was chairman of the ball committee and did an excellent job. I was also on the committee, which was worth a free ticket to all the other balls on the same evening, but I was in no mood to stray from Queens' that night. Joan Marjason, a recent friend from Oxford, was my partner. By this time I had lost my social inhibitions and the evening passed in a golden haze of delight! My dancing had improved astonishingly and I adored every girl in sight, including Joan. We finished up with breakfast under the trees at the Orchard in Grantchester. I think I must have seen Joan off to Oxford before going to sleep until the second performance of *As You Like It* in the early evening. There was yet another party after that.

The final university event of that summer was the degree ceremony. My mother came for it and was very impressed with all of us strolling along King's Parade to the Senate House in our evening gear and borrowed hoods of rabbit fur. John Silverlight endeared himself to her by tying my bow tie for me. Following the ceremony, Mother bullied me into the photographer's studio to have the occasion recorded. Since John had no relatives in England, he came to stay with us at Rotherhithe for a time. It was while he was with us that he met his wife Pamela through my sister Betty.

The future

With all these heady things happening, it was easy to think that life would always be a student idyll. In fact I had been worrying about the future from the middle of my time at Cambridge. I had gone up to the university sure that I wanted to continue with journalism. But as my university career progressed the Christian faith became more and more important to me. When L.J. Potts asked me at the end of my second year what career moves I proposed to make, I told him that I had begun to think that I should be ordained, though I wasn't sure whether it had to be in the Anglican or the Roman Catholic Church. He murmured some mildly discouraging things about the Catholic option – didn't I realise that the Catholics don't believe in married priests? I did realise that but perhaps I hadn't pondered it sufficiently. I was inclined to think 'in for a penny in for a pound', as long as it wasn't just yet. It was easy to put the issue of the ministry to sleep with all that was going on and it was only in my last term that I turned to face the decision. I decided to offer myself for the Anglican priesthood. Our dean and chaplain were both approving. I was too late to get into Westcott House at Cambridge, my first choice of theological college, but Wells in Somerset accepted me for September 1948. I must have passed the various selection hoops that summer. Ian Taylor and I had entertained the idea of going to an American university for a year. This was a very alluring prospect for many undergraduates at the time. I think our third-year tutor, Arthur Armitage, who subsequently became the President of Queens', would have made this possible for both of us. But having cast the die for Wells, I dropped the idea.

Berlin during the blockade

One other adventure occurred that summer. Charles Parker was involved in the Cambridge University Marlowe Society's summer productions. These were serious theatricals and most of those already signed up had a particular talent for the theatre. There were, however, a few places left for 'walk-ons'. After performing the plays at the Arts Theatre in Cambridge (sufficient glory in itself), the company was to take them to Germany. We had been signed up to perform the plays in the renowned Renaissance Theatre in Berlin which had survived the destruction of the city. Berlin was in the grip of the Soviet blockade at this time and we were to be part of a show of cultural solidarity with the West Berliners instigated by the Foreign Office. Charles thought I might like to join the company. The plays were Shakespeare's *Measure for Measure* and John Webster's *The White Devil*, a Jacobean horror story. I was duly accepted and was allocated the parts of a friar in *Measure for Measure* and clerk of the court, second poisoner and 'a boy' in *The White Devil*. As 'a boy', I had a line: 'This is not true, Madam!' A critic commenting on a London production of *The White Devil* had said that, for him, the most moving moment of the play was when a young innocent stepped forward amid the carnage and said, 'This is not true, Madam!' It was said that after this remarkable plaudit the lead players put 'the boy' behind a pillar to say his line. It was now my line and I was proud of it.

Our company included a trio of King's College dons, all of whom were established Cambridge thespians. These were George Rylands, Donald Beves and Noel Annan. There was also Camille ('Pop') Prior, an elderly lady who had adorned Cambridge theatricals for many years. Also in the party were some notable undergraduate players, including Richard Baker of later broadcasting fame. Charles Parker's best part was Abhorson, the executioner in *Measure for Measure*. Phyllis, his wife, was also in the party, a minor

77

player like me. Two other veterans of *As You Like It*, James and Monica Beament, were in the company with more substantial parts. Each play ran for three days at the Arts in Cambridge; we drew good audiences and received flattering notices.

The trip to Berlin was what we were all looking forward to. We were flown in to Gatow airfield in a Dakota with seats all along the sides. Our scenery and costumes were also packed on to the plane. The aura that pervaded post-war Vienna in Carol Reed's film *The Third Man* also typified Berlin at this time. Large areas of the city had been destroyed. In the western sectors the rubble had been cleared away but there were still mountains of it in the east. The Berliners were in hourly fear that the Russians were going to attempt a complete take-over of the city; they were entirely dependant on the western airlift for supplies of food and medicine. Individuals had been snatched by the Russians in the Potsdamer Platz where the British, the American and the Russian sectors all met. This intersection was the crossroads of Europe. From the British side, one could see heavily armed Russians just a few hundred yards away. In the side streets off the Platz there were units of our military police ready to react to any trouble.

Berliners, especially the younger ones, greeted us as saviours, but the British Control Commission people were scarcely polite about our arrival. When aeroplane space was so precious, the authorities had flown us in! No doubt many of the Control Commission officials were doing a good job, but some of those we met seemed little better than thugs left over from the war. They had unlimited power and privilege and enjoyed humiliating the Germans.

We performed our plays to full, but I fear largely un-comprehending, audiences. We went to a number of official receptions and were particularly sought out by Berlin students. A young Berliner, Wolfgang Hanel, attached him-self to us. He was desperately keen to establish some sort of western solidarity. He gave us a copy of *Hamlet* as we left, with the English text and a German translation on opposite pages. He wanted that to be a sign of the common destiny of our two cultures. The war was too recent for us to be very sympathetic, but I have often wondered since what became of Wolfgang.

We took in quite a lot of the Berlin scene. We had a close-up visit to the Russian war memorial which had been built in the British sector quite near to the Brandenburg Gate. We also got as near as we could to Hitler's bunker in the Tiergarten, also in the British sector. Some of us ventured into the Russian sector to go to the Comic Opera, which was sumptuous. We also found our way to a night club in the French sector and had a very lively evening. We did a lot of thinking among ourselves about the menace of Russia and the future of Europe. These great world issues were to be the background to much of our future lives.

Back we came to England from this fascinating but very disturbing experience. I never met the other members of the party again except for Charles and Phyllis Parker and James Beament. For me, the scene was shortly to shift from the crossroads of Europe to the English backwater of Wells in Somerset.

4
Wells and Woolwich

At Cambridge, I had lived on the crest of a rising wave and had tasted the sweetness of success. Almost anything had to be a come-down after that. I think this was true for all of us who had shared the intoxicating days of the Queens' Quincentenary. It was certainly my experience at Wells. I had arrived at a beautiful little place with an historic cathedral but it was in the back of beyond. The atmosphere of Wells was pure Anthony Trollope. Even the pubs seemed vaguely ecclesiastical. I did not take to my fellow students at the theological college very readily. The only one I already knew was Arthur Dodds who was one of the Queen's, Oxford, footballers. It was he and his wife Letty who had invited me to the Oxford Commemoration Ball. Arthur and Letty were great Moral Rearmers, or Buchmanites. These were a kind of religious Rotary movement with a great commitment to certain moral absolutes. They were sometimes known as the 'Oxford Group' because their American founder, Frank Buchman, found his first support in England at Oxford. Arthur and Letty seemed more wedded to 'The Group' than to the Church of England. Although we were good friends, we were not exactly soul mates in religion.

Vocational angsts

I was also suffering a reaction from my decision to train for the ministry. At Cambridge, I had entered an expansive and glamorous world. Now, at Wells, I felt cut off and restricted. I had an acute attack of this on my way back to London for one of our vacations. The coach stopped at the bus station in Reading and I went into the buffet for a coffee. As I sat there alone, the sound system played Glenn Miller's 'Moonlight Serenade'. This tune seemed to typify everything that I had passed up by going to Wells. At that moment I was very tempted to pack it all in.

However, I did stick it out. I was never comfortable at Wells and never completely sure that I was on the right track. But I did feel strongly that the call of God was urgent and that if I really did have a vocation to the ministry I would be wrong to turn away from it. I also had a very un-Anglican attitude towards the ministry and marriage. I had no theological convictions about the celibacy of the clergy – indeed, I would have been quite unable to grasp that concept at this stage of my life – but I was reaching a suspicion that not getting married was part of the package. I have mentioned this already apropos of the conversation I had with L.J. Potts when he asked what I proposed to do about my career. Years later, I learned that John Henry Newman had had an early intimation of the same kind.

The problem was compounded for me because I was now very attracted to women and some seemed to be interested in me. This would produce a crisis in my life a few years later when I had to choose between the ministry and my love for someone whose name I have already mentioned, Cita Quigly. The crucial problem to come was that Cita was a Roman Catholic and an ardent one. For the moment, however, it was my freedom that was at issue, and the bright lights.

Still, we are bidden to count the cost and at Wells I did a lot of cost counting. The example that registered in my mind was that of the Duke of Windsor. How could he have sacrificed his vocation for the sake of private happiness? Many years later, I learned about Thomas More and the vocational battles of his early life. He made the opposite decision, deciding that his vocation was to marriage and family life rather than the priesthood. He became a saint!

At Wells, I pondered a great deal about the nature of 'vocation'. Was it a specific thing, as if God should say, 'I want you, Charles Walker, to be a priest'? Or was the call more general, on the lines of 'The Church needs priests – what hinders you from being ordained?' I wriggled on the end of this hook, but it did seem that hooked I was. I came eventually to the conclusion that the call of God, at least as far as human beings could apprehend it, was both general and particular. At first it was an invitation but as one began to respond it became part of one's very identity. I was persuaded that there was a Providence in all the stages by which I had arrived at Wells and that the same Providence was perfectly capable of redirecting me elsewhere. 'Thus far the Lord has guided me, surely he will guide me still.' So I continued at Wells doggedly but I never had a feeling of blessed assurance.

As for the choice between the Anglican and Catholic ministries, I suppose the cultural distance between the Anglicanism of my upbringing and the Catholic intimations I was just beginning to receive was much too great for me to bridge at that time. My head was very alert to the claims of the Catholic Church but as a possible alternative belonging it was much too far away. The Catholics were on the edge of English life, slightly mysterious and alluring but really quite foreign. It was easy to think of the Church of England as the custodian of the soul of England and that it was her job to look after our people. In any case, some of the most precious things in my life were by now associated with the Church of England: my attachment to St Mary's, Rotherhithe, and my regard for Canon Daniels. My family came into the reckoning too, and especially my mother. And the Anglican presence in Cambridge had been very persuasive. Finally, I did belong to the Church of England by baptism and upbringing – should one deny one's spiritual roots?

The college at Wells

I gradually came to terms with life at Wells. To begin with, I was billeted at the YMCA with two other students because the college numbers were inflated and there was a shortage of accommodation. Fred Honey, Glen Owen Jenkins and I quite enjoyed living in an outside lodging. Being ten minutes' walk away, we panted in and out to services and lectures but otherwise followed our own rules, and we made friends with a lot of young people who used to frequent the 'YM'. After about a term, space was found for us in houses in Vicars' Close. Wells was unique among theological colleges in its students' living arrangements: Vicars' Close was a mediæval street with houses on either side and a little chapel at the end. The houses were once the individual quarters for the singing men of Wells Cathedral. The mediæval character of the Close was still intact, though some of the single houses had been joined to their neighbours to become double-fronted. I was allocated to number 16, which was the largest. There were about ten of us in it, including a member of staff, the Revd Lewis Clark, and a married couple who used to look after all the domestic arrangements. Several other houses were used for students and there were married quarters for two other members of the college staff. The Close Chapel at the end was a little mediæval jewel. It could take about twenty of us at a time. My memory is that we used to have two 'sittings' for Evensong there every day at which students officiated. The variable prayers at the end were chosen by the officiating student and would sometimes reflect his particular concerns. One of our number used to call these the 'axe-grinding prayers'. A high Tory member of the college once started off, 'Let us pray for all anarchists, revolutionaries and other discontented people …'!

Each day began with Morning Prayer and meditation in the Lady Chapel of the cathedral. The Principal, the Revd Kenneth Howarth, would be there long before the earliest of us. I was among those who found it difficult to be consistently early. It was customary to apologise to the Principal whenever one was late. He had a number of apologies from me. The Lady Chapel gradually insinuated itself into my consciousness as a place of great beauty and holiness. There was a modern figure of the Virgin Mary as the centrepiece of the reredos. I came to cherish that figure very much. The cathedral, of course, was a daily delight and sometimes a wonder. It became an abiding presence in our lives. We were very casual about the mediæval clock and the throngs of tourists who queued up to see it. When the Dean and Chapter decided to make a small charge for viewing the clock with its hourly jousting match, the finances of the cathedral were immediately transformed. Happily the clock was in the north transept and, at that time, the rest of the cathedral was open and still free. Wells Cathedral had other remarkable features, notably the west front and the inverted arches separating the nave from the chancel. In the years I am speaking of, the west front was filled with figures, some defaced at the Reformation and others decayed. A splendid restoration took place during the 1990s and the west front is now more glorious than it has been for half a millennium.

Hugh Walpole in *The Cathedral* has described how such a building can brood over a small city and dominate its life. This was true of Wells. The cathedral could be seen from any part of the city and all roads seemed to lead to it. It had different moods. At times it would look simply picturesque; at other times it could be awesome.

Wells also contained the glorious perpendicular parish church of St Cuthbert's. Shortly after I arrived, students of the college performed *The Castle of Perseverance*, a mediæval morality play, there. Another handsome feature of Wells was the moated bishop's palace with its resident swans. By tradition the swans were supposed to ring a bell with their beaks at feeding time. They had got out of the way of it during the war and one of the students of my time taught them the trick all over again. This too had great tourist appeal.

Its people

I have mentioned that the college numbers were high in the summer of 1948. Most students were graduates and the majority of these were from Oxford or Cambridge. As I got to know the others better, I began to realise that there were a lot of very choice men among them. A considerable number of students had wives and children and there were married quarters all over the city. The wives too were often very estimable people. The majority of our students were ex-servicemen and some had had a very rugged war. Arthur Dodds, for instance, an RAF flyer, had been shot down over the western desert. He had been taken prisoner and had escaped from a camp in Italy. His wife Letty had been a WAAF. Nearly all of us were in our twenties but there were a few older men. One of our more senior members had been highly placed in the Sudan Civil Service; another had been a Methodist minister.

The wives, guided by the Principal's wife, took a prominent part in the life of the college. All the feminine parts in *The Castle of Perseverance* were taken by students' wives and they were very much involved in the social life of the college. Some chose to attend lectures and seminars. Letty Dodds was brilliant at auctions. These occurred fairly frequently in and around Wells and complete household effects would normally be up for bids. Letty would do a brisk but concentrated tour of all that was on offer and when the bidding began she knew exactly what she wanted and how much she was prepared to pay. I saw her garner armfuls of bedding for a few shillings in the old money and on another occasion she collected virtually a shedful of garden tools for less than a pound.

We used to have morning lectures and sometimes early

evening ones. These would cover biblical studies, Christian doctrine and morals, church history, liturgy and pastoral practice. The intellectual level wasn't quite as high as that of a university nor was it speculative and critical in the same way. The training was meant to be a professional one, and as such it was of good quality. We all had to pass the General Ordination Examination – GOE – which included a paper in New Testament Greek. I had a struggle with the Greek; in fact I think I was allowed GOE without passing it. The students, like the staff, had varying ecclesiastical perspectives and priorities. Some were high church, revealing themselves as such by genuflecting during the Nicene creed at the words, 'and was incarnate by the Holy Ghost of the Virgin Mary'. Others were more evangelical in their sympathies and stood by the classical principles of the Reformation. And there was a broad band of middle opinion, sometimes high, sometimes low, for whom doctrines mattered a little less than their particular enthusiasms. I have mentioned that Arthur and Letty Dodds were keen Moral Rearmers. There was a considerable group who were interested in particular causes like racial justice in South Africa and industrial mission in Britain.

A great deal of the intellectual and 'special causes' sparkle centred in our chaplain, John Robinson, later Bishop of Woolwich and of *Honest to God* fame. John Robinson came on to the staff at Wells at roughly the same time as I started as a student. He had previously been curate to Mervyn Stockwood, a notable Anglican, in Bristol. John shared Mervyn Stockwood's left-of-centre political opinions and like him was very impatient with conventional religion. Under John's stimulus, some of us became especially interested in the French experience of coping with a post-Christian society. We were absorbed in Abbé Michonneau's *Revolution in a City Parish*, Abbé Godin's *France Pagan?* and Abbé Perrin's *Priest-Workman in Germany*. For a few of us, these preoccupations at Wells were to shape our future ministries. It is curious that such continental ideas should have been taken up in an English ecclesiastical byway like Wells.

There were opponents to John Robinson and his ideas. He was denounced in a sermon by the Dean of Wells, Richard Malden, for speaking for the Labour Party in a general election. He also incurred the wrath of another member of staff for making a great deal of 'house churches' in apostolic times. There are references in St Paul's letters to 'the church that is in their house'. John was inclined to conclude from this feature of early Christianity that maybe house churches were a unit of the Church that we could do with again. He made the case in a Friday night Compline address which was normally followed by the weekly 'night silence'. The address caused such a stir that some found it difficult to contain themselves and the silence that night was punctured a little. Compline the following Friday produced a refutation by the sceptical member of staff. He thought the championing of house churches was a recipe for the fragmentation of Christian communities. Again the night silence suffered. The dispute rumbled up and down Vicars' Close for a few weeks. Not everybody was aligned, but a good number saw it as a prime example of new wine and old bottles.

With such stresses occurring from time to time, our Principal's policy seemed to be one of vicarious suffering. He would avoid adjudicating on the issues. He would give everyone credit for trying to do their best for God and would bow his own shoulders to bear the consequences of the trouble. Soon, everyone would forebear to cause him any more pain and the college would resume its even tenor. We were, in fact, very well served by the four or five staff members in my time. Kenneth Haworth, the Principal, was universally admired by the students, even if we did feel slightly protective towards him. The others became good friends and valued mentors. John Robinson stands out in memory both for the influence he exercised on some of us at the time and for his subsequent history.

Ordination

I was due to be ordained – strictly, to be 'made deacon' – in September 1950, the church season of Michaelmas. I was being sponsored by the Anglican diocese of Southwark so I was going to be working somewhere in south London. In the final terms at Wells, the GOE exams had to be negotiated, the man from Wippell's (the ecclesiastical outfitters at Exeter) came to measure us up for cassocks and suits, and there were various legalities to be initiated. The latter included a fee to be paid to the legal officer of the diocese in which we were to be ordained. One of our number, Alfred Harrison, took a fierce objection to this fee – 'Why should I pay some lawyer for the privilege of doing God's work?' Alfred held out for quite some time. I believe certain people were prepared to pay the money for him. But no – it was the principle of the thing! He decided eventually that he had made his point and gave way. The lawyer got his money and Alfred got ordained.

For each of us, a more crucial question was the parish we were going to sign up for. The proper phrase was 'serve a title'. Vicars needing curates were writing in to the Principal all the time and there were certain parishes which regularly had curates from Wells. My fellow students were considering parishes all over England and Wales. Indeed, we had a few who were going overseas, including our American comrade, Charles Bradshaw, who was heading back home to Boston, Massachusetts. Several of us were bound for south London. I chose to go to St Mary Magdalen's, Woolwich, a Thames-side parish like the one I had belonged to at Rotherhithe. St Mary Magdalen's had a rector, the Revd Ronald Thompson, for whom I came to have a high regard, though we were scarcely kindred spirits.

The ministry and marriage

Throughout my time at Wells, my relationship with Cita Quigly had been maturing, but as a devout Roman Catholic it was no pleasure to her that I was set on becoming an Anglican priest. She did, however, agree to come to my deacon's ordination at the Anglican Southwark Cathedral. She had observed Catholic discipline of the time by asking her parish priest's permission. With Cita present at the ordination, it really did seem that marriage to her and my Anglican ministry might be reconcilable. I had, of course, taken advice about it and the judgement on both the Anglican and Catholic sides was that it was an either/or situation – either I married Cita or I entered the Anglican ministry; I couldn't do both. Even so, on the day after I had been ordained a deacon, I did ask Cita to marry me and she agreed. It was a beautiful moment.

From then on all Cita's expectations were that we would be married within a year or two. We met each Friday, which was my day off, and spoke on the telephone every evening. But I was inhabiting two entirely different worlds. Cita did not fit into my Woolwich picture at all and that part of my life was entirely strange to her, though I did tell her all that I had been doing when we talked on the telephone. I moved into her world every Friday – indeed, I came to think of myself that day as 'Man Friday'. I seemed acceptable to her family and I met a number of her friends. We talked a good deal about religion. It is interesting that I never had any expectation that Cita would become an Anglican to facilitate our marriage, nor did I want this of her. Through her, I was having a glimpse of a world that fascinated me but was still very alien. If we went out for a meal on a Friday evening, she always took great care that if soup was on the menu it was a soup that didn't contain meat. We met one evening on the Feast of the Epiphany, a Catholic holy day of obligation, and Cita hadn't been to Mass. We had to visit St Patrick's, Soho Square, before doing anything else. The church was packed and we just got in the porchway with Mass having started. Cita was absorbed in the proceedings and seemed to forget about me. I marvelled at the great crowd filling a West End church on a weekday evening and the blaze of light around the distant altar. This was pre-Second Vatican Council Catholicism and it impressed my Protestant soul.

When I first met her at the Caius May Ball in 1947, Cita was a student at the Architectural Association (the 'AA') nearing the end of her course. In the year that followed, I restored the link between Queens' College and Queens' House in Rotherhithe. Cita was interested in all this and she chose to do an architectural study of Queens' House, a riverside youth centre, as her thesis for her final exams. She clambered over barges to draw the riverside elevations and the work she produced was highly praised.

After graduation, Cita went to work for Architects Co-Partnership (ACP), among the most exciting firms in British architecture during the immediate post-war years. ACP was allocated part of the Festival of Britain project, and all during 1950 Cita was working on the decorative screen along the York Road part of the site and on the 'mining block' which simulated a mine shaft. This was done by constructing a tapering structure above ground, and as people looked up it from the inside it felt as if they were looking down the shaft. I was fascinated by what she was doing, and when the Festival opened in 1951 I took a great pride in the part she had played in its success.

St Mary's, Woolwich

At the same time, I was getting more and more absorbed in the parish. St Mary's Church was an undistinguished eighteenth-century preaching box with a Victorian chancel added on. Its position, however, was splendid. It was built on a rise overlooking the Thames with fine views up and down Gallions Reach. Looking across the river, one could see the big ships berthed in the Royal group of docks. In the foreground were the terminals of the Woolwich Free Ferry with the ferry boats constantly looping to and fro. On the landward side the church was obscured by the large bulk of the Odeon cinema.

In terms of churchmanship, St Mary's was a mixture. Ronald Thompson, the rector, came from an evangelical background but had acquired some Anglo-Catholic sympathies as time went on. He was very well connected with the Anglican Franciscans and we had two Franciscan-led 'missions' during my time at Woolwich. One was a special effort for the parish alone; the other was a Woolwich-wide spiritual campaign led by Fr Michael Fisher of the Franciscans with a large contingent of university clergy and undergraduates from Cambridge.

Another of Ronald Thompson's enthusiasms was Lee Abbey, the evangelical Christian centre in Devon. This link had originally been forged by his predecessor at Woolwich, Cuthbert Bardsley. Cuthbert, as he was known to everyone including the choirboys, was Rector of St Mary's during the middle years of the war before becoming the Provost of Southwark Cathedral. After that, he became Bishop of Croydon and then Bishop of Coventry. Quite a number of St Mary's people were keen Lee Abbey frequenters and a St Mary's girl had become its resident administrator. I did not pick up this particular enthusiasm. Lee Abbey struck me as too 'folksy' and soul-searching, though I was impressed by the qualities of its people.

Ronald Thompson was a most zealous parish priest. All the services were well conducted and he was constantly looking for ways of building up the St Mary's community, both in numbers and in spiritual fervour. He used to put a great deal of effort into his sermons and expected me to do the same. He had a Bible study and prayer group which used to meet on Thursday evenings and he would spend most of Thursday preparing for it. But he was almost completely enclosed within the parish. He seemed to have very little sympathy with the life of Woolwich in general. He was also a shy man, not a great relater or communicator. He had a good mind, however, and was well abreast of current theological thinking. He and I used to get on well even though we were different sorts of people, both temperamentally and in terms of our enthusiasms. I admired his commitment to the parish and his steadfastness. I think he approved of me because I worked quite hard and had something to show for my efforts with the children and young people. Women mystified him. He was unmarried and had little natural rapport with the womenfolk of the parish. There was a long-running dispute between two of the leading ladies of the parish and trying to hold the ring between them nearly reduced him to despair.

My personal dilemma

I did, however, present him with a major problem. Newcomers to the Anglican ministry usually serve one year as a deacon before being ordained priest. This is what Ronald Thompson expected of me. But I was firmly fixed on the horns of my dilemma. Nearly a year had passed since I had asked Cita to marry me and nothing was happening about our marriage except that we met each week on my day off from the parish. Cita was getting very fed up and her family were questioning the situation too. I had gradually to face up to the fact that I would have to sacrifice Cita or the ministry. No one gave me any encouragement to think that an Anglican priest could be married to a Roman Catholic. 'It would mean that the person closest to you wouldn't believe that you were a priest' – these were Canon Daniels' words. But I was not yet ready to part with Cita or to give up the ministry. In later years, I was asked to advise a young couple in the self-same situation. An Australian Anglican clergyman wanted to marry an Italian Catholic girl. This was in the years following the Second Vatican Council and such was the change in the ecumenical climate that a highly placed Catholic dignitary made it his business to facilitate the marriage. What seemed impossible in the 1950s happened almost easily in the late 1960s.

But for Cita and me in 1951/2 there seemed to be no such solution. There were subsidiary problems. I had no money. I couldn't even afford to take my MA degree at Cambridge when it became due in 1951 (there was a fee of £5) until one of our St Mary's churchwardens gave me the money. There was also the background suspicion in my mind that the ministry involved the sacrifice of marriage anyway. This was a kind of undertow in my mind but it was not strong enough to deny me the actual relationship that I had discovered with Cita. The unresolved issue became increasingly burdensome. I took refuge in delay. I avoided going forward for the priesthood after my deacon's year was over. Various pressures were put upon me. I had to go and explain myself to the bishop and Ronald Thompson arranged for me to be counselled at Mirfield by a member of the Community of the Resurrection, one of the Anglican religious orders. The problem was clear enough in my mind – I was just not ready to choose.

Cita for her part had decided to cut the knot by going to live in Italy. In the summer of 1951, I went to see her there – in Florence – accompanied by my brother Ian who was by now an undergraduate at Oxford and not very happy there. Cita was somewhat distant from me and she had in fact met the man she subsequently married. Nevertheless, our relationship was still alive and I think could have been fully restored if I had been able to be more positive. The visit was a fraught one in that my brother Ian was showing incipient signs of a nervous breakdown. Having met Cita for the first time in Florence, his advice was simple: 'Why don't you lick the Pope's boots?' This wasn't the most gracious assessment of the issues involved but it was a robustly English and Protestant reaction and left me in no doubt where he stood in the matter.

Throughout the ensuing year, we corresponded frequently. Cita acquired a well-paid job at a NATO base near Florence and was evidently getting more and more Italian-orientated. She did not write much about her relationship with Adriano Milani, her future husband, but I gathered that it was maturing. I had bought time at Woolwich, but long before my second year in deacon's orders was up I had to grapple with the decision to stay or not to stay in the Anglican ministry. I did not know whether Cita had turned the page by this time but on my side I was still desperately reluctant to abandon all hope of marrying her. If I had been unhappy at Woolwich it might have been easier to pull out of the ministry, but I doubt if this was so. I think by this time I was convinced that I was meant to be a priest and that I had to continue for better or for worse. Ronald Thompson wasn't much help – he had the idea that what I needed was an ultimatum. Eventually, I made a lonely decision to write to Cita abandoning all hope of us being married. At the same time, I agreed to go forward to priest's ordination the following September. Even if Cita had already made up her mind that we had no future together, for me the decision to abandon the hope of marrying her felt like a great sacrifice.

I had an abiding sense of failure in my relationship with Cita and all thought of marriage disappeared from my mind for many years. When she and Adriano were married some years later (they were stuck with a long drawn-out annulment process because Adriano had contracted a previous marriage), I was very glad because her happiness now seemed to be assured. Adriano, a medical man, became a very distinguished specialist in cerebral palsy. His clinic in Florence became an international centre for research and treatment. He and Cita had two daughters. There is a sequel to this story that ended so unsatisfactorily in 1952 but it was a long way over the horizon.

Final years at Woolwich

With the decision made to proceed to the Anglican priesthood, I became more and more absorbed in my work. I
stayed at Woolwich until the summer of 1955, which was a
bit longer than most first curacies, so I could be said to
have compensated the rector and the parish for my extended
diaconate. I became very absorbed in the work I was doing
with children and young people. I used to run 'Children's
Church' on Sunday afternoons and I was the supremo of all
the cubs, scouts, brownies and guides. We had cohorts of
cubs and brownies and a fair number of guides but the
scouts were weak and I made these my special concern.

My other major commitment was the Youth Fellowship. This already had considerable momentum when I
arrived and it built up steadily as time went on. We had
a splendid crowd of boys and girls from fifteen years
upwards. A lot of the activities were social and recreational
and some were educational, but we also had a considerable
spiritual programme. Most of those who stayed for any
length of time became confirmed and we had retreats
and quiet days, as well as a summer holiday and lots of
outings, including rambles in the Kent countryside on all
the Bank Holiday Mondays. I have vivid recollections of
many of these boys and girls and am still in touch with
some of them. I was happy to conduct several of their
weddings. They nearly always married within the Youth
Fellowship.

The message of Charles de Foucauld

Another interest that began at Woolwich and would prove
significant for the future was my first encounter with the
message and spirituality of Charles de Foucauld. There was
a house near St Mary's Church which had formerly been the
headquarters of a lady who had done notable Christian social

service in Woolwich for many years. She had died a little before I arrived on the scene. The house was vacant and another lady, Mary Every, moved in. We soon discovered that Mary was a very remarkable person. She had been head of the Lady Margaret Settlement in east London but she had come to Woolwich to try out an entirely new kind of life. She gave us a sheet of paper outlining the life and message of a French Catholic priest called Charles de Foucauld whom none of us had ever heard of. Evidently he had lived among an obscure tribe in the depths of the Sahara Desert and had inspired a new kind of religious life.

Neither Ronald Thompson nor I had much inkling of what it was all about. Mary was obviously a highly competent person and could have been immensely helpful as an activist in the parish. But that was not her idea at all. She was happy to belong to the St Mary's community and play a part in parish life, but her main purpose was to get a job in a local factory and make friends with her workmates. At the same time she would devote a great deal of her leisure hours to prayer. I could not realise at that time that in Mary's endeavour I was in touch with a very early Anglican experiment in a way of life that had already taken firm root in the Roman Catholic Church on the Continent, especially in France. It was to become a broad movement in England in later years, bringing Anglicans and Catholics together in a common belonging. The new vocation that Mary Every brought to Woolwich was my first encounter with the Jesus Caritas ('Jesus Love') movement which was to become a major influence in my life.

Cambridge again

While I was still at Woolwich, Queens' at Cambridge invited me to be the college missioner when Michael Ramsay – then Bishop of Durham but later Archbishop of Canterbury – was to lead an official Anglican mission to the university in 1954. These special efforts took place from time to time at Cambridge, as at other universities, and generally lasted a fortnight. A leading figure in the Church of England would come and preach the mission in the university church and there would be contributory programmes in each of the colleges. Bishop Ramsay, I thought, was a splendid preacher. He had a fine presence, a fine mind and a well-tuned understanding of life in an English university. He was also a man possessed by the gospel. His wit was delicate. A joke would be signalled by a fluttering of his eyebrows and a slight stammer, and would conclude with a great beam.

My participation in the university mission actually led to my return to Cambridge. One of the Anglican Franciscans, Fr Edward (formerly the Revd Christopher Lee-Smith), had looked after Peterhouse very notably during the mission. The Dean of Peterhouse, Joseph Sanders, had suffered a heart attack and needed to shed some of his tasks. Although Peterhouse had no more than three hundred undergraduates and would not normally have rated a chaplain as well as a dean, the governing body were prepared to make an appointment for the sake of easing the Dean's burdens. I think the college would like to have appointed Fr Edward, but being a Franciscan with multifarious tasks elsewhere he was not available. I think it was he who recommended me. He certainly counselled me to accept the job when it was offered to me.

By the early part of 1955, it was time for me to be moving from Woolwich anyway. The prospect of becoming Chaplain of Peterhouse was immensely attractive. I went to the college to be scrutinised for the task. Joe Sanders seemed already to have made up his mind that I would do. The Master, Dr Paul Vellacott, gave me a friendly interview and it was all settled. I would come into residence for the May term, 1955.

I made my farewells at St Mary's and came away laden with gifts and mementos. In spite of my personal difficulties, it had been a happy five years and I had learned a great deal from Ronald Thompson and the people of the parish. I would see a lot more of the parish and of Woolwich in the years to come; indeed, some of the friendships of those days have endured to the present time.

5

Peterhouse

I was just short of thirty-one when I arrived at Peterhouse. This made me about ten years older than the most senior of the undergraduates. So in terms of age I was well placed to make friends with them. I was to remain Chaplain of Peterhouse for the next five years – until the summer of 1960. My time there proved to be a very rich chapter of life though it culminated in a great upheaval.

The college

Peterhouse is the oldest of the Cambridge colleges. The foundation dates from 1284 when the Bishop of Ely, Hugo de Balsham, decided to set up in Cambridge a college 'like unto Merton at Oxford'. Both universities were emerging from the informal days of masters gathering groups of poor scholars around them and setting up hostels to accommodate them. Andrew Dockett created the College of St Margaret and St Bernard, which became Queens' College, out of one such hostel – St Bernard's – as late as 1448. Peterhouse was created out of two existing hostels located on the road to Trumpington. The first collegiate building to be added was the Hall in 1286. The college ramified in the centuries that followed and the original hostels were demolished in the seventeenth century to make way for a new chapel and eventually for the eighteenth-century Burroughs building. The Hall, much restored by George Gilbert Scott and handsomely embellished by the Pre-Raphaelites, was one of my constant delights at Peterhouse. It has a fine oriel window, a beautiful Tudor fireplace with William Morris tiles, and above the west gallery there is a stencilled scroll by Morris praying that we who shared our 'commons' in the Hall at Peterhouse would one day share in the celestial banquet of Heaven. I could always breath 'Amen' to that. Another special feature of the Hall is a series of sixteenth- and seventeenth-century wooden panel portraits of college alumni, including Hugo de Balsham.

The original college chapel had been the Church of St Mary-the-Less (always known as 'Little St Mary's') which was previously dedicated to St Peter. This dedication gave the college its name – 'St Peter's College' for several centuries, and then 'Peterhouse' since the early part of the nineteenth. Little St Mary's is still a Peterhouse living: that is, the college has the right of appointing the vicar. It is one of the most beautiful mediæval churches in Cambridge. In 1632, however, Matthew Wren, Master of Peterhouse, built the new chapel which, in defiance of the strong Puritan sentiment in the university at that time, incorporated such high-church – 'Laudian' – features as an altar, a crucifix and painted angels.

In 1643, the new chapel attracted the malign attention of William Dowsing, the inveterate destroyer of all such 'Popery'. Most of Matthew Wren's liturgical features were destroyed. 'Wren's nest', as the new chapel was known to its Puritan critics, was later renovated and embellished with Baroque facings at the charge of his successor in the master-ship, John Cosin, another high-churchman. John Cosin was ejected from the mastership by Parliament in 1644 but became Bishop of Durham at the Restoration of King Charles ll. It was as Bishop of Durham that he saw to the renewal of Peterhouse Chapel. His most notable achievement in the religious ferment of his day was the part he played in compiling the Book of Common Prayer of 1662. Peterhouse under the dean I worked with, Joseph Sanders, remained faithful to this gift of our illustrious seventeenth-century master – we used the 1662 Prayer Book in Peterhouse Chapel and nothing else.

My task was the pastoral care of the undergraduates. I also felt a responsibility for the college staff in all departments and for those of the Fellows who were active Christians. I was strictly an employee of the Master and Fellows. I was not a Fellow myself and had no academic role. My immediate boss was the Dean, who was a Fellow and a university lecturer. He was also Junior Bursar with control of the day-to-day running of the college. Joe Sanders was a very considerable scholar. He was an expert in New Testament studies and was writing a commentary on St John's Gospel which was going to flutter the dovecotes of the Theology faculty very considerably. Joe was a splendid figure. He was short, bearded and burly in stature. He could be described as an earthy country parson with a lot of brains. He was also a very good administrator and in argument he was extremely keen. Few of the other Fellows would lightly dispute with him. He would puff away at his pipe and if challenged about the health hazard of smoking he would growl, 'Well, you've got to die of something.' Another of his throw-away remarks at the time of an election was, 'Don't bother me with the facts, I've made up my mind!' I became very fond of Joe and his wife Dorothy and their three children. The eldest, Ruth, was a very clever girl and became a theologian like her father. She used to call me 'Charlie Chaplain'. Catharine, the youngest, became another of my god-daughters and Timothy became a pop musician after being a chorister in King's College choir.

The dons

Although Peterhouse was the smallest society in Cambridge its Fellows were among the most distinguished in the university. Paul Vellacott, the Master who appointed me, had died by the time I arrived and the college was presided over by the historian Herbert Butterfield. The new Master was a non-drinking Methodist. At table when it came to choosing a wine he would ask the nearest Fellow, 'What's the right thing to drink?' Then the high table butler would pour him out a half-pint of ginger beer in a silver beaker. Herbert Butterfield was a puckish person, a chain-smoker and something of an iconoclast. As a young Fellow of the college he had advocated selling the chapel to some institution in the United States. Besides being Master of Peterhouse, he was Professor of Modern History in the university. He had written a study of eighteenth-century English politics called *The Whig Interpretation of History*. This work had pioneered a fresh form of historical enquiry which became known as 'historiography'. This was the study of history and historians in relation to their ideological and cultural contexts. His mind was diamond-like and he had no tolerance for woolly ideas. But he was capable of great compassion, as I discovered when he became aware that I was very worried about my younger brother who was suffering from a bad bout of mental distress. The painter Ruskin Spear did a portrait of him while I was at Peterhouse which I thought captured him marvellously. It portrayed him as a little gnome-like figure, seated in a deep armchair, about to explode into laughter. Mrs Butterfield – and possibly some of the Fellows too – were horrified by it and it was not placed on public display.

History was Peterhouse's strongest academic suit, followed by engineering. In addition to Herbert Butterfield, we had three other history professors and at least four teaching Fellows in history. David Knowles, whose lectures I had attended when I was an undergraduate, was now the Regius Professor of History and a professorial Fellow. I have mentioned that he had been a monk of Downside Abbey, and was regarded with great curiosity both in the college and in the university at large. While I was at Peterhouse, he was completing his monumental work on the religious orders in Britain up to the time of the

Reformation. Denis Brogan, another of my undergraduate mentors, was the Professor of Political Thought, and Michael Postan occupied the Chair of Economic History. We also had a theological professor, Dr H. Farmer, and the Professor of Archaeology, Graham Clark. The Professor of Greek, Keith Guthrie, was one of our number until he became Master of Downing College. Among the scientists, Fellows and Honorary Fellows, there were two who became Nobel Prize winners, John Kendrew and Max Perutz. There was plenty of other distinction too among the total Fellowship of less than thirty.

Such company was rather intimidating for me, certainly to begin with. I once made the mistake of engaging one of the Fellows on an esoteric aspect of his subject, and found the conversation very difficult to sustain! But in general, the Fellows were very welcoming and kind to me. I discovered after a while that the staples of conversation, apart from current events, were investments and hi-fi equipment. Occasionally, however, there were really absorbing conversations. I remember listening in while some of the scientists discussed the possibility of there being life on other planets. And on another occasion I heard Denis Brogan enlarging on the French Algerian crisis. Denis used to complain that he could never forget anything. He certainly had an encyclopædic knowledge of both French and American affairs.

Soviet visitor

We had a constant succession of visiting scholars. There was a strong link between Peterhouse and the National University in Dublin. Quite a few of its leading historians had spent time at Peterhouse. I became friendly with several of these, including an Augustinian Friar, Fr Frank Martin, who was writing a thesis on his notorious sixteenth-century confrere, Martin Luther.

Another visitor who became a good friend was a Soviet historian, Victor Israelyan, who came to England just after Kruschev had denounced Stalin. No doubt the Foreign Office had a hand in his coming to Peterhouse. As far as we could see, there were no KGB restraints on him. He lived in college, moved about freely and accepted hospitality from all and sundry. I used to help him with some of the conundrums posed by English life in general and Cambridge life in particular.

Victor had a nice line in humour. He would look through the newspapers in the Combination Room and would murmur, 'What has my terrible country been doing to-day?' He was set upon by all the Marxist sympathisers in Cambridge, but seemed to have little affinity with them. Although he was a member of the Soviet Foreign Service as well as an academic, he was not really an ideologue. I learned that in the Soviet Union, all historical interest was in modern history, and history was a branch of foreign affairs. His purpose in coming to England was to research into 'Anglo-Russian Co-operation in the Second World War' – he would roll these words round his tongue in engaging self-mockery.

We made a number of expeditions together. I took him to choral Evensong in King's College Chapel – both the building and the singing impressed him enormously. He came with me when I went to Ardingly School in Sussex to preach at a Sunday evening service. The educational advantages of a boarding school made a strong impact upon him; and he was very taken, too, with the imposing middle-class residences in the vicinity of Ardingly. He wasn't at all put off by the fact that this was a glimpse of affluent and privileged England.

We went to the FA Cup Final. He was more admiring of the Royal Marines band than the actual football match. The standard of play he was used to in Russia was more than the finalists of that year could rise to. One day, I went with him to a curious dust-covered office near

Charing Cross in London where the organisation which had opposed the intervention by the Western Allies against the Bolsheviks in Russia in 1918/19 kept its archives. I don't know how germane that particular historical throw-back was to his research, but he came away with an armful of files.

I asked him to take part in two encounters. One was with the undergraduates of Peterhouse on something like 'The Soviet System'. The young men crowded into my sitting room in large numbers because the opportunity of engaging with a real live Russian was at that time un-precedented. We had a great time with the undergraduates attacking on a range of freedom issues. Victor, whose English was good but not perfect, answered their questions with considerable diplomatic skill and good humour and we all parted good friends.

The other encounter was at a pub in Greenwich in south-east London. During the Cambridge vacations, I was visiting several south London factories under the auspices of the South London Industrial Mission. One of them was G.A. Harvey's metal works at Greenwich where I had got to know some of the shop stewards and where, by a strange chance, the personnel manager, John Roberts, had been a classmate of mine at school. When I told the stewards about Victor, they were all very keen to meet him.

Victor knew next to nothing about industry or industrial relations but he agreed to come to Harvey's to please me. We met in a pub opposite the main gate of the factory. There were about ten stewards present, including Jack Berlin who was known to be a card-carrying Communist. John Roberts the personnel manager was also there – an eloquent testimony to the trust that the trade unionists had in him. Most of the stewards were honest-to-God working men who had grown up to think of Russia as the Promised Land. I was a small hero for giving them this chance of discussing the situation of the working class in the Soviet Union with an actual Russian citizen. When one of the

Harvey's lads asked Victor how they got on if there was a strike, Victor produced the bland reply, 'How can you strike against yourself?' The lads tried to conceive a situation in which there was only one side in industry and, of course, Victor had given a textbook rather than an existential answer. Jack Berlin saw the conversation as a propaganda opportunity towards his fellow stewards and he started to play 'in off the Russian' with such leading questions as 'Is it not a fact that …?' We drank quite a few pints and the stewards were well content with the meeting. It is poignant to contrast working-class fascination with the Soviet Union in the 1950s with the almost complete discrediting of the Communism system in the late 1980s.

Victor returned to Moscow after six months with a large crate of things he had acquired in England. He had invited me to visit him in Russia and in the following summer of 1958 I managed to scrape enough money together to do so. The visit proved to be a fascinating experience. I met his first wife Marina and his daughter Jane and visited his elderly parents in their *dacha*, or country retreat. Jane was a remarkable ten-year-old and with a little prompting she could tell me Russian folk tales in English. Victor took me to Zagorsk, the great fortress/monastery near Moscow and to the circus, the ballet and a football match. The whole experience was a huge mind-stretch. I began to apprehend the collective ideal which Russia seemed to embody and I tried to grapple with the spiritual prospects for the Russian people. The Russian Orthodox Church seemed to be an antique survival in the face of, at that time, a massively confident secular reality. I came away with two impressions of the Russian Orthodox Church. One was the deep cultural kinship that Orthodoxy had with the Russian people, so much so that all traditional Russian folk song seemed to be an echo of the Orthodox liturgy. I had the feeling that the singing in church, though the worshippers were few in number, was an effusion from the very soil of Russia. The other impression contrasted with this. It was my friend

Victor who took me to Zagorsk. I knew he would never have gone there except for my sake. I for my part saw Zagorsk partly through his eyes. When the country folk approached the bearded priests in their black robes and pill-box hats for blessings, he clearly recoiled from the whole proceeding. When I asked him in the car afterwards what he thought of Zagorsk, he said that for him it was all so 'uncultured'.

I pondered over the visit. Simply on the evidence of this glimpse of Russian religion, I doubted if the Orthodox Church would ever be able to re-evangelise the Russian people.

Peterhouse Chapel

I had arrived at Peterhouse at the start of the May term, 1955. My first set of rooms was at the top of the Burroughs building where the eighteenth-century poet, Thomas Gray, had 'kept'. (Residence at Cambridge is traditionally described as 'keeping terms' and one's place of residence is where one 'kept'.) Thomas Gray had two great phobias: one was drunken and aggressive neighbours and the other was fire. Gray had a bar fixed outside a window with a long length of rope attached so that he could escape in case of fire. There is a college legend that Gray's thuggish neighbours raised a hoax fire-alarm, whereupon Gray made a panic-stricken escape by means of his bar and rope straight into a butt of water that his persecutors had placed beneath his window. The legend maintains that Gray was disgusted with Peterhouse after this and migrated across the road to Pembroke. The bar, believed to be Gray's original, was still there during my occupancy. However, after just one term, I moved from the aura of Thomas Gray into the first floor of adjacent B staircase which was to be my home for the next five years.

Although I overlapped by just one term with the third-year people who were 'going down' in the summer of 1955, I tried to get to know as many of them as possible. The university mission of 1954 had had a considerable effect on a number of those who were about to leave. These men helped me to understand my job.

My first full year began in October 1955. I interviewed all the freshmen and then invited them to tea in twos and threes. These were useful first acquaintances and I gradually built up a picture of the student body. There were quite a few who were keen Christians, but there were all sorts of sub-groups among them. We had some Roman Catholics who gravitated towards Fisher House, the RC Chaplaincy centre, presided over by Monsignor Alfred Gilbey. The practising Anglicans, Methodists and Presbyterians resolved themselves into two main groups: the evangelically minded who tended to join the Cambridge University Christian Union, and the others, who were more liberal in outlook and were interested in Christian aspects of a wide range of secular affairs. Some of the latter joined the Student Christian Movement (the SCM). As a result of the 1954 mission, the Peterhouse Fellowship had been formed. This was basically an alliance of all those who attended the college chapel. There was a programme of talks and discussions each term in addition to the chapel services.

Each Sunday, we had Holy Communion at 8 a.m. which we sang to the Merbecke setting, and then choral Evensong at 6.30 p.m. between the two Hall sittings. Joe Sanders and I would alternate as celebrant and preacher in the mornings but we often had a visiting preacher in the evening. We had Robert Runcie one evening. He was then Dean of Trinity Hall and later, of course, he became Archbishop of Canterbury. He preached on Adonibezek in the Book of Judges who used to cut off the thumbs and great toes of his enemies. Eventually Adonibezek was defeated and suffered the same fate as he had meted out to others. His words were, 'As I have done to others, so it hath been requited unto me!' The preacher's point was that in the world at large you indeed get what is coming to you, but in the Christian dispensation, sinners, even thumb and great toe removers, can find forgiveness rather than retribution. It was a very entertaining sermon and went down very well with our young men.

I have precious memories of Peterhouse Chapel. At Evensong, the Senior Fellow, Roy Lubbock, would always read the Old Testament lesson and did so memorably. The Master, Herbert Butterfield, who always attended morning and evening, would generally take the second reading from the New Testament. The Dean was a most thoughtful and edifying preacher. I had my moments. I managed to catch the mood of the Suez crisis in Cambridge with a sermon on the text from the prophet Malachi, 'What does the Lord ask of you but to do justly, love mercy and walk humbly with your God.' There was a profound 'end of an era' sense in Cambridge at the time of Suez in 1956. We were close enough to the great events of the Second World War to think of Britain as one of the leading players on the international stage. At the same time there was an undeniable 'smell' about the whole Suez proceeding. On both patriotic and moral grounds, we all felt greatly diminished. My sermon tried to thread a way through these feelings.

It was my job to settle the Sunday liturgy in discussion with the organ scholar. We had a choir of undergraduates – all volunteers, though some received a small bursary for their services. One Advent we recruited some boy choristers for a carol service but rehearsing them proved such a hassle that we didn't repeat it.

We had our chapel high spots. A number of undergraduates became practising Christians while at the university and this sometimes entailed their being confirmed either in Peterhouse or in some other college. I negotiated with the Master about one such confirmation for which I proposed to invite the Bishop of Ely who was the college's official 'Visitor'. Herbert Butterfield was very happy for the bishop to come but he was very insistent that the Bishop should be absolutely clear that he was not exercising ecclesiastical jurisdiction in the college. All the mediæval colleges had taken great care to make themselves independent of the Bishop of Ely, and Herbert Butterfield was not going to allow the current bishop to 'lord it' in Peterhouse. I had to ask the Bishop not to bring his pastoral staff – the symbol of his jurisdiction. Of course, the Bishop had no such claims in his mind and was content simply to come and confirm two undergraduates.

I was Acting Dean for one academic year while Joe Sanders was away on sabbatical leave. During this year we had a mission in the college lasting two weeks. We had signed up Canon Joe Fison, who later became Bishop of Salisbury, and the Revd Ronald Spivey, a distinguished Methodist, as the missioners. It turned out to be a very good college effort. The majority of the undergraduates were not practising Christians and some were not Christians at all. But the college, and Cambridge in general, presented them with a great Christian tradition and a lot of our active Christians were very good advertisements for the faith. I made it my business to make friends with all our men and not simply those who came to chapel. In spite of some sectarian excesses, Christianity in Cambridge had a good reputation and exercised considerable influence. These were days when all the college chapels were thriving.

Our mission at Peterhouse was well conceived and well carried through. There was a twenty-minute gap between First Hall and Second Hall on weekdays and this was a peak time in the Sexcentenary Club. This was the college's Junior Common Room. It derived its name from the 600th anniversary of the college in 1884 and was inevitably known as 'the Sex Club'. The Club committee sounded out opinion in the college and then agreed that there could be a short talk and questions in the Sex Club during the interval between Halls by one of the missioners on each of five weekdays. The topics chosen were 'Faith', 'Hope', 'Love', 'Joy' and 'Peace'. These talks went down very well indeed and stimulated a lot of thought. In the course of the mission fortnight, active Christians got their friends together for coffee, tea or drinks and invited one of the missioners along. Altogether it was a good evangelistic enterprise. No one was arm-twisted or pressurised, but a large proportion of our men did make some sort of Christian encounter during the fortnight. All the events took place within the interchanges of college life; there were no special services or big meetings.

Religion in the university

It was otherwise with a special Billy Graham effort put on by the Cambridge University Christian Union in Great St Mary's, the university church, in 1956. The Christian Union movement in all British universities is very evangelical and some of its members are Protestant fundamentalist. The Billy Graham mission was preceded by a great deal of razzamatazz which had the effect of provoking a lot of scorn. What had this American evangelist to say in an ancient English university? However, it was remarkable how Billy Graham's preaching brushed aside a great deal of youthful scepticism. A lot of young men made 'decisions for Christ' during this mission. Some lived to regret them; for others, however, there was a lasting beneficial effect. Several of us college chaplains became concerned about the effect of powerful preaching on undergraduates with existing inner distresses. We didn't feel that Billy Graham's message was liberating for all; for some it was coals of fire on their heads. Such young men needed a lot of counselling afterwards.

Just before the Billy Graham mission, Mervyn Stockwood had become vicar of Great St Mary's following his very notable ministry in Bristol. Although he was outshone by Billy Graham on his arrival, Mervyn took centre-stage thereafter and a remarkable era of influence at Great St Mary's began. Sunday evenings at Great St Mary's

111

became a major university event. People like Aneurin Bevan, the radical Labour Minister of Health, would grace the pulpit, and there would be queues to get into the vast church.

Mervyn Stockwood was an inspired choice for Great St Mary's. Flamboyant, imaginative, very amusing and very kind, he was bound to go down well with undergraduates. He quickly became the standard bearer for Christianity throughout the university. He made friends with an astonishing range of people. I have mentioned in a previous chapter how he encouraged F.A. Simpson, the Trinity recluse, to come back to life. There was an agnostic don to whom he would send a Christmas card wishing him 'a happy winter solstice'. And while all his much publicised events were going on at Great St Mary's, Mervyn would quietly be visiting a retired college servant he had once known. From Cambridge he went on to be Bishop of Southwark and a number of Cambridge people went with him, including John Robinson. John had been Mervyn's curate in his Bristol parish before he became Chaplain at Wells Theological College where I first knew him. He was Dean of Clare College when Mervyn came to Great St Mary's and went with him to south London and became Bishop of Woolwich in 1959.

The Cambridge clergy of the 1950s were a very interesting body. Nearly all the colleges had an academic dean and a pastoral chaplain, though some deans were active pastorally and some chaplains had claims to scholarship. There was an alliance of chaplains which used to meet regularly with Professor Charlie Moule as our mentor. Some of us also formed a deans and chaplains 'gang of eight' and would meet to bounce ideas off one another and to engage in spiritual exercises which often had hilarious moments. Of that group, three became bishops and two became Roman Catholics!

Various intimidating tasks came my way. I had to preach before the assize judge on one occasion. This assignment entailed being part of a procession from the judge's official lodging in Trinity College to the university church, led by the university mace-bearer. In my sermon, I reminded his lordship that, like the centurion in the Gospels, he too was a man under authority. As far as I could tell, the judge took my invitation to humility in good part. I also had a turn as select preacher for the official Sunday afternoon sermon before the university at Great St Mary's. Attendance at this traditional event from Reformation times was once mandatory for all the office holders of the university. By the mid-twentieth century, only the Proctors with their constables maintained the tradition. If there were a couple of dozen others in the congregation, the preacher could be said to be 'a draw'. Sometimes the sermon was reproduced in *The Cambridge Review*. Mine wasn't, though a few people liked what I said.

The Peterhouse Commemoration of Benefactors was also a considerable challenge. The sermon had to be no more than ten minutes and it was preceded by a set bidding prayer which included a long list of benefactors. Without due care and attention, it was easy to mispronounce some of the names. I nearly came to grief with 'Lord and Lady Dewar'. I was about to make them rhyme with 'cigar' when I realised that the proper rhyme was with 'skewer'.

I became acquainted with Shaftesbury House at Royston, ten miles or so south of Cambridge. This was a residential school for maladjusted boys in the care of the Greater London Council. I accepted the task of giving these youngsters a weekly religious lesson. They were a turbulent lot and I don't know how much religion got through, but by stages I managed to form some sort of a relationship with them. The necessary grace was to understand the deep human need behind their delinquency. The visits to Shaftesbury were a bracing experience but they had the singular benefit of bringing me the friendship of the headmaster and his wife, Ike and Gwynneth Ingham. They were marvellous Anglican Christians. Years after, when they had retired to Cornwall, some of their former boys were still searching them out and coming to see them.

Summer schemes

There were various Christian enterprises in the summer which mobilised a large number of undergraduates. In line with my industrial mission interests in south London, I organised several industrial working parties of young men and women undergraduates who worked in factories for a fortnight and thus had a glimpse of working-class life. The influence of SLIM (South London Industrial Mission) and the reputation of Cambridge were sufficient to gain fifteen or more temporary jobs and I knew enough working-class families to be able to ask for lodgings for them. These working parties were an eye-opener for our Cambridge people. Even more important were the sympathies they discovered and the friendships they made. Some of the undergraduates who took part thought that these working parties were one of the most important 'life-lessons' they had gained during their undergraduate years.

Another Christian summer undertaking that I cherished was the Hopping Mission. Each September sixty or more undergraduates, again both men and women, volunteered to spend three of the four weeks of the hop-harvest in Kent with the Londoners who traditionally came to do the picking. Although this had always been a very warm and human encounter, it did have a slight hint of the 'conscience of the rich' about it. During the 1950s the social gap between the students and the Londoners narrowed greatly. This was partly due to a greater spirit of identification with one another and partly because the harvesting became mechanised. Of the three farms we were concerned with – all in the Goudhurst area – two installed machines which stripped the hop vines mechanically and turned the hopping into a process of machine tending. Our undergraduates signed up for the machines along with many of the Londoners, and after one has been a machine slave for a few hours – sitting beside a moving belt picking out leaves and stalks – the social differences between subjects of higher education and working-class Londoners began to evaporate.

To begin with, the machines handled only part of the crop and there were constant design modifications to make them more efficient. A large part of the harvesting continued in the traditional manner. The hops were stripped by hand into large bins which were set up in the hop gardens between the rows of vines. The London womenfolk were marvellously adept at stripping the vines. The family bins gradually moved up the rows as the picking progressed. Men with long hooks – the 'pole-pullers' – brought down the vines and draped them across the bins for the people to pick. The farmer's tally-men came round regularly to measure out the contents of the bins. As they did so, the women would 'fluff up' the hops with great arm movements to make their hops score better in the bushel measure. All this was the characteristic hopping scene. We missioners had a bin too, and although we did our picking we were nothing like as zealous and skilled as our London friends. We tended to use our bin as a base from which we could meet the people – we would spend a lot of time picking at their bins.

Eventually the machines were improved sufficiently to take over the picking completely and this signalled the death of the hopping, except for a few who still came from London for the money they could earn at the machines. Near the end, one of our farmers set up a single bin beside a machine for Mrs Jeffreys from Deptford to pick by hand. Mrs Jeffreys was an old lady by this time and it was a touching sight to see her there – a last survivor of a great London tradition. She had been hopping every September since she was a child and the farmer intended to accommodate her for as long as she still wanted to come.

The Hopping Mission always felt like a good human

and spiritual undertaking. Our Cambridge people developed a great appreciation of the Londoners and we became genuine friends. Some of our hopping pals used to come and see us in Cambridge and members of the mission used to visit some of the folks at their homes in London. During the hopping in Kent, we used to go in for overt evangelism. We had services and Sunday schools, we put on plays and we showed films. We also maintained a very disciplined spiritual life among ourselves which included a daily Eucharist. With a very early start, a full day's work and evening activities, one of our problems was exhaustion.

I had already experienced the spirit of Charles de Foucauld through Mary Every in Woolwich, who had come to identify with workers in Woolwich in the same way that Charles de Foucauld had identified with the Touareg people in the Sahara. As I learned more about the Jesus Caritas movement initiated by de Foucauld, I realised the extent to which our Hopping Mission approximated to some of its key values. There was an identification, albeit temporary, with the life of our London friends. There was friendship and appreciation alongside our specific evangelistic purpose. We took prayer seriously and we were poor. We lived as workers earning our living and having all things in common. Needless to say, we laughed a lot and we became almost like brothers and sisters. Years later, I became very involved in the Jesus Caritas movement and I always look back on the Hopping Mission as my first experience of its way of life. It was marvellous to be a priest among such young people. There were two of us who had this good fortune, myself and Murray Irvine, Chaplain of Sidney Sussex College. Professor Owen Chadwick, the Master of Selwyn College no less, used to visit the mission most years. He had been an enthusiastic hopper in former years.

One particular hopping incident is worth relating. On the biggest of our farms, a group of travelling families used to set up every year. While picking at our bin, I got a message that one of these families had some business to discuss. It turned out that a middle-aged couple with three children wanted to get married – could I couple them together properly before the hopping was over? I was very apprehensive because a clergyman I knew had appeared on the front page of the *Sunday Mirror* for conducting a wonky marriage! I established that there was just time to get the banns read for three consecutive Sundays in the village church and the vicar was willing for me to conduct the ceremony. I launched carefully into the pre-marriage enquiries, collected evidence of baptism and freedom to marry. The day came for the marriage. The bridal party left for the church in the bridegroom's lorry with me scuffing a horde of youngsters off the tailboard. It would have been mayhem if they had been let loose in the church. The marriage was duly solemnised with the bride and bridegroom's two daughters as bridesmaids, and afterwards we all repaired to the George and Dragon at Lamberhurst for the reception. The pints mounted up, and the final moment of glory came when the village policeman stepped into the bar at closing time to make sure that the party, including his reverence, drank up and went home.

High moments

My original engagement at Peterhouse was for three years but in 1958, when I was thirty-four, this was extended for a further two. During my final years, notable events took place in the college. An old alumnus, William Stone, died in 1958 aged a hundred and one. In the previous year, the college had laid on a special celebration to mark his hundredth birthday. He had intimated that he meant to make the college the chief beneficiary of his will. The benefaction proved to be one of the largest ever received by a Cambridge college and the ashes of the old gentleman were reposed in the college chapel. The Stone Building rose in a corner of the Scholars' Garden: this was a small tower block but big enough to accommodate eight Fellows and twenty-four undergraduates. In addition, further Fellowships were endowed. William Stone had never married. He had lived in Albany in Piccadilly for the greater part of his life. This was said to be the most exclusive block of flats in London and over the years he had acquired nearly the whole block. Indeed, Albany was the basis of his fortune. It is a poignant thought that in all his long life, nothing mattered to him more than his old college.

The years 1959/60 were a period of sensational achievement by some Peterhouse scientists. A special unit in the university was engaged in what was often referred to then as 'the Protein Study'. It was led by two Peterhouse scientists to whom I have already referred, John Kendrew and Max Perutz. Both were awarded the Nobel Prize for scientific achievement. The study was bent on establishing the structures of the myoglobin and haemoglobin molecules in blood. It became dubbed as an enquiry into 'the secret of life'. Related to this study was the research of James Watson and Francis Crick into the DNA molecule, 'the thread of life'. It was during these years that the great resolutions occurred. The teams engaged in the study had party after party to celebrate the latest success. Even at a distance, one could appreciate the unique excitement of these discoveries. It was all a splendid Cambridge experience.

Burdens of decision

For me, however, my final year at Peterhouse was a troubled time. The academic year 1959/60 started well because I was offered a Fellowship at Queens' if I would like to return to the college as Chaplain. It was a splendid compliment and a most tempting offer. Queens' realised, of course, that I was not a scholar and so would not have reason to stay in Cambridge for ever. But the role of Chaplain and Fellow would certainly have extended my time by several more years. I think I knew from the beginning that I would not be able to accept the invitation. By this time, I had formed the general intention of going back to south London when my Peterhouse engagement was over and working full-time in the Industrial Mission. I was one of those caught up in the euphoria of Mervyn Stockwood's appointment as Bishop of Southwark, though my south London affiliations, of course, went back much further.

However, my south London plans became problematical. The slot in the Industrial Mission that I had been asked to fit into seemed to put me back into the status of a curate and I was very loath to accept this. I don't think I ever regretted my decision not to go back to Queens', but I was singularly unattracted to the prospect of what faced me in south London. Eventually I resolved to grit my teeth and take up the Industrial Mission job. Life was further complicated by another attack of matrimonial longing. I was approaching thirty-six and Joe Sanders was recommending me to find a wife. I had lost Cita, of course; by this time she had married Adriano Milani. Soon I was in the position of pursuing somebody who didn't want me. My sad state was compounded by my being very worried about my brother Ian, who had come to a full stop with a nervous breakdown. Ian had gained an athletics Blue in his first year at Oxford, winning the long jump in the annual contest with Cambridge. He represented Great Britain in several international athletics meetings. With a Second in Greats, his academic form was also good. The whole gruesome contradiction between Ian's great talent and his inability to cope with life contributed to my dark night of the soul.

My last six months at Peterhouse were a period of cumulative depression. I had no relish for the future, yet I had made up my mind about it. Cambridge had given me a taste for position and success but now it was all slipping away from me. I had little prospect of marriage. For these months, as soon as I awoke in the mornings, a dark cloud descended on me. Nevertheless, I was still able to cope with my work and there were still things that I could enjoy. For one thing, I was due to go to America that summer and the prospect pleased me.

I gradually realised that more than my immediate future was at issue. It seemed that nothing that lay ahead could make me happy. Somehow, the thought of becoming a Roman Catholic re-emerged into my consciousness. I had entertained the idea before, as I have recounted, but this time it was insistent and immediate in a new way. At first I was aghast. The idea felt like a death wish. How could I set aside a ministry of ten years with all its precious relationships? How in particular could I disappoint the Dean of Peterhouse and all the undergraduates who trusted me? Surely I was deceiving myself. This was simply a way of avoiding a job in south London that I didn't want to do.

There were various concomitant considerations. One of the Fellows of Peterhouse, also an Anglican priest and a former dean, had defected to Rome just as I had come to the college. One of the Master's sons had also become a Roman Catholic. I knew what a bitter blow my demise to Rome would mean to Joe Sanders whom I regarded as a dear friend. I nursed all these dire thoughts in solitude. I did talk to two former 'convert clergymen' I knew in Cambridge and they tried to counsel me. But their approaches to the issues were so different from mine that I couldn't gain a line of action from them. I read a great deal. Alex Vidler's book on Lamennais, the French Catholic philosopher of early nineteenth century, interested me enormously. I also discovered the writings of Yves Congar, the French Dominican theologian.

My head was moving steadily away from Anglicanism but I was still gripped by its culture and relationships. My study of Catholicism was now a desperate bid for life. It still seemed as if there was a great chasm to leap across. One specific thing that held me back was the Catholic understanding of the priesthood. I could not easily relate to the men in black suits that I saw flitting around Cambridge, nor could I understand the priesthood as a kind of caste. It was Congar's book on the laity that turned this corner for me. He showed me the difference between the lay and the ministerial vocations in the Church and helped me to come to terms with the 'sacerdotal' aspect of the priesthood. I still didn't like it but I understood it better.

All this turmoil was going on in my mind and heart as I was preparing to leave Peterhouse that summer. My declared intention was still to take up my role in the Industrial Mission in south London. The undergraduates were having a collection to give me a parting gift and were naturally interested in my next move. My hope was that I could avoid a disclosure until after they had all gone down for the long vacation. Then by the following October, my demise would be months in the past.

But I still couldn't make up my mind. I went through the closing events of the May term almost in a trance. Eventually, it became sufficiently clear that I was never going to get to the job in south London. My Anglicanism had died and the only hope I had was the Roman Catholic Church. It was now the thing I believed in. I went to see Canon Colin Cuttell, the head of the South London Industrial Mission, to tell him that I wouldn't be joining the Industrial Mission that summer. That disclosure was bad enough. My breaking of the news to Joe Sanders was excruciating. Other friends had to be told. Some were understanding, others were critical. I wrote to my mother and had a marvellously supportive reply. Nearly all the undergraduates were away by this time, so I had no call to announce my intentions to them. The Master was sympathetic but businesslike. I was paid up to the end of August, but I was deemed to have finished my engagement in June. My first step towards Rome was to go and see the head man of the Dominicans in Cambridge, Fr Arthur Gilbey OP (not to be confused with Monsignor Alfred Gilbey, the university Catholic chaplain), and it was agreed that I would begin the transition in London.

I spent some time preparing records for my successor

who had already been appointed. Two of my sisters and a brother-in-law came to help me pack up my things. I left Cambridge with a heavy heart, almost by stealth, and I was exhausted. My great good fortune was to be going to America within a few weeks. Having declared my intentions to everyone who needed to be told, I found the prospect of leaving the problems behind for three months a blessed relief.

6
Rome

My 1960 visit to the United States (the first of two) is a separate story. I was at Harvard University for six weeks during its summer vacation, taking part in an international seminar run by Henry A. Kissinger, who was then a professor of political thought at Harvard with the signs of his subsequent world fame just beginning to show. Both the seminar and the opportunity to experience the United States were a marvellous boon to me.

I returned to England after a total absence of three months to a very bleak prospect. I had no job, no income, no home. I managed to survive because my youngest sister Betty and her husband Peter took me into their north London home. After several attempts to break into journalism, I eventually found work as a supply teacher. My second teaching job was particularly worthwhile. I worked for nearly a year at Forest Hill Comprehensive School, one of the two earliest comprehensives in south London, and found it a fascinating window on the world.

During this time, I had applied to the Catholic archdiocese of Southwark as a candidate for the Catholic priesthood. Once again my lack of a right arm proved a problem, but I was grateful to the Archbishop of that time, Monsignor Cyril Cowderoy, for taking up my cause and obtaining a dispensation from the Vatican for me to go ahead. He also secured me a place at the Beda College in Rome where I was to do my 'conversion course'.

I arrived in Rome in October 1962 just as the Second Vatican Council was starting. One of my first excursions from the Beda College was to St Peter's Square to see the long line of bishops from all over the world ceremonially entering the great basilica on the day of the Council's opening. They were all robed and mitred and Pope John XXIII came at the end, borne aloft on the *sedia gestatoria*, the great papal throne which is reminiscent of the pomp and glory of Imperial Rome. He was escorted by cohorts of the Swiss Guard, resplendent in their blue, yellow and red uniforms originally designed by Michelangelo. This was a most striking introduction to the majesty of the Catholic Church. I was to see many more papal ceremonies, including a number of ceremonies of canonisation. Some residual Protestantism lurking in my breast reacted initially against such manifest 'popery', but by stages I came to *feel* as well as to *believe* that these were evidences of the innate splendour of the Church. I felt that I really had discovered the Church as a divine reality as well as something all too human, and these great ceremonies were a celebration of it. This came home to me acutely during the first canonisation that I attended – it was that of St Vincent Pallotti. I realised that with all the pomp and circumstance – the great banner depicting the saint hanging in front of St Peter's, the dressed pillars inside, the Palatine Guards with their guns lining the nave (this was a shock!), the music and the pageantry – the Church was rejoicing in its real treasure, which is holiness of life.

The Second Vatican Council

In coming to Rome to begin my conversion course, I was scarcely aware that such a momentous event as the Council was about to take place. It continued until December 1965 so it was the background to nearly all my four years at the Beda College. Moreover, a number of the English bishops lived at the college during the Council sessions. This circumstance was enough to make us students feel witnesses to history. More particularly, our philosophy teacher, Fr (later Canon) W.A. Purdy, covered the Council for *The Tablet*, the English-language Catholic weekly review published in London. W.A. Purdy was highly knowledgeable about the Vatican and an acute observer of all that went on during the Council sessions and behind the scenes. He was closely associated with the *Times* correspondent, Peter Nichols, and together they were able to transform the way that the Council secretariat was proposing to deal with the media. I had many conversations with W.A. Purdy about the great Council themes, notably the vexed question of freedom of conscience and about the contents of the famous *schema tredici* which eventually became '*Gaudium et Spes*', *The Pastoral Constitution of the Church in the Modern World*. This document and '*Lumen Gentium*', *The Dogmatic Constitution of the Church*, were the two great fruits of the Council. '*Lumen Gentium*' gave a marvellous vision of the nature of the Church; '*Gaudium et Spes*' charted the relationship of the Church to the secular order.

Purdy wrote a very good book about the Council, *Church on the Move*, showing how Pope John's spirit of *aggiorniamento* changed the climate of the Church's thinking and feeling. He demonstrated too that all the Council's reforms were rooted in developments that were already taking shape in the Church before the Council was called.

Each working day of the Council a coach arrived at the Beda College to take our contingent of the English and Welsh hierarchy to St Peter's. The Council Fathers, as the bishops were properly called, converged on St Peter's from religious houses all over Rome. The rest of the bishops of England and Wales were lodged at the English College, the Venerabile, in downtown Rome, where many of them had been students in their youth. The huge nave of St Peter's was lined with tiers of seats for the 2,500 bishops who took part. There were places for auditors – some of them Catholic lay people, others clergy of non-Catholic denominations who had been specially invited. And there were the *periti* – theologians and other advisors of national hierarchies or individual bishops. The language of the plenary sessions was Latin. A lot of the bishops needed help with that. It is said that when one of the American cardinals was told that all the speeches would be in Latin, he offered to install simultaneous translation equipment at his own expense – or, rather, that of his diocese! When informed that this could not be, he asked Pope John's leave to go home!

Considering the huge number of Council Fathers and the kaleidoscope of races, cultures and ecclesiastical traditions that they represented, it is amazing how cohesive the Council quickly became. Of course, there was a great deal of mystification on the part of many individual bishops and moments of general disarray. The Fathers, however, did sort themselves out into working groups, language groups and study groups. This could only have been achieved so quickly because there was a great common determination that the Council should succeed. The Fathers were soon grappling with the substantive business of the Council. They moved quickly into considerations of the Liturgy, closely followed by 'schemas' on the 'Sources of Revelation' and 'Ecumenism'. For all the bishops, these early sessions and the numerous encounters that went with them were enormously educative. European bishops could be forgiven for supposing that they were the hub of the Church, but the North Americans quickly made a huge impact as did the bishops of the Third World. 'Catholicity' took on a very profound meaning. Some of the English bishops gave clear indications of a broadening of mind even to students at the Beda College. They would often come and chat with us after the evening meal. I remember one bishop, knowing that I was a former Anglican priest, revealing how disorientating he found the ecumenical discussions!

By stages, Council celebrities emerged and acquired labels. Cardinal Ottaviani was deemed to be the archconservative, though there were many who were well to the right of him. He was an endearing figure, however, because he was manifestly a 'man of the people' – indeed, he was a product of Trastevere, a working-class district of Rome which had a fascinating history and a tremendous communal personality. Archbishop Thomas Roberts, an Englishman, a Jesuit and a former Archbishop of Bombay, was one of the most prominent liberals. He was not an accredited Council Father because he had resigned his diocese in India to make way for an Indian successor and he was not given leave to speak at a plenary session. Nevertheless, he raised his voice in Rome on a number of issues including ecumenism and birth control. He was admired by many and denigrated by some. Our own Cardinal Heenan had a moment of prominence: he sponsored and presided at a lecture given by another English Jesuit, Fr Francis Clark, which proved to be an indictment of Anglican deficiencies in Eucharistic doctrine and a discouragement of ecumenical enthusiasm. The lecture was a great attraction for the seminarians of Rome and hundreds of us crowded into the largest *aula*, or hall, at the Vatican. But it was generally judged to be a disappointment. The lecturer had nothing positive to say and he was clearly out of harmony with the spirit of the Council. The occasion, not very significant in itself, was something of a commentary on the early mind-set of the English bishops. This changed as the Council progressed.

I was in Naples, taking a Whitsun break from Rome, when Pope John died. Immediately death notices and black palls went up all over the city and there was manifest mourning on the part of ordinary people. Back in Rome, I went to his lying-in-state at St Peter's with my friend Dan Williams from the Beda College. It was poignant to see him laid out on the ornate bier as unending lines of people filed past. He was still discernible as a little round figure and, though arrayed in magnificent papal robes, he still looked like a humble servant of God. He had brought the Church to the Second Vatican Council and had opened a hugely important chapter in the life of the Church. Pope Paul VI would succeed him and take the Council through to its conclusion in December 1965. It was also to be the unenviable lot of Pope Paul to cope with the negative fall-out from the Council.

Vatican II lasted very much longer than most of the bishops expected. The first phase, until December 1962, was a time of tremendous excitement and expectation. In the ensuing years, the Council settled down to a steady grind, punctuated by the promulgation of successive epoch-making enactments, with impressive ceremonies in St Peter's to inaugurate them. As I had seen Pope John open the Council in 1962, so I saw Pope Paul close it at the end of 1965. It was marvellous to have been in Rome for the whole period. I had joined the Catholic Church when it seemed very much a sub-culture in the English context, and a foreign one at that. The Catholicism of the Council was an all-embracing reality. And with a vernacular liturgy, the Bible restored and fresh respect for freedom of conscience, it all began to feel much more like the Anglicanism I had left behind. This did not dismay me one little bit. This sort of Catholicism looked as if it really could enter the mainstream of English life.

An event took place at the Council which was to have a bearing on my future Catholic ministry, although I was to hear about it only subsequently. The Council Fathers decided that they would like to give some of the lay auditors an opportunity to address the Council in plenary session. The first to be asked to speak was Patrick Keegan from England. He had been first the leader of the Young Christian Workers (YCW) in England and Wales and then the leader of the world-wide Young Christian Worker movement which was known in the French-speaking world as the Jeunesse Ouvrière Chrétienne, or JOC. Keegan, among the foremost of the Church's lay apostles, suggested to the assembled bishops that there was an apostolate that belonged to lay people as of right, simply by virtue of their baptism and confirmation. While it had to be exercised in collaboration with the Church's hierarchy, it was not to be thought of as a privilege conceded by bishops and priests. The speech made a very powerful impression. The evidence behind the speech was the great corps of apostolic men and women that the YCW/JOC was creating among working youth throughout Europe and beyond.

I was told that I ought to meet Pat while he was in Rome. I did so early in 1966 and invited him to come to the first Mass I was to celebrate as a Catholic priest and to the lunch party afterwards. Pat was moved to make a speech at the lunch and declared that I should come and be 'our priest'. Seven years later this very thing happened. In 1973, after two parochial appointments, I became national chaplain of the YCW in England and Wales. Pat was head of the adult development of the YCW, the Family and Social Action Movement, whose offices were in the same building as the YCW at 106 Clapham Road in south London. We were in constant contact with one another for the following five years.

The Beda College

Although there was a narrowness to the English Catholic outlook at the start of the Council, pre-Conciliar English Catholicism had the vitality and ruggedness of a fighting minority church. The generality of English Catholics, whether from the minor aristocracy, the professional bourgeoisie or the working class, were from the same mould as the sixteenth- and seventeenth-century martyrs. The student body of the Beda College reflected the Catholic community of England and Wales in both its virtues and its limitations.

The Pontifical Beda College was founded in the latter part of the nineteenth century to train 'late vocations' for the Catholic priesthood. There was reason to think that there might be many 'convert clergymen' coming from the

Church of England's Oxford Movement and there were in any case a growing number of men from other avocations who were offering themselves for ordination in their middle years. The numbers of former Anglican and other clergy seeking the Catholic priesthood never amounted to a flood, though there was to be a considerable surge in the 1990s when the Church of England decided to ordain women priests. During my time at the Beda, there were about eight former clergy, including an American Episcopalian and a Welsh Baptist. Other previous avocations included the armed forces, the law and teaching, and there were a fair number who would have described themselves proudly as 'British working class'. Most of the students were British by birth but we had strong contingents of Americans, Irish and Australians and representatives of other Commonwealth countries in a total student body of around seventy. There were a few 'foreigners' but they were all due to be ordained for an English-speaking country. Most of the staff were from England but we had a Dutch Dominican who lectured us engagingly on the Old Testament and an Irish Dominican who gave us learned lectures on the New. In age, we spanned the late twenties to the early sixties. I was thirty-eight when I began.

My particular friend at the Beda was Dan Williams. He had been a Baptist minister in South Wales and he and I shared a lot of reactions to the life of the college and to Rome in general. We had to deck ourselves out in cassocks and shovel hats and neither of us felt the part. In fact we began to describe ourselves as a couple of strangers in paradise. Dan had had a far greater cultural distance to travel than I, and I always marvelled at the integrity and determination that his conversion to Catholicism signified. On one occasion, we walked through the centre of Rome together in our cassocks and carrying our hats with Dan expounding the Catholic doctrine of Purgatory, which had hit him with all the force of revelation. On another occasion, we both underwent the Blessing of St Blaise – the saint who specialises in sore throats – with neither of us knowing what it meant. We queued up in the chapel with the rest of the men, knelt down at the altar rail and someone placed a couple of candles against our necks. Dan lingered outside the chapel for me afterwards and in his rich Welsh accent said, 'What did you make of that?'

The Beda ethos

Ecumenical enlightenment was slow to dawn at the Beda College. We had a maverick canon law lecturer who used to refer to the then Archbishop of Canterbury as 'Mr Ramsey'. On the part of the students, scarcely any recognition was given to those of us who had previous ministries. As far as the Beda College was concerned, all of us who had been ordained in other communions were laymen like the ex-soldiers, solicitors and schoolmasters. Many of these, it was true, were marvellous Christians and very good examples for such as me. But I was never reconciled to this non-recognition of my Anglican ministry and it soured my attitude to the college for most of my time there. The Rector, Monsignor Jeremiah Curtin, and I were wary of each other for most of my Beda career, but we both belonged to the Southwark diocese and when we were back in England we became good friends and, eventually, fellow canons in the Southwark Cathedral Chapter.

Some of us were sporty. There was a keen quoits school on the little court at the back of the building which had originally been set up for volleyball. I ran a football team which used to compete on unequal terms with the younger fellows in other colleges. We had a home ground opposite the Beda on a dust patch belonging to the local St Paul's youth club. I made friends with a splendidly gnarled Italian priest called Padre Libero; he exercised a benevolent tyranny over a small army of boys who crowded into the St Paul's centre throughout the week. In a confiding moment, Padre

Libero showed me a picture he had been given which he thought might be a Titian. It was quite a small canvas, the subject was the woman taken in adultery, and it certainly had the honey-coloured look of a Titian painting. He asked me if I could take it to London and get it auctioned so that he could use the money to build more workshops for the boys! I had to point out gently that the Italian authorities were very unlikely to allow the export of a painting by Titian, if indeed it was a Titian. He agreed that I should get the painting evaluated in Rome. With the help of some people I knew, I was able to take the painting to a lady who was an expert in such matters. She decided that it was certainly a Venetian painting of Titian's time but it was not the work of Titian and the drawing and brush-work made it of limited value. When I told Padre Libero that the lady thought it worth just the lire equivalent of £500, he wanted to give it to me!

We also played cricket. The Rome Cricket League used to consist of the Beda College, the English College, the British Embassy (for whom an Indian Ambassador sometimes played!), the Australian Embassy, the Imperial War Graves Commission and, at times, the Food and Agricultural Organisation of the United Nations (FAO) could field a side. We used to play each other on a concrete slab with a matting surface in the grounds of the Villa Doria Pamphilj, owned by one of the most ancient and illustrious families of Rome which by the 1960s had become three-quarters British. Donna Orietta was the daughter of Don Andrea Doria Pamphilj and his Scottish wife (both deceased) and in the 1950s she had married a British naval officer who was always known in the British community as Don Frank. He and Donna Orietta were the epitome of Britishness in Rome. Don Frank was naturally President of the Rome Cricket League.

We used to have very amiable contests at the Villa. The English College and the Australians used to vie with each other for the top honours each season, but the Beda team was sometimes formidable. We used to field some young Oblates of Mary Immaculate, several of them Sri Lankans, who were skilled enough to confound any opposition if they were all available at the same time. I gained a brief renown playing the Australians one Sunday afternoon. I was fielding near the long-off boundary when the star Aussie batsman, Ken Gillard, took a huge swipe at a loose ball. It came straight at me in a very low trajectory. I scarcely had a chance to get out of the way. Without moving my feet, I managed to pluck the ball out of the air and hold the catch. I was acclaimed by friend and foe alike.

The school of Barbiana

I was falling in love with Italy and the Italian people. We always had a week or so off after Christmas, Easter and Whitsun and these were chances to travel further afield. Amalfi was one of the places where several of us spent one such holiday. This was a magical place not very far from Naples with a remarkable maritime history. On another occasion a group of us went to Assisi, but more often than not I travelled on my own. In this way, I saw Pisa, Bologna, Ravenna, Padua, Verona and Lake Garda. I also paid another visit to Venice in company with my Blackheath friend Benedicta Whistler and her mother. I went to Florence several times and called on Cita, my former fiancée, and her husband Adriano Milani and their two small daughters Valeria and Flavia. It was on one of these visits to Florence during my last post-Christmas break in Italy that I first went to Barbiana.

Cita's husband Adriano had told me about his brother Don Lorenzo who was a priest of the Florence diocese. I gathered from Adriano and Cita that Don Lorenzo was a very gifted but very controversial priest. During my visit to Florence after the Christmas of 1965, Adriano volunteered to take me to meet him in his parish of Barbiana, a remote village in the Mugello Valley, north of Florence, where Don Lorenzo ran a remarkable school. Adriano drove me to Barbiano one evening with his two small daughters who went to sleep on the way, curled up like puppies on the back seat of the car. We drove into the hills on very bumpy roads and the last bit – the actual approach to the parish house – was a precipitous track round the side of a little dip actually constructed by Lorenzo and the boys of his school.

As we arrived, a number of boys issued from the house and greeted Adriano. They picked up the two girls, put them on their shoulders and carried them into the house, with Adriano and me following on behind. We had arrived in the midst of a discussion. Don Lorenzo presided over the proceedings dressed in his cassock. The room was filled with young people, most of them boys aged from eight to eighteen. Also taking part were the parents of two of the youngsters who lived in part of the parish complex and farmed the land. *Nonna* (Grandmama) was there, likewise Adele, who was a school teacher from a nearby town who helped Lorenzo with the school whenever she was free. Also part of the circle was Eda the cook who had come with Lorenzo from his previous parish.

When there was a break in the discussion, Lorenzo turned to his brother and with a glance in my direction said, 'Who's he?' Adriano explained that I was from England and was learning to be a Catholic priest in Rome having previously been an Anglican one. 'Why did you change?' was Lorenzo's immediate question. In halting Italian I began to try and explain the great issue of my life. He interrupted me – 'You can speak in English,' he said, 'most of the children know enough English to understand you.' This was shock number one – the fact that these boys and girls in a rural corner of Tuscany could handle English. It was also my introduction to the learning process at Barbiana. Lorenzo would conduct discussions on complex matters of politics, religion, morality, literature and other subjects and each youngster would be expected to participate.

Before Adriano took me away that evening, Lorenzo invited me to come again. Evidently he had judged me to be *simpatico*. The next opportunity was the Easter holiday of 1966 by which time I was ordained a Catholic priest. I went again at Whitsun. On the first occasion I took with me an English poet friend from Rome but for Lorenzo he proved to be the opposite of *simpatico*. Lorenzo did not like him and made little effort to hide the fact.

At my Easter visit, I was able to take in the beauty of Barbiana. The parish plant – the church, the parish house and the farm buildings – was located on a spur in the Apennines with magnificent views on three sides. It was beautiful beyond words and in the few moments of solitude I was able to steal at Barbiana I would sit in the shade of an olive tree and feast my eyes on the hills and the valley below. All around were scattered farmsteads, some of them derelict. Those farmers who persisted scraped a living out of vines and olives and a few animals. But the adjacent farms were important to the school of Barbiana because they were lodgings for Lorenzo's pupils. Every morning at about 8 a.m., the children would converge by farm tracks on to the parish house and school would begin. From then on, it would be purposeful activity until between 6 and 7 p.m. There would be a great variety of lessons, lots of learning in groups, sometimes under the guidance of an older pupil, and there would be plenary sessions run by Lorenzo. Adele would come as soon as she was free from her school in the valley and she would always be there on holidays, of which there are very many in Italy.

Don Lorenzo

Lorenzo had leukæmia and was really a very sick man. He conducted most of his classes from his bed but this was the only concession he made to his failing strength. He behaved like a man with a great deal to do and too little time to do it. He was a great critic of Italian education. He had no patience with the standard regimentation of children in Italian schools and the learning by rote which was still normal at that time. The school of Barbiana was genuinely a process of 'education' – a drawing out of understanding from within his pupils. Teaching was an invitation to which youngsters responded with their own individual hearts and minds. Lorenzo himself was a heaven-born teacher. He could make everything interesting. Issues and problems were pursued at remarkable depth. Each afternoon he would gather all the youngsters around his bed and he would take them through a daily newspaper, discussing the religious, political or social implications of a number of items. Sunday morning Mass was prepared in similar fashion. The youngsters would study the Gospel of the day with copies of the Synoptic Gospels in parallel columns before them. Lorenzo would lead a discussion on the meaning of the Gospel. Some of the youngsters' comments were amazing.

One of the older boys had been to England and had stayed with a Baptist family in Essex. When it was time for him to return to Italy, the family gave a farewell party for him which included some hymn singing. The party was recorded on a tape which the boy in question played for my benefit and as the strains of 'Jesu, Lover of my Soul' came over, I murmured, 'What a lovely old Protestant hymn!' Lorenzo came back at me at once, 'Why Protestant?' I enlarged on the Reformation doctrines contained in the hymn – the sense of the total wretchedness of human nature and the desperation of man's upward reach to God. There ensued a remarkable discussion with all the youngsters joining in about the difference between Protestant and Catholic understandings of salvation. The conversation would have given credit to any group of seminarians.

My role at Barbiana was to give English lessons to a group of three sixteen-year-olds which included Eduoardo, whose family lived in Milan, and Carla, whose parents farmed the parish land. The four of us would find a little spot in the fields and talk about absolutely anything. Lorenzo had taken them through George Orwell's *Animal Farm* and Carla was particularly taken with the chorus 'Beasts of England' which she pronounced 'Bits of England'. They were very interested in what I could tell them about the life of young people in Britain. When I returned to London that summer, I took Eduoardo back with me at Lorenzo's request. I found him lodgings and a job and saw quite a lot of him during his six months' stay. He joined the Young Christian Workers group I started in the Brixton parish where I was working. This was the nearest approximation I could offer him to the values of Barbiana. Carla came to London a little while afterwards and I fixed her up with a family in north London in which the mother was Italian. Alas, Carla never settled and I had to arrange for her to go home as a matter of urgency.

Don Lorenzo had acquired a national reputation by the time I discovered Barbiana. He was known by unfriendly people as a *prete rosso* or red priest. The label was quite unjustified. He certainly identified with working people and was a fierce critic of a number of Italy's leading politicians, including many of the Christo-Democrats. He also had a bad relationship with the Cardinal Archbishop of Florence at that time. But he had a great reverence for Pope Paul who sent him money for the school and special medicines for his leukæmia. There were some politicians whom he trusted – Signor La Pirra, a mayor of Florence, was one. He would come and visit Lorenzo at Barbiana.

Some notoriety attached itself to Lorenzo because of his tilts at the establishments of Church and State. While he was serving in an urban parish, he wrote a book called *Pastoral Experience* which was an exposure of certain unreformed aspects of Italian church life. When he was told that the Vatican was not pleased with the book he dutifully withdrew it. During the Second Vatican Council discussions about freedom of conscience, the Tuscan military chaplains issued a statement to the effect that young men had a duty to accept military service and that those who pleaded conscientious objection were cowards. Lorenzo discussed this issue at great length with the children of Barbiana and the result was an open letter to the military chaplains denouncing Italy's involvement in a whole series of meaningless wars. The letter was sent to all the newspapers in Florence but only the Communist one printed it. Lorenzo had to answer a civil charge of subverting the allegiance of military personnel. The force of the charge, however, was somewhat blunted because the Second Vatican Council was showing evident signs of upholding the principle of freedom of conscience, including the right of conscientious objection from military service. The matter was still unresolved when Lorenzo died in 1967.

At my second stay at Barbiana, Lorenzo had a little over a year to live. During my visits, he conducted nearly all his business and teaching from his bed. The scene was quite unforgettable. He would be propped up on a pile of pillows always wearing his black soutane. The children would gather round for the discussions and Marcello, the youngest who was also a retarded boy, would lie at the foot of the bed. There would be great animation throughout the discussion; Lorenzo would be highly involved even as he engaged with young immature minds. He was exhausted after these sessions and would lie back for a while to recover. When school was over for the day, Eda would produce a meal for all who were in residence in the parish house. She was devoted to Lorenzo and he delighted in her pithy unsentimental remarks. On one occasion, Eda stirred up a large bowl of pasta and pushed it into the middle of the table, saying in Italian something which might translate into English as 'part this among you', a rather gracious expression. Lorenzo was delighted with Eda's remark. He turned to me and said, 'Only three people could say what Eda has just said – one, Eda herself, two, the Professor of Italian at Florence University, and three, Dante!'

After supper, Lorenzo and I would often chat over a brandy. He was always kind enough to speak English for my benefit. I learned a considerable amount about him during these conversations. He had been a student of fine art as a young man and his decision to enter the seminary had been a great surprise for all his family and friends. But as a priest, he valued painting only as an aid in teaching. He had been deeply hurt by the distrust his archbishop showed towards him. He must have been one of the ablest priests in the archdiocese – even in Italy – but here he was exiled into a country parish with scarcely a congregation to look after apart from his children and the few adults in the attached farmhouse. In his lifetime, Lorenzo was known and admired by some of the choicest people of Italy; his posthumous reputation has been huge. Books have been written about him and films made. Although he was denigrated by right-wing politicians and churchmen as a red priest, Lorenzo was never a crypto-Communist. His Christian motivation was far too deep. His particular kind of ministry among working people effectively stood Communism on its head. He showed that there was a Christian motivation for working people that was more human, more thoroughgoing and more persevering than that displayed by most Communist politicians.

The ultimate testimony to the school of Barbiana was published shortly after Lorenzo's death in 1967. Eduoardo, back in Italy from his stay in London, was among the youngsters who kept vigil at Lorenzo's bedside as he lay dying. He and others composed their tribute to Lorenzo and the school of Barbiana in *A Letter to a Lady Teacher* (*Lettura alla Professorezza*). Many years later, I revisited Barbiana and was again uplifted by its beauty. Lorenzo lies in the little walled graveyard with Nonna, Clara's grandmother, beside him. The house and church were locked but looked otherwise in good order. The whole place for me was peopled with ghosts. I could visualise my English class chatting under an olive tree. There was the pergola by the side of the house where the boys and girls used to eat their lunch. It wanted just a little imagination to see them all again. And I found the small piscina which the boys had made for bathing. I once asked Carla if she ever went for a swim in it. She answered me with utter finality, 'I am a girl'!

Ordination

As my ordination to the priesthood approached, I became increasingly disturbed by the prospect of being Catholicly ordained without any account being taken of my Anglican ministry. I have mentioned previously that the regime at the Beda College gave no recognition of previous ministries. Other former clergy seemed not to be bothered by this. Some were simply content that they would now be receiving 'valid orders'. I was asked by some whom I consulted whether I wanted to be 'conditionally' ordained. I did not – I had no conviction that my Anglican orders might be the equivalent of Catholic orders. What I did want was a formula that would recognise the value of my previous Anglican ministry. I was looking for a form of words such as: 'In fulfilment of the ministry that you have already exercised, I ordain you ...' I felt sufficiently strongly about this to raise the question at the Secretariat for Christian Unity, the new department at the Vatican devoted to ecumenical matters. The priest I saw referred the matter to Cardinal Willebrands, then head of the Secretariat, and he was generous enough to give me an interview. The Cardinal proved to be very sympathetic. He even allowed that the matter might one day be taken up on the lines I was suggesting. But in the meantime, he thought it right for me to go ahead and be ordained a Catholic priest without qualification. Thinking forward to the 1990s and the considerable numbers of Anglican clergy who came into the Catholic Church over the issue of women priests, I am very happy that this principle of recognition was adopted in the Catholic Church. There were clear statements that

Anglican clergy do not come empty-handed and those receiving Catholic ordination would have their previous ministries fulfilled and not repudiated.

So I moved forward to my Catholic ordination. The ceremony was to take place in the Basilica of St Paul's Outside the Walls on Saturday, 26 March 1966. Cardinal Cicognani, the Papal Secretary of State, was the ordaining prelate – he was the Cardinal Protector of the Beda College. My brother Ian came from London to support me and he performed the ceremony of binding up my hand which is the office of a close relative, generally a parent. Monsignor G.A. Tomlinson, Administrator of Westminster Cathedral, also paid me the great compliment of coming from London for the ceremonies. He was to be assistant priest at my First Mass the following day. The role of an assistant priest at a First Mass is to make sure that nothing goes wrong. It is customary to invite someone who has been an important mentor in one's approach to the priesthood. For my First Mass, I had asked for the hospitality of the Church of San Onofrio al Gianiculo because it was the Rome headquarters of the Franciscan Missionaries of the Atonement who had Anglican links in both Britain and America. Monsignor Tomlinson had been a very good friend to me in London. He was a former Anglican priest himself and had been a student at the Beda.

Various other friends came to the First Mass. I have related how Pat Keegan came to be there, and how at the lunch party afterwards he foreshadowed my future role in the Young Christian Workers movement. W.A. Purdy, philosophy teacher at the Beda and one of my encouragers, also came and made a gracious speech about me. There were a number of Beda friends present and also some from the English and the North American Colleges. The Rome cricketers were well represented and there were some other Rome friends, including Dorothy Hanson, an American lady who was a devoted member of her national church in Rome, Santa Suzanna. We had a merry lunch party afterwards at a very attractive restaurant called the Horti Galateae near the Porta San Sebastiano.

In my final weeks in Rome, a two-line letter from the Vicar-General of Southwark diocese came, appointing me the parish of Corpus Christi, Brixton Hill, in south London. The name Brixton immediately rang up the image of the prison, and indeed the Catholic chaplaincy of this was soon to be an important part of my job.

7

Brixton

I arrived in Brixton on 26 July 1966, the day that England beat Germany in the Football World Cup. I watched the match on the television and England's victory seemed an excellent omen.

In the parish of Corpus Christi, Brixton Hill, I was in the bosom of the Irish. It would be more accurate to say that we were an Anglo-Irish community, because there were a lot of native spouses and most of the children spoke with cockney accents. We also had quite a few converts to Catholicism. But the predominating mores were Irish. I found this entirely congenial: somehow I had developed a feeling for Ireland on the strength of one visit when I was an Anglican curate. My Irish friends at that time had all been members of the Church of Ireland and I had been able to observe Catholic Ireland only from the outside. I remember being vastly impressed when I popped into a Catholic church at the end of a Dublin bus route and observed some busmen saying their prayers before starting the next run. I had also enjoyed the company of a number of Irish fellow students at the Beda College.

In the late 1960s, however, the large congregation at Corpus Christi was scarcely a reflection of all the ethnic diversity of the district. Every third face in the streets outside was black but we had very few black families in the church on Sundays. There were a number of Polish, Maltese and Italian families and a few Goan and African ones. We also had a group of families who had come to Britain from Libya after the Second World War when Britain had control of that country. An elderly man of this small community used to pray devoutly in the church every day, making a tour of our numerous statues and always blowing kisses to the statue of Our Lady.

But Caribbean people, who abounded in the streets outside, were notable by their absence in church. The easy assumption was that very few of them were Catholics. This was decisively disproved by the fact that our Saturday morning catechism classes for children who weren't able to get into our Catholic primary school were full of children from Caribbean families. By this time, West Indian parents had despaired of getting their children into Catholic primary schools, but they still wanted them to be prepared for First Holy Communion and Confirmation. The paucity of black children in our day school was a classic instance of unconscious racism. Without there being a deliberate policy of exclusion (though there may have been an element of this), black children did not get into Catholic schools unless their parents made strenuous efforts to gain them places. There was massive over-subscription for Catholic schools in those days. In general, black parents did not know the processes of admission, especially the need to register a child's name shortly after birth. They also needed to get the endorsement of the parish priest and very often he did not know them. Once the eldest child had gone to a state school, it was certain that subsequent children would follow. The conclusion had to be drawn that Corpus Christi, like most other inner-city Catholic parishes of south London, was not ministering adequately to Caribbean Catholics. This had to be studied as a pressing pastoral problem.

My Irish induction

With such an Irish ethos in the parish, I had first to learn more about Ireland and the Irish. This came easily to me and it was not too long before I felt like an honorary

Irishman. People used to ask me, 'What part of Ireland do you come from, Father?' Michael Breen was one of those I became very fond of. I said something that he approved of one Sunday as he was driving me to Mass at one of our outstations and he exclaimed, 'Spoken like a Wexford man!' I took this as Michael's gift of honorary citizenship.

The parish priest at Corpus Christi was Fr Patrick Bailey, a Kerry man. What apprehensions he must have had about the new curate who was being foisted on him can only be imagined! He was acquiring a former Anglican priest of early middle age who was English and short of his right arm. Whatever his misgivings, he gave me a warm welcome. Later I discovered on a visit to one of our parishioners that she had in her flat a large statue of the Sacred Heart with one hand broken off. When I asked her about it, she told me shyly that the statue used to be in the sacristy at Corpus Christi but Fr Bailey, when he knew that I was coming, had asked her to take it away and hide it in case the sight of it would embarrass me. Later, Fr Bailey and I had lots of tussles but I don't think we ever lost respect and affection for one another. After a long tenure at Corpus Christi, he finished his days as parish priest at Blackfen on the margins of Kent. In September 1983, I drove three Corpus Christi parishioners to his funeral at Blackfen and we swapped stories about him all the way there and all the way back. We celebrated his life and his ministry with laughter and love.

My fellow curate was a young man called John Kiely, on loan from the Waterford diocese in Ireland. Fr John was a tall, slightly taciturn priest with a delightful and sometimes surprising turn of humour. Shortly after my arrival, he was showing me how to lock up the church at night. I was to look in the pulpit and all the confessional boxes (we had three) to make sure no vagrants had tucked themselves in for the night. Then he added without any change of tone, 'But if you see any of the little people, you're not to disturb them.' I blinked and looked at him in wonderment. This was my introduction to the lore of the leprechauns.

John Kiely also inducted me into our ministry in Brixton Prison. At this time, the Catholic chaplaincy to the prison was a parish responsibility and was mainly carried out by the curates. I duly ascended Brixton Hill to the prison with him one morning. We reported at the fearsome gates where, having been recognised and admitted, he drew a large bunch of keys reserved for 'the RC priest'. John showed me which key opened which gate and we did a tour of the wings. As we went round, he greeted various prison officers and a number of inmates. I marvelled at the innate authority that this young man showed in his relationships within the prison. He was in fact a shy man and yet he clearly had great certainty in his role as a priest. It was all the more remarkable because he came from a very rural part of Ireland where crime was almost unknown. 'Sure,' he told me confidingly, 'someone stole a watch in the next village a few years back.' This was his previous acquaintance with crime. In Brixton Prison, he was moving among men who were accused of the most hair-raising misdeeds.

Our work in the prison is a story on its own. John Kiely was recalled to his diocese in Ireland within a month of my arrival; I had rapid promotion to senior curate and immediately found myself the lead man in the prison. Other young priests came to us from the Waterford diocese which seemed to have forged a link with Brixton. Fr Charles Scanlon, John Kiely's successor, was another Waterford man. He too was very well trained and professional but he did not stay long. Fr Walter Walsh followed and he and I were together for most of my time at Corpus Christi. Walter was older than the other Waterford men, having been a technician in the Irish air force before becoming a priest. This made him very handy in managing parts of the parish plant. He was also very adventurous, building a catamaran by the side of the parish hall and sailing it from somewhere in Wales across to Waterford. One of his singular achievements in the parish was the creation of a youth club for black youth. He built the sound system himself and was forever constructing security cages under the stage to protect the gear from thieves. Alas, he laboured in vain – the club lost the lot at least twice!

I enjoyed the interplay with our Irish parishioners. Their humour and humanity appealed to me enormously and, of course, most Irish people love the Church and would do anything for it. And being a priest among the Irish, even an English one, is very ego-boosting. You can easily believe that you are at least as infallible as the Pope. We had lots of splendid Irish and Anglo-Irish families. Their children filled the parish school and many of their young people were enthusiastic members of the Legion of Mary and the Young Christian Workers. Irish immigration into Britain had been continuous for many generations; in the late 1960s it was in spate. Several successions of brothers and sisters became good friends of mine – the Guiheens, the Friels and the Monaghans in particular. I conducted the first four Guiheen marriages (one to a Friel) before I was moved from Brixton, and we have remained friends ever since. In 1992, I began the same office for the second generation.

The troubles in the north of Ireland began to boil over while I was at Corpus Christi. One of our girls was a student at Coleraine and took part in the early civil rights marches. Republican collectors appeared outside the church on Sundays and naturally the sympathies of a lot of our people ran with them. At that time, the appeal was for the relief of those injured or homeless as a result of the civil strife. Moved by these events, I became a student of Irish history and of Irish affairs. I acquired some camping gear and, having learned to drive in Brixton, I took to touring and camping in Ireland for my summer holidays. I found a fresh location each year in the west of Ireland, and each one seemed more beautiful than the last. Of course, Ireland gets more than its fair share of wet weather and I spent quite a few hours peering out of my tent into mist and rain.

Always there were families of our parishioners to visit. This, together with my being a priest, helped me to discover something of the inwardness of Irish life. In a very remote village on the coast of Donegal, two people recognised me from Brixton. One of them had worked on the tunnels of the Victoria line in London and had made enough money to buy the farm next to that of his elderly father. The former tunneller was happy to be able to work both farms and so relieve his father. Later, I was to see a great deal more of Ireland in the 1970s as National Chaplain of the Young Christian Workers (YCW) in Britain. I travelled widely in Ireland in co-operation with the Irish YCW. Another joint cause was the Jesus Caritas Fraternity of Priests – this is the diocesan priests' section of the international spiritual family inspired by Charles de Foucauld.

Black Brixton

Brixton in the late 1960s was not the powder keg that it later became. It says something for the old Londoners that they had moved over to make room for the large influx of black people without the degree of public agitation that some politicians predicted. Of course, there were plenty of murmurings and some outright hostility, and a lot of white people simply moved out. There were certain persistent abrasions – loud music was one. When I was at Corpus Christi, there was just the beginnings of a crime problem among black lads and there was only a sprinkling of black men in Brixton Prison. Black people were not the large proportion of the total prison population that they are now. I am convinced that one at least of the black prisoners whom I got to know had been gaoled simply because his motives were misinterpreted by the court that sentenced him.

The mood began to change with Enoch Powell's 'rivers of blood' speech. I remember a black lady telling me that she was not conscious of racial hostility until then. Black people began to develop a defensive mentality, and among white people racist attitudes began to be acceptable in a new way. In the late 1960s, Notting Hill was the most racially disturbed part of London. The police raided a café frequented by black men because there was evidence of illegal drinking there, and the raid led to some ugly disorders. Brixton was peaceable in those days. While I was at Corpus Christi, the Council for Community Relations in Lambeth (CCRL), the first such body in London, was inaugurated. This CCRL was an assembly of local council-lors and other politicians, church people, trade unionists and representatives of various community organisations including ethnic ones. Some heavy politics centring on racial issues were to come in Brixton, but in the late 1960s these were a cloud no bigger than a man's hand.

Both the main political parties participated in the CCRL and it became the focus of a lot of honest effort on the part of ordinary people to right wrongs and encourage multi-racial development. It has to be said that the churches took a leading part. The first chairman to be elected was the Revd Graham Smith, then vicar of St John's, Angell Town, where there were many black residents. Among our early enterprises was a shot at a 'mediation service'. I remember marching on to a housing estate in company with a black Baptist minister to try and make peace between an Irish family and their black neighbours. Such efforts were a small overture to a much more carefully thought-out and successful mediation service which was inaugurated in the late 1980s. The inspiration for this came from a Quaker lady, Mrs Greta Brooks, and it was another 'first' for Lambeth.

The Brixton Hostel Scheme

There were two other church-led initiatives, one of which was linked with the CCRL. I had started driving lessons at the time with a small garage on Brixton Hill and the manager told me that a young black lad they employed had taken to sleeping in the cars at night. It appeared that he was not getting on with his step-father and had left home. Enquiries among other clergy and in schools uncovered the fact that a lot of young black youngsters, mainly boys, were homeless in varying degrees. A group of us – various sorts of clergy and some lay people – got together to set up a Brixton Hostel Scheme. Lambeth Council was very helpful. When we found a suitable house, the Housing Department bought it for us and members of the Architect's Department drew up plans for its conversion. We could accommodate about ten boys and three staff.

We negotiated with Dr Barnardo's Homes to see if they would come into partnership with us. We needed their expertise in finding and sustaining residential staff. All was going well until we were told that Dr Barnardo's would insist on the hostel warden being an evangelical Christian. Some of our committee were unwilling to agree to this, and so we parted company and decided to advertise for our own warden. We were very unwise. Among the applicants for the job was a youngish black candidate who looked promising and we appointed him. It was an error in positive discrimination. Our error was compounded by the kind of lads we admitted to the hostel. We had originally intended to accommodate those who were simply homeless, not those with other problems. But when it came to balancing the books, we had to take lads who had local authority grants behind them, and most of these were either on remand from the courts or had psychiatric problems. It gradually became clear that these youngsters were beyond the capacity of our warden and his helpers to handle. By this stage, too, I – the chairman of the committee – had been posted to another parish. Much as I tried to keep up my Brixton commitments, I had eventually to hand over the chair to another member of the committee, though I remained a trustee. The hostel suffered considerable damage and disorder and we had to close. When we found that we had a deficit at our bank of several thousand pounds, I was one of the small group of trustees who had to go to our bank manager to ask him to petition his head office to write off our debt. The bank did cancel the debt, but it was a humiliating experience.

So the Brixton Hostel Scheme was a sad failure. We were right about the need and great trust had been showed to us by Lambeth Council. But we were not capable of managing such a demanding business as residential care. We really did need a partner such as Dr Barnardo's. In years to come there were several other attempts at hostel provision for black young people, for girls as well as boys. Some of these collapsed even more resoundingly than ours.

Tate Housing Association

In the late 1960s, the housing situation in Brixton was excruciating. Much of the housing stock was sub-standard; there was a chronic shortage of accommodation and lamentable over-crowding. Somerleyton Road and its adjacent streets were the horror story of the time. These streets were lined with big Victorian family houses on four floors with a basement. All were in multiple occupation and in recent times many of the basements had been drinking dives. Most of these basements had been bricked up by the council by the time I got to Brixton. I estimated that one of these houses accommodated forty souls. The landings commonly featured a cooker and piles of household impedimenta. I talked with a black lady on one of these landings during a visit to the house. She was trying to do some washing up in a bowl of water with two wide-eyed children clinging to her skirts. White and black people shared each other's poverty. I was called one night to an Irishman I knew who had died in a nearly empty room.

There were contrasts, however, even in Somerleyton Road. I was asked to visit a Caribbean couple one evening. I made my way to the house and climbed over the grime and rubbish of the stairs up to the top flat. The door was opened by a smiling face and I stepped into a little three-roomed palace, spotless and cosy. It was an amazing contrast with the dreariness of the staircase and of the street outside.

The Tate Housing Association, which was a small Christian challenge to Brixton's fearsome housing problem, started in a ludicrous fashion. The Catholic Housing Aid Society (CHAS) was already active in north London and I and my associates began by trying to persuade its management to extend its operations to south London. The people concerned were unwilling to take on further responsibilities and they simply advised us to launch out and learn housing management in the process of doing it. By this time, there was a certain amount of public money going into voluntary housing schemes and we fell in with a group of people whom we thought could help us. It turned out that this particular group had seen that there was money to be made in voluntary housing and so they tried to ride on our backs. Eventually it became clear even to us innocents that we were being used. Following a crisis meeting, our putative partners departed with the original name and certificate of recognition and left us a £10 donation towards our restart! We had to find enough money to re-register as a bona fide housing association and to choose a new title. We adopted the name of a Brixton benefactor, Sir Henry Tate, the nineteenth-century sugar magnate, whose munificence set up the Tate Gallery on the Embankment and also the central library in Brixton. We thought the Tate Housing Association would establish our Brixton credentials.

The Tate committee was made up mainly of Corpus Christi parishioners but we had some Anglican members. We used to meet in the home of one of our number who was a solicitor. Our meetings were sometimes fraught and sometimes very funny. I was the one who looked for the houses and negotiated with the council's housing department. We actually acquired two houses which were converted into seven units of accommodation, ranging from a three-bedroom flat to a commodious bed-sitter for a single person.

We were persevering amateurs, and as such we staggered from crisis to crisis but somehow we did manage to stay on our feet. We had all the problems that beset housing management: blocked drains, bad payers, warring tenants and on one occasion a flash flood. A water main burst two doors away from one of our houses. The deluge that ensued by-passed our neighbours and gushed into our basement flat. We had to find emergency accommodation for our tenants and have the place dried out. We had just about got the Tate on to an even keel when I was posted to the parish of Abbey Wood. Nevertheless, we all carried on until it became quite clear that the Tate Housing Association was not going to develop any further and that the remaining committee members faced a lifetime of mortgage repayments, rent collecting, crisis management and tenant welfare. We managed to negotiate a take-over by a much larger voluntary housing association that had moved into our area, the London/Quadrant. We bequeathed them our houses and our seven units in a good state of repair. They also inherited our tenants and some cash in the bank. For a long time I held the last remaining memorial of the Tate, which had a lifespan of about five years. This was a name board painted by the daughter of one of our committee stalwarts. I regard this as a special memento of a quaint but rather splendid little bit of social endeavour.

Work with young people

Corpus Christi Parish was notable for the vitality of its Legion of Mary. Legion groups undertake any task asked of them by the clergy. They visit the sick and housebound, instruct some who want to become Catholics, conduct a parish census and help set up a wide range of parish activities. We had a parishioner who was housebound with multiple sclerosis. A succession of our junior legionaries of primary school age would call each week to do her shopping and some of her housework. Our teenage group organised a meeting on one of our housing estates to give an early warning to their fellow youngsters about the perils of drug addiction. My young adults decided for themselves that they wanted to reach out to the black community. When permission to celebrate Mass in people's homes came through, we initiated a programme of house Masses in the Somerleyton Road area. These brought us into contact with a lot of Catholics who had got lost.

Our Legion of Mary members had splendid commitment and reliability. As the name suggests, the spirituality of the Legion is very Marian. A criticism often made is that it is slavishly dependent on an outmoded handbook. The devotion of the Legion is certainly traditional but if we judged our Corpus Christi legionaries in the 1960s by the Gospel test of 'by their fruits you shall know them', they came through impressively.

Although our Legion of Mary activists were so numerous and so effective, I had come to the parish wedded to the ideas of the Young Christian Workers Movement – the YCW. I had learned about it in Rome and thought it enormously attractive as a means of educating ordinary young people to become missionary-minded Christians in day-to-day life. The specific difference between the Legion and the YCW can be described in these terms: the Legion exists to help the priest do his job; the role of the priest in the YCW is to help young people to do theirs. Generations of YCW boys and girls in Britain and huge numbers in other countries have learned how to develop their faith in relation to their working life, their families, their relationships and their leisure activities. The priest takes part in the YCW as a friend, encourager and educator. It is sufficient to say here that our Corpus Christi YCW, though not as disciplined as the parish Legion, engaged in some very effective social action and produced a number of splendid active Christians, including a missionary priest, Fr Eddie O'Connell, who has done remarkable work in South America and in Britain.

Anti-abortion campaign

A most singular effort was about to take place in the parish just as I arrived. This was our anti-abortion campaign. To his undying credit, Fr Bailey the parish priest was deeply dismayed about the impending legalisation of abortion in Britain. While the Catholic bishops hesitated to give a lead, partly because they did not want the cause to be branded as an issue for Catholics alone, Fr Bailey organised a national campaign against the abortion bill from Corpus Christi parish. A room at the presbytery became our campaign headquarters. Troops of parishioners came in to address and dispatch vast piles of petition forms to doctors all over the country. We had a campaign committee which included local doctors, one Catholic, one Jewish, one Presbyterian. We also drafted in a Catholic gynæcologist from Wimbledon and a moral theologian who was one of our neighbouring parish priests.

I telephoned the picture editor of *Life* magazine in New York asking for the use of some remarkable photographs of the human embryo by a man called Nielson. We were sure that these pictures of the human fœtus, tracing its development from its earliest beginnings, would be most persuasive for our cause. I told the *Life* man why we wanted the pictures and he refused to entertain the idea. With Fr Bailey and some other members of our campaign committee, I went to the British Medical Association for an interview with one of its leading doctors. We had hoped to encourage the BMA to declare itself against abortion but found ourselves closeted with a member of the Moral Rearmament movement who was in favour of goodness in general but who had no strong feelings either way about abortion.

155

Our campaign had a double climax. We had collected a very large number of doctors' signatures from all over the country against the bill and Fr Bailey assembled our campaign committee at a tea party at the presbytery to present them to the MP for Central Brixton who was then Sir Marcus Lipton. Along with cups of tea, sandwiches and cakes, there was a bottle of whisky on the table. Sir Marcus was subjected to some very hard persuasion. He was inclined to agree with abortion; we had to try and change his mind. To help him think straight, Fr Bailey topped up his tea from the whisky bottle. Fr Bailey, it should be noted, was a strict teetotaller. Sir Marcus left the tea-table that evening with an armful of petition forms and a more open mind on the evils of abortion.

The other climax was a mass meeting in Lambeth Town Hall which our committee spared no effort to advertise as a great south London anti-abortion rally. Our Wimbledon gynæcologist was to be the main speaker and our moral theologian from the next parish was to support him. Fr Bailey wrote a song to give the campaign some added emotional appeal. When I murmured some doubts about the song, he referred me to the plethora of songs that had lifted Irish hearts during their independence struggle. 'People have forgotten the cause,' he said, 'but they all remember the songs!' A huge crowd turned up for the rally, so much so that I had to lead a couple of hundred people to an overflow meeting in our parish hall about half a mile away. I had to conduct this meeting as a solo effort. I cannot remember what I said or how we managed. I do remember, however – very vividly – that a lady came up to me after the meeting and told me that she was the mother of two handicapped children. In spite of this, she said, she couldn't countenance the deliberate termination of human lives. Her words and her quiet demeanour gave me an added sense of the weight of the issues.

The parliamentary bill was duly passed, as we all know, and the toll of human lives in this country alone now runs into millions. Our Brixton campaign waned with the passage of the bill but the general campaign will continue until we are able to persuade enough of our countrymen and women to perceive the great evil that is being perpetrated in our society. Our Brixton campaign had its entertaining side as well as its high purpose; it had all the limitations of a spontaneous homespun effort. But Fr Bailey and Corpus Christi parish, Brixton Hill, ought always to be remembered in the story of the British anti-abortion campaign.

The prison

In the 1960s, Brixton Prison housed just over a thousand men, most of them on remand awaiting trial. Of these, roughly a quarter were Catholics. For my first two years at Corpus Christi, the spiritual care of these men was a parish responsibility. After this, a Jesuit priest was appointed full-time to look after the Catholic prisoners. This was a great relief to the clergy of the parish. I used to spend a large part of Wednesdays and a few hours at other times in the gaol. My fellow curates also gave it time and we shared the Sunday services. The best we could do was to see all the men who had asked to see 'the RC priest'. This was the official designation of the Catholic man; 'Chaplain' was reserved for the Anglican minister.

I have described my introduction to the prison by Fr John Kiely. I soon got the hang of all the keys and began to find my way around the wings. Security levels were modest at this time compared with later, but nevertheless there were areas of higher security than others and there were men 'on patches' (they had coloured patches on their grey battledress) who were deemed to be escape risks. Most of the hard men were kept on 'D' wing or in the prison hospital at this time. Another of the wings had a large number of men who were, in varying degrees, psychiatric cases.

Habitual offenders accommodate themselves readily

to prison routine, but it can be devastating for a man who arrives there for the first time. A prisoner has certain rights, but the regime doesn't emphasise them. He is shouted at, sometimes sworn at, and if he is timid can easily be persecuted by other prisoners. His most important concerns have to wait until a prison officer has time to listen to him. At Brixton, men were locked up for as much as twenty hours a day, often three to a cell. There was morning and afternoon exercise walking round the prison yard and a weekly bath. 'Slopping out' was a daily routine. Men kept three to a cell had to do their business in front of each other and in the morning there was a queue to empty the chamber pots. The smell which pervaded every inmate was perhaps the most humiliating of all the prison indignities.

I developed a rough rule of thumb in categorising the men: there were the hard men who normally did not bother the priest very much – at least not in a remand prison like Brixton, though occasionally they would have a family problem for which they wanted help. Many more of the men were unfortunates for whom prison was scarcely the right answer. Such men generally had anti-social tendencies which society could not ignore, but they needed treatment rather than punishment. There was psychiatric provision in the gaol, but it was very sketchy. Many remand prisoners were innocent of the offences they were charged and would be released after their trials. And there were others who were eminently redeemable. These men needed a encouragement to preserve their self-respect and to have hope for their future.

The prison had its entertaining side. I was given a lesson in pick-pocketing (the 'dip') by one prisoner. Another – one of our chapel 'red bands', sometimes known as 'trusties' -- gave me a fairly comprehensive account of who was who in the London underworld of that time with ribald and amusing character sketches of some of the notables. I arrived one Sunday morning to find all the chapel benches stacked up on one side. Our chapel red band, who was in prison for defaulting on a fine, had disappeared without trace. Someone had called the previous afternoon and paid his fine and he was gone like a shot. It was too bad that he was preparing the chapel for Sunday Mass at the time.

However, my predominating memory of Brixton Prison is of a heartbreak house. So many men simply ate their hearts out there. They were trapped in their way of life outside and their prison sentences were simply an interlude before their next clash with the law. There were a lot of men who, at their discharge, walked through the gates into a world where nobody cared whether they lived or died. I was called one evening to an old con called John who had just died in his cell. I knew him already and had seen his prison record. It was about two inches thick. He had spent a total of thirty years in gaol. Now it was his sad fate to die there. I gave him the last rites and arranged for his funeral to take place at Corpus Christi Church. One of the assistant governors came, with some prison officers. I also asked the undertaker's men if they would stay and take part in the service and they readily agreed. It was thus that John took leave of this world. We did our best to give him a decent send-off into the next.

My next posting

Mindful of our poor pastoral showing with the Caribbean community in Brixton, I and others began to petition our archbishop of that time to create a specialised West Indian chaplaincy. It was clear to us that our Caribbean people had distinctive needs and constituted a special pastoral opportunity. But our diocese was not quite ready to create a new role of Caribbean chaplain at that time. Three years later it was, and I was appointed to the task. But in the meantime I was sent to another parish, Abbey Wood/ Thamesmead on the margins of Kent. One of the welcome aspects of my move to Abbey Wood was that I would be joining two other Jesus Caritas priests.

8
Abbey Wood

I was very reluctant to leave Brixton. As a community it had a tremendous personality and, as I have indicated, I was deeply involved in various enterprises, notably the Brixton Hostel Project and the Tate Housing Association. I was also anxious about my Young Christian Workers because it was not clear when I left who would be their chaplain. In the event, my fellow Brixton curate took up the task and the boys and girls continued to flourish for several years.

The deployment of clergy in the Catholic Church was becoming a little less arbitrary. I was consulted about the move to Abbey Wood. I made it clear that if I was given the option I would choose to stay in Brixton. But Archbishop Cowderoy took the trouble to explain his reasons for the transfer and I was not disposed to question his judgement. A Corpus Christi parishioner came round with his Ford Transit van and delivered me and my things to Abbey Wood.

Housing estate territory

The parish of Abbey Wood/Thamesmead was tucked into a corner of south London bounded by the Thames to the north and the Kent border to the east; Plumstead lay to the west and Bexleyheath to the south. It was about ten miles down-river from my birthplace at Rotherhithe. Old Abbey Wood, containing the little church of St Benet's, was a housing scheme built by the Royal Arsenal Co-operative

The young Charles Walker as a junior newspaper reporter on the Mid Sussex Times, 1943.

The quincentenary visit to Queens' College, Cambridge, of Queen Elizabeth (the late Queen Mother) in June, 1948. Charles Walker standing on grass.

The marriage of Michael and Barbara (Sheila) Munoz at Brixton, 1966.

The Young Christian Workers' national team outside our Clapham Road headquarters, 1978.

Society (RACS) in the first decade of the twentieth century. Some of the roads were named after Co-op notables – McLeod Road, Broderick Grove, etc. – and the whole neighbourhood was imbued with Labour movement values. By the 1970s, however, nearly all the houses were in owner-occupation and the RACS were in the process of selling off the last of the freeholds. St Benet's Church, named after the Saxon saint Benet Biscop, had been built in 1909 as a chapel-of-ease to the Plumstead parish. It became the centre of the independent parish of Abbey Wood after the Second World War, and was augmented first by a new council estate across the North Kent railway line and then by the beginnings of the very large housing development of Thamesmead.

At the time of its conception, Thamesmead was expected to occupy the whole of the Plumstead and Erith marsh and to be the largest urban housing scheme in Europe. The original grandiose scheme for a new town with 100,000 inhabitants was gradually scaled down to a suburban housing area for something like 40,000 people. Even so, it was still a very large development and posed a major challenge to the Catholic and other churches.

The parish plant

Phase One of Thamesmead was nearing completion when I joined Fathers Frank O'Sullivan and Tony Castle at Abbey Wood in June 1970. The tiny presbytery next to St Benet's Church could just about accommodate two priests upstairs. The front room downstairs was the parish office and inter-viewing room, and there was a small kitchen and a dining room. The church itself was not much more than a large room and the sacristy served as a print shop as well as a vesting room for servers and clergy. A small parish hall occupied most of the back garden. As far as clergy accommo-dation went, the situation was saved by the allocation to the parish of a flat in one of the new tower blocks on Thames-mead. Fr Frank moved into the flat and Fr Tony and I shared St Benet's presbytery – 31 Abbey Grove.

The Abbey Wood estate across the North Kent railway line was built in the 1950s and we had a church there of the same vintage, called St David's. When I arrived, the Abbeymead social club was just about to be built. This was a large and very smart facility alongside St David's Church. Such social clubs are a feature of Catholic parish life up and down the country, but especially in the north of England. Their ethos reflects British working-class life with a touch – sometimes more than a touch – of Ireland in it. When it was completed, the Abbeymead had a very large bar-lounge on the ground floor and an equally large function room upstairs. At weekends both were thronged with people. The whole place was attractive and folksy and it quickly became the hub of the Abbey Wood estate, virtually killing two pubs in the process. Not only were the drinks cheaper, but there was a lot of entertainment, including, occasionally, all-in wrestling. Membership was open to all local people and complete families were encouraged to join, though there was, of course, no under-age drinking. Along with the social purpose of the club, the parish hoped it would make enough money for the church development that was going to be necessary on Thamesmead.

The Abbeymead brought together a large number of people under a Catholic umbrella, but drinking Catholic beer is not really a prescription for true religion. Nevertheless, as priests the three of us were in very favourable contact with a lot of men and women – some non-Catholics, others lapsed Catholics – whom we would not easily have met otherwise. Always in the general conviviality drinks were generously pressed upon us, and it was easy not to realise just how much one had taken. Fr Frank, the parish priest, was the official proprietor of the club and most of the committee were very keen parishioners. The Abbeymead was a financial success from the beginning. The capital outlay was recovered in very few years and there were considerable surpluses thereafter. But social clubs have a marked capacity for distorting parish life. The affairs of the Abbeymead were a big preoccupation for Frank O'Sullivan as parish priest; a lot of money was involved and there were always human imbroglios to be sorted out. The sort of problems that occurred were often very embarrassing from the pastoral point of view. An instance of this was the poor welcome that some of the habitués gave to black and Asian people. From the 1980s onwards, there has been a general disenchantment among the clergy with social clubs, certainly in the south of England. Frank O'Sullivan's successor as parish priest had no taste for the Abbeymead at all and in his time the place was sold.

We also had a primary school on the Abbey Wood estate, St Thomas-a-Becket, headed by a remarkable La Sainte Union sister, Sister Mary Pius. More commonly she was known as Madam Pius, the 'Madam' being a traditional usage in the order. St Thomas-a-Becket was certainly one of the most successful primary schools in south-east London. The children were beautifully turned out in a very smart uniform, they were very well cared for and disciplined and the staff, both teachers and support staff, were devoted to the children. It was the Eton among primary schools on the estate and for a long way around. In admitting a child to the school, Madam Pius was bestowing a privilege. The parents had to come up to scratch as well as the children. One mother applying for her child remarked to Madam Pius, 'I hear you are very strict.' 'You heard right,' barked back Madam Pius! It could be argued that St Thomas-a-Becket's excellence was a little out of key with the rumbustious character of the Abbey Wood estate but, with few exceptions, neither the parents nor (retrospectively) the children would have had it otherwise.

On Phase One of the new development of Thamesmead, we had Mass every Sunday in the old people's home to begin with. Our first objective was to have another primary school which could also be the place of worship on Sundays. The Thamesmead part of the parish crossed the educational border between London and the borough of Bexley so we had to negotiate with the Bexley Education Authority for our new school. Bexley eventually agreed that there was a need for a Catholic primary school on Phase One and St John Fisher School opened in a splendidly designed open-plan building. Another member of the La Sainte Union order, Sister Mary Benignus, was appointed head and the school soon emulated St Thomas-a-Becket in excellence.

Sunday morning Mass in St John Fisher School gradually built up in numbers. In the years that followed, Phases Two and Three of Thamesmead were built and a third primary school, St Margaret Clitheroe, came into being, and also another church, St Paul's. This new church was a significant ecumenical innovation because it was designed to have two worshipping areas, a Catholic and an Anglican one, within the same building

The Thamesmead Christian Community

The Thamesmead Christian Community was a co-operative venture deliberately entered into by the Anglican diocese and the Catholic diocese of Southwark. There was Methodist participation too. It attempted to create a single ecumenical Christian community for the whole of Thamesmead, including, to begin with, Old Abbey Wood and the Abbey Wood estate. Frank O'Sullivan on the Catholic side was an enthusiast for the arrangement and so was the Anglican rector, the Revd Jim Thompson, who was later to become the Bishop of Stepney and subsequently of Bath and Wells. Jim Thompson was a very able and likeable man and he developed a considerable congregation at the Anglican centre which he built on Phase One – the Church of the Cross. There were regular prayer meetings for all the clergy involved in the Community. Ted Byrnes, one of our elderly

Catholic parishioners who used to prepare St Benet's for these meetings, used to refer to them as meetings of 'the brethren'. There were also a good number of other joint ventures, including carol services and a procession of witness on Good Friday, and we all tried to support one another's events. The ecumenical team of ministers aspired to elect its own leader and to vet any new priest or minister who was to be appointed to Thamesmead. The Catholic diocese never quite conformed to this plan. Our archbishop personally chose his men to work in Abbey Wood and Thamesmead and that was that. In fact, for most practical purposes, the Catholics pursued their own objectives.

The ecumenical aspiration of the Thamesmead Christian Community reached its apogee with the creation of the St Paul's Christian Centre to serve Phases Two and Three. The goal of ecumenical relations is sometimes seen as Eucharistic intercommunion. The Anglicans want this but the Catholics cannot make an equivalence between Anglican and Catholic ministries, nor between Anglican Holy Communion and Catholic Mass. The accommodation to these realities at St Paul's was to have a single church partitioned in the middle. For most Sundays, the two congregations, Anglican and Catholic, worship separately. But on one Sunday each month, the first part of the Eucharistic service – the Liturgy of the Word – is celebrated together; then Anglicans and Catholics separate for the central Eucharistic rite when the focus moves to the respective altars and where understanding of the meaning of the service most clearly diverges. The St Paul's experiment was one of the most advanced ecumenical endeavours in the country of that time. There was a certain imbalance at St Paul's because there were more Catholics than Anglicans. There was also the problem that a number of Thamesmead Catholics did not like the arrangement and chose to go to Mass elsewhere. Nevertheless, the Catholic archbishop continues to endorse the experiment and he chooses only priests who are its sympathisers to serve at St Paul's.

I was not as enthusiastic as Frank O'Sullivan for the Thamesmead Christian Community. I was more than ready to engage in joint social ventures with other kinds of Christians and there were special occasions in the year when united sevices were appropriate – such occasions as Christmas and Good Friday. But attempts at approaching common Eucharistic worship when there was too little community of belief seemed to me to be bad ecumenism. Perhaps my personal history of crossing over from the Anglican to the Catholic Church was bound to make me unsympathetic. But I do think my reservations went beyond prejudice. In my judgement, profitable ecumenism begins with a recognition of the differences between the churches. Mutual respect and friendship is crucially important, but attempts to overlap the boundaries of belief end up either in confusion or in meaninglessness. I am not sure how St Paul's has settled down under its subsequent Catholic incumbents but, in my view, the monthly Eucharistic sharing was an experiment – as we say – too far.

The Catholic parish

We had three priests and three distinct pastoral areas. I looked after Old Abbey Wood and Tony Castle the estate. Frank O'Sullivan both lived in and served Thamesmead. As parish priest he was, of course, responsible for the whole parish. We used to alternate at our three centres of worship. Before I arrived, a section system had been set up which divided the parish up into a number of localities, each with a lay team and a section leader. By means of house Masses, discussion evenings and visiting, the section teams would reach out to as many of their neighbours as possible, both lapsed Catholics and non-Catholics. The priest of the area would celebrate the house Masses and attend as many of the other meetings as possible.

The sections mobilised very considerable evangelistic

zeal on the part of our people and took up a lot of clergy time and thought. We also had a number of parish organisations . The Union of Catholic Mothers ('the Mums') was very thriving. Tony Castle already had a Young Christian Workers Section. I started up a junior branch – the Pre-YCW – for boys and girls in secondary school. We had a Friday night youth club which the Pre-YCW initiated as part of its sphere of influence. Later on we started another club for younger boys and girls, most of them in primary school. This was called the Junior Grove and was run by a parishioner always known as Mac, with the help of a group of mothers. Frank O'Sullivan and I also created a Sunday night Political and Social Action Group (PASAG). We had a number of active trade unionists in the parish and PASAG was an attempt to work out a Christian apostolate in social affairs. Its high spot was a public meeting on the topic of 'Inflation'. We held this long before inflation became a great issue of public debate. My Cambridge friend, Ralph Harris (later Lord Harris), who by this time had become a market economist of international repute, led the proceedings and got a very good hearing in spite of the Labour sympathies of most of our activists.

All three of us worked hard at Abbey Wood but Frank O'Sullivan could work himself to a standstill. On occasions he would fall deeply asleep in the church while saying his prayers late at night. He was a south Londoner born of Irish ancestry. He had been a navigator with RAF Coastal Command during the war and ever afterwards his hairstyle declared him to have been a 'Brylcreem boy'. No idea was too outlandish for him to entertain, at least for a while. He was a great believer in UFOs and would advance biblical evidence for their existence. He was always teeming with ideas for the parish and sometimes his schemes were adventurous and courted the displeasure of the diocese.

Tony Castle came from Dover and had trained for the priesthood from the age of twelve. He was the youngest of the trio, being around thirty when I joined the parish. Frank

O'Sullivan and I were in our late forties. Tony had very considerable communication skills and was very effective with young people. His innovations included all-night youth vigils. He and his collaborators would turn St Benet's Church upside-down and there would be talks, discussions, prayers and music culminating with Mass at dawn. The youngsters loved these events and took part with great seriousness. Frank O'Sullivan and I were sometimes roped in to give talks – mercifully before midnight. Tony was a keen teacher. He and I both did spells of RE teaching in our local state secondary school on the Abbey Wood estate until we were persuaded that it was more profitable to support the Religious Education department in our nearest Catholic secondary school, St Paul's in Plumstead. Tony Castle was in fact given charge of the RE department at St Paul's and he made a very good job of it. This experience encouraged him to ask our archbishop to let him do the professional course at one of the two teachers' training colleges that belonged to the diocese at that time. He was given leave but, sadly, while he was studying there he decided to get married and so leave the priesthood. He cherished the idea that one day it might be possible for him to be both married and exercise his priesthood. It was a sad day for the parish when the news of his departure was made known. He had been very popular and had done lots of good work.

The archbishop was unable to supply another priest when Tony Castle began his teachers' training course so Frank O'Sullivan and I had to manage the parish between us. I took on the estate as well as Old Abbey Wood and Frank had to cope with the ever expanding Thamesmead. We both worked even harder that year and just about managed to keep all the balls in the air and retain our sanity. Some years after, when Phases Two and Three of Thamesmead had been completed and Frank O'Sullivan had also moved on, the parish we knew was divided into four separate parishes with a priest in each. This was a luxurious allocation of manpower compared with what we had known.

Pastoral initiatives

I have used the word 'we' a good deal because most of the pastoral programme in the parish was worked by the three priests in unison and frequently in consultation with our parishioners. The three of us were united in outlook, which isn't always the case in parishes. From time to time we would go and spend twenty-four hours together at Allington Castle. This was a time to relax a little, catch up with our prayers and confer about the life of the parish. Each of us took responsibility for different things and each of us took initiatives of our own with the agreement of the others.

Tony Castle ran a successful folk music club. Quite a few of our young people were competent guitarists and most often a semi-professional group, one of whom was a parishioner, would be the main billing of the evening. These sessions took place on Sunday evenings in St Benet's hall. Subdued lighting, wall posters and candles in bottles would create an intimate atmosphere. A lot of our young adults used to look forward to these evenings.

Marriage Encounter became an important specialism for Frank O'Sullivan. Its objective was not to rescue wobbly marriages but to make good ones better. The programme came from America and had a number of keen psychological insights. It recognised that very many couples were in fact strangers to each other despite the intimacies of marriage and the upbringing of their children. Often they did not really converse; they were insensitive to each other's needs and seldom prayed together, even when they shared the Faith. A Belfast man once told me how a Marriage Encounter weekend had transformed his relationship with his wife. 'We've been married for twenty-five years, had eight kids and I never knew her!' Frank O'Sullivan became a very keen and valued counsellor in Marriage Encounter and it had a great influence on his own spiritual life. After he left the Abbey Wood parish, he took on a responsiblity for Marriage Encounter throughout the south of England in addition to his new appointment as Director of the Southwark Catholic Children's Society.

I retained an interest in industrial mission from my Anglican ministry. We had a cable factory called Day's in the parish, employing about a hundred people and I took to visiting it most Wednesday mornings. The main technology was extrusion. There was a large shop with several long machines which extruded plastic covering on to a wide variety of wire cores. Day's would tailor-make cable to suit all sorts of industrial purposes. The firm's original product was army lanyards and there was still a little section of factory turning these out. The 'anatomy and physiology' of the factory used to interest me a great deal – how all the departments fitted into the overall manufacturing process. The machine shop which serviced all the machinery was a curious little hugger-mugger of its own. There were various milling and drilling machines. Everything was coated in oil and grease but the few men in blue overalls who worked there obviously regarded themselves as the firm's elite. I also explored the offices and learned about the development department. I was shown a piece of coiled cable suitable for standard telephone handsets that was incapable of developing kinks. It was beautiful and completely effective, but it cost too much.

The Day's management appreciated me as a welfare adjunct to the personnel department. I was happy to take up individual needs as they occurred. But it was also clear to me – as it had been when I worked with the South London Industrial Mission in my Anglican days – that there is a role for a priest in a factory, office or store as a 'guide, philosopher and friend to all on board'. (This is how the Royal Navy has traditionally described the role of its chaplains.) A workplace is a community of human beings with a network of relationships, functions and responsibilities and there is a 'cure of souls' within it. It is not an easy ministry to exercise because the work force, both management and workers, contains many different dispositions and outlooks. But if there is a reasonable level of acceptance, a lot of good can be done even among those who do not practise any religion.

One bizarre episode is worth relating: for some reason which nobody can now remember, the parish gave hospitality for an Easter weekend to a coachload of young French workers who came to London to 'do the town'. All they asked was to camp out in St Benet's hall and make us their base for trips to the West End. Their coach was in fact an old Paris bus with a platform at the back, psychedelically painted up. It was an incongruous sight parked outside the church in Abbey Grove. Most of the group were young fellows but there were three girls. The lads had to cope as best they could with the limited facilities of the hall but we invited the girls to use the bathroom in the presbytery. They had an older man with them who seemed to have some sort of responsibility for the party. After a while we guessed that he might be a worker priest who had identified himself with the group. All went reasonably well until some of the party got left behind in the West End after one of their trips. We were rung up in the middle of the night to hear a heavy French accent saying, 'Please tell them to send the bus back.' We had to tell the voice, 'No can do.' The next day we waved them off with considerable relief.

Jesus Caritas

As members of the Jesus Caritas Priests' Fraternity, all three of us were wedded to the spirituality of Charles de Foucauld. Brother Charles, as we always called him, was a French aristocrat and army officer who underwent a radical conversion in Paris in 1886. He became a Cistercian monk for a while and later was ordained a priest. Eventually he devoted his life to the people of Saharan Africa, first at Beni Abbes on the border of Algeria and Morocco and later at Tamanrasset in the depths of the Algerian Sahara. He did carry out a little medical work but the novel vocation he discovered was simply to be with the strange unknown people of the desert – to be their friend, to study their culture, to compile a dictionary of their language and to pray among them. He was shot and killed at Tamanrasset on 1 December 1916, during a Bedouin raid on the oasis where he lived with the Toureg people. The anniversary of his death has been reverently observed by his followers ever since.

Europe was preoccupied with the First World War so his death was unnoticed except by those who already cherished him. However, a biography of him by René Bazin was published in France in 1921. In the 1930s some newly ordained priests in Paris discovered his plans for a new kind of religious order. They were moved to study Charles de Foucauld's experience and translate his plans into a workable form of the religious life. The leader of this group was Fr René Voillaume and the religious congregation they started was the Little Brothers of Jesus. In 1936, Mother Madeleleine Hutin founded the Little Sisters of Jesus in Algeria. She had already felt a call to give her life to the poor and to the Muslim world.

Both the brothers and the sisters gathered many recruits, especially the sisters, in the post-war years. Their vocation had a universal appeal. Although France was the seed bed, young men and women soon began to join them from elsewhere in Europe and beyond. They lived in small groups called fraternities in the midst of poor and neglected communities. Indeed, wherever there were poor people outside the ordinary scope of the Church, the Little Brothers or the Little Sisters might make their home with them. There were brothers who became deep-sea fishermen. Some of the sisters became travelling people, others became voluntary prisoners in gaols. In Britain, fraternities of brothers and sisters have been set up on housing estates and in run-down districts of London, Leeds, Birmingham and Glasgow. Their business is to identify themselves with their neighbours, to make friends and to pray, very much as Charles de Foucauld did among the Toureg people at Tamanrasset.

The life of the Little Brothers and Sisters and the message of Brother Charles has also caught on among lay people – those with jobs to do and families to bring up – and the appeal has spread beyond the Catholic community. Such lay people also form small fraternities and try to live as much of the life of Brother Charles as is consistent with their existing responsibilities. There are also some lay-women who live out their responsibilities in ordinary life and yet make a commitment which approximates to the life of the Little Sisters.

Diocesan priests – broadly speaking parochial clergy – have also been inspired by the prophetic life and message of Brother Charles and the example of the brothers and sisters. The Little Sisters set up their first fraternity in England in the cathedral parish of the Southwark diocese, just south of Lambeth Bridge. Contact with the sisters was enough to interest some of the cathedral clergy, notably Fr John Morris, who started the first Priests' Fraternity in Britain. The first British Lay Fraternity started at roughly the same time but quite independently. John and Jacqueline Ross discovered the idea from friends in France and launched a fraternity in London.

I have related already how I first heard about Brother Charles while I was an Anglican curate in Woolwich. This was when Mary Every came to live in St Mary's parish and mystified us all by being an educated and ardent Christian who chose to work in a motorcycle factory. Some of us at Cambridge also became interested in what we knew of the movement and I was an avid reader of the English edition of the *Jesus Caritas Bulletin* which came in those days from France in brown paper covers. I did go and visit the Little Brothers in France in 1961, but my first real contact was with the Lay Fraternity of John and Jacqueline Ross during summer leaves from Rome while I was studying at the Beda College. It was during my time at Brixton that I was introduced to the Priests' Fraternity (then known as 'the Union') which was ramifying from the original group formed by John Morris in the Southwark Cathedral parish.

At Abbey Wood, Frank O'Sullivan and I belonged to a fraternity that met in a convent at Bexleyheath; Tony Castle went to another fraternity in south-west London. The ingredients of our meetings were an hour of prayer, a convivial lunch, study of the Bible and a review of life in which each of us would share problems and conundrums, both personal and pastoral, and encourage and support each other.

The governing ideal of the Priests' Fraternity, as for all the different sections of the Jesus Caritas Association, was the Spirit of Nazareth. Brother Charles' experience among the Toureg, a life hidden among a remote and unregarded people, echoed the first thirty years of Our Lord's own life. During this time, Jesus simply lived among the people of Nazareth. He belonged with them, shared their particular language and culture and felt their common heartbeat. Yet all the time he was the Son of God, our Divine Saviour. This would be revealed when he began his public ministry but it was hidden during the Nazareth years. Nazareth then, for all Charles de Foucauld people, means identification with those around us and especially those most in need. It also signifies the importance of the ordinary things of daily life. In addition, there is the call to be 'delegates of prayer' for all 'neighbours' in the Gospel sense. The prayer of adoration before the Blessed Sacrament is especially precious for all followers of Brother Charles. He himself used to spend long hours before the Blessed Sacrament, sometimes through the night when the comings and goings at Tamanrasset occupied all his daytime hours.

In the Priests' Fraternity, we aspired to pray for an hour a day ('the Hour') before the Blessed Sacrament. We also attempted to live as simply as possible, being prepared to give away any surplus income we might have. The most undemanding and needy parishioners would be our special care. We would also cultivate brotherhood with all other priests, especially any we knew to be in difficulties. Every month we would try to spend a 'Day in the Desert' – a whole twenty-four hours if possible – which we would spend on our own trying to be available to God. At least once in a lifetime we would take part in a 'Month of Nazareth'. This normally meant the sacrifice of one's annual holiday. The Month would be an extended adventure into the spirituality of Brother Charles. Those taking part lived a common life in very simple conditions for the period of a month. Manual work could be a feature of each day. There would be a lot of Gospel enquiry and sharing of pastoral and personal experience. Always the month would include a week's retreat led by one of our brothers, very often someone from another country.

The Lay Fraternity shares fully in the spirit of Brother Charles but has to adapt its practices to suit lay life. The annual retreats have to be vacational as well as spiritual for the sake of their children and young people as well as for the 'recreation' of all concerned.

In the years that have followed, I have been to many Months of Nazareth and a number of other European and international encounters. In the 1970s, I became the 'Responsible' (the French word translates awkwardly into English but we try to retain its concept) for the Priests' Fraternity in England and Wales. During this time, we developed a close link with the Irish Fraternity and used to hold our Months of Nazareth on alternate years so that they could be shared. These occasions were an opportunity to explore the intricacies of the Anglo-Irish relationship.

An all-Anglican fraternity had developed in Nottingham with the help of one of our Catholic brothers in the north of

England. Their Responsible began to come to national and European events, and by stages we were made to confront the question, 'On what terms could Anglicans be members of the Priests' Fraternity – should they be a parallel organisation on their own like the Anglican Franciscans or Benedictines or is some sort of common belonging possible?' We wrestled with this issue for nearly a year and finally decided that the Spirit was directing us towards a common belonging. We had to think through the consequences of this. We had no brief from the Church to advance the frontiers of ecumenism. If we could be clear that our common belonging was based on our sharing in the message and spirituality of Brother Charles, it was then our task to go on and manage the anomalies involved step by step. We resolved emphatically that we would do nothing that might offend our respective authorities. So we never attempted Eucharistic sharing. We did, however, try to envisage the possibility that all members of the Priests' Fraternity in Britain – both Catholic and Anglican – might want to choose an Anglican as the national Responsible. It was a very hypothetical possibility because of the small numbers of Anglicans involved and because an Anglican could not preside at a common Eucharist, but the very fact that it had been raised was enough to disaffect some of our Catholic brothers. For a while some of them detached themselves, but it was a dispute between brothers and, though it took some years to resolve, harmony was eventually restored. In our eagerness to extend the hand of fellowship to our Anglican brothers a mistake had been made. Once again it was a case of an ecumenical step too far, but this time I was the culprit!

9
Young Christian Workers

In the summer of 1973, I began to get intimations that I was going to be moved from Abbey Wood. During my time there, I had been elected by the priests of the Greenwich deanery as one of their representatives on the Diocesan Senate (later Council) of Priests, one of the new consultative bodies that had been set up in the aftermath of the Second Vatican Council. Though I had no immediate responsibility for the black community at that time, I used the opportunity to run the cause of a specialised ministry to our black people in the presence of the then archbishop, Monsignor Cyril Cowderoy, and a lot of my fellow priests. Maybe my airing of the proposal had some effect because I was now hearing that the Archbishop did mean to set up a chaplaincy to 'the immigrants' and that he was going to give the job to me.

No formal appointment had been made, however, when I received an approach from the national headquarters of the Young Christian Workers. They would like me to become their National Chaplain. This prospect was enormously attractive to me, but I did feel heavily committed to the chaplaincy to the black community, if indeed that role was going to come my way. Michael McCann, then leader of the YCW national team, and Frank Lane, the headquarters administrator, made the approach. After I had explained what might be in the offing for me in the diocese, I agreed that they should go to the Archbishop and enquire of him. It did indeed prove to be the case that the Archbishop had got me lined up for the new role of 'immigrant chaplain', and shortly afterwards I received the official news.

The appointment to look after the black community was the fulfilment of what I had hoped for since my years in Brixton. At the same time the YCW was one of my great enthusiasms and to work for the movement full-time was an opportunity I was very reluctant to pass up. I conceived the idea of running the two jobs together. I can't remember anybody giving me any encouragement for this, but I asked the Archbishop to agree to it and he did so, somewhat unwillingly. Thus in July 1973, when I was forty-nine years of age, I became National Chaplain to the Young Christian Workers Movement of England and Wales and Chaplain to the immigrant communities of Southwark diocese.

The YCW movement

I had first heard of the movement in Rome and Pat Keegan, perhaps the most distinguished product of the British YCW, had come to my First Mass as a Catholic priest in March 1966 while he was attending a meeting of Pope Paul VI's Commission on the Family, of which he was a member. Monsignor G.A. Tomlinson, who was then Administrator of Westminster Cathedral and had come to Rome to be the assistant priest at my First Mass, had suggested that I should invite him. At the reception after the Mass, Pat Keegan had enthused about me though it was the first time we had met. He went as far as to say (speaking for the British YCW) that I should 'become *their* priest'. His words were very flattering for me; they also proved to be prophetic.

From my experience as a YCW section chaplain at Brixton and at Abbey Wood, I well understood that building up a new local section was hard work and fraught with disappointments, but I had seen a little of what could be achieved. I had also acted as chaplain at a London-wide training weekend at Aylesford in Kent which gave me a small glimpse of the movement at the regional level. Now at the national level I needed to improve my grip on YCW principles and practice.

The founder, Josef Cardijn, was a Flemish priest heavily involved in Catholic Action in the early part of the twentieth century. This was a very broad movement in the Catholic Church stemming from *Rerum Novarum*, the great encyclical letter of Pope Leo XIII written in 1891. This letter, addressed to the universal Church, reflected upon the profound human, social and spiritual consequences of industrialisation in the nineteenth century. It also contained a critique of the 'Socialist' (really Communist) interpretation of industrial society contained in the *Communist Manifesto* of 1848. In April, 1925, Cardijn launched a movement of working youth in Belgium which he called the Jeunesse Ouvrière Chrétienne, quickly dubbed the JOC. Cardijn's movement was later described by Pope Pius XI as 'a perfect form of Catholic Action'. After many years of painstaking ministry among young working people, Cardijn had brought to birth a movement which accurately expressed the life-realities of young workers in their late teens and early twenties and had shown itself capable of motivating and training them to be apostles for Christ within the world of work.

The JOC quickly took off in both the Flemish- and French-speaking parts of Belgium and after a year had spread to France. It was a unique creation: it proclaimed the God-given dignity of each working boy or girl and declared that each of them could be an apostle of Christ with an individual vocation. 'No pope, no prime minister, can replace you – John Jones or Mary Smith – in your unique vocation!' Such words were a revelation to young working people who had never acquired much self-esteem. Nor had they ever been shown that the life and work of a factory, shop or office was a sphere of Christian apostolate. So the JOC liberated generations of Belgian and French young workers and mobilised them as Christian apostles within working-class life. When the tenth anniversary congress of the Belgian movement was held at the Heysel Stadium in Brussels in 1935, nearly 100,000 working boys and girls from Belgium and France, and a few from England, took part.

Josef Cardijn had created a mass movement of working youth. He had also given them a remarkable educational tool in the See–Judge–Act method of enquiry. The discussions of most young people (adults too, for that matter) are a jumble of facts, impressions, opinions and a desire to do something. Cardijn's method gave shape, purpose and cutting edge to serious enquiry. 'We start with life' was one of his great axioms – not doctrines, slogans or book knowledge. Each enquiry in a JOC group would begin with the actual experience of the youngsters. They were the world's experts on the experience of young people, but they had to be trained to notice what was happening to them, perceive its importance, and learn to evaluate it.

Thus, if the topic under consideration was drug addiction among young people, the first thing to share was first-hand knowledge. 'Have any of us been close to the drug scene?' 'Who do we know that has?' 'Where are the places that drugs can be obtained?' All this is the 'See' part of the enquiry. The 'Judge' part might well start with the question, 'Do we know enough about the consequences of using drugs?' 'How serious a problem is drug use in our locality?' 'What do we know from the gospel or Christian tradition that helps to evaluate the situation?' Having established the facts of the matter (very often after taking pains to get more accurate information) and having made a careful judgement, the enquiry should move on to a decision for appropriate action – something reasoned and something within the power of the group. Once they had grasped the See–Judge–Act method, relatively uneducated young workers could develop a keen ability to analyse and remedy complex human situations.

The first sprouting of the movement in Britain was in Bristol during the mid-1930s under the auspices of the

Dominican Fathers. The early recruits used the name JOC for their group and called themselves the 'Jocists' of Britain. It was they who represented England at the Belgian tenth anniversary congress in 1935. The tap root of the British movement, however, was at Wigan in Lancashire in 1937 where Fr Gerard Rimmer and Pat Keegan were the great pioneers. Very shortly after this beginning, the name 'Young Christian Workers' was chosen for the movement in England and Wales and this was progressively adopted throughout the English-speaking world. The movement began in Ireland at roughly the same time and there too it became known as the Young Christian Workers. The movement made less startling progress in the British Isles than in Belgium and France, partly because the Catholic bishops here were much slower to pick it up. In Ireland, the YCW was rejected by the Dublin archdiocese as 'Communist', but flourished in Belfast under the patronage of the Passionist fathers in the Ardoyne district. The YCW of England and Wales and of Northern Ireland made impressive progress in the pre-war years and became a very broad movement in the Catholic community after the war. Its signal achievement lies in the large numbers of informed and committed apostolic laymen and laywomen it has produced over the years.

The British YCW of the 1970s – the national team

I began work with the YCW in the autumn of 1973 as a man with two hats. At the beginning, I spent nearly all my time with the YCW. It already had a structure and a programme into which I had to fit and I was soon very busy catching up with events. As far as my new 'immigrant ministry' was concerned, I made a start whenever I was in London at weekends. I quickly decided that I had to concentrate my activities on the Caribbean community and began to call myself the Catholic Caribbean Chaplain of south London.

The wisdom of my taking on the two roles can be questioned. As time went on, some of my West Indian friends resented the time I spent with the YCW; my YCW comrades occasionally referred to me as their 'part-time chaplain'. It seemed to me that I was, in fact, doing two full-time jobs and life was very strenuous. Later the balance of my activity tilted more and more towards my West Indian ministry, especially after the opening of our chaplaincy centre in Balham in December 1977.

My first task in the YCW was to get to know the members of the full-time national team. We had our headquarters at 106 Clapham Road in south London, very near the Oval tube station, and that became my base of operations. Indeed, '106' was almost as famous a door number in the international YCW as 'Number 10' in international politics. We had a constant stream of visitors from all over the world.

Michael McCann from Middlesborough was National President and leader of the team. He was a married man with four children and was resident in Birmingham where he had been promoting the movement for a number of years. He was the undoubted leader both of the national team and of the YCW of England and Wales. He was a very good speaker and debater and his experience ranged beyond the national movement to the international dimension. The term we used for members of the national team was 'national organiser'. It was a great compliment for a YCW to be invited on to the national team and very few declined the opportunity, though nearly all of them took a cut in salary in leaving their previous jobs. Each one was responsible either for a headquarters role or for an area of the country where he or she would reside. The headquarters organisers also did spells 'in the field'. Michael had conspicuous organisational gifts – he had rebuilt the Birmingham YCW from virtually nothing.

Julie Prescott from Liverpool was just completing her

contract as National Secretary when I arrived. Julie was a splendid example of a YCW girl leader. She was tough, clear-headed and blunt. Like Michael, she was a very committed but unsentimental Catholic. 'By their fruits you shall know them' could have been her motto. The London organiser when I joined was Tom Caluori. Tom was as authentically a Londoner as Michael was a Yorkshireman and Julie a Scouser. Both Julie and Tom left the team shortly after I arrived. Julie was married soon afterwards and Tom began training as a teacher. The Faith always meant a great deal to Tom; at one time he had hoped to be a priest. He has, in fact, become a first-class Religious Education teacher and is now married with six grown-up children.

The team was eight strong in October 1973 when I joined them. Apart from Michael, Julie and Tom, there was Paul McGee from Gateshead at headquarters in London. He was mainly concerned at that time with publications and our organisation for boys and girls still at school. When Michael McCann left after two further years, a reorganisation of the national structure made him Michael's successor as leader of the team with the new title of General Secretary, paralleling trade union organisation. Paul was a man of relatively few words but he was an inspirational speaker when he chose to be. He was also passionately committed to working-class values and when roused he did not mince his words.

Peter Bussy was also at headquarters as Training and Development Officer, a role specially created for him because he was already a teacher. Peter came from the Kent fringe of London. He master-minded many successful events, including summer schools in Germany. South Wales was one of his areas of fieldwork. He singlehandedly created an entirely new group in Cardiff in a district known as Splott. Thereafter, Splott and its characterful boys and girls were part of Peter's patrimony. Peter is also remembered for his guitar-playing – the folk song 'Streets of London' will always whisper his name to us.

Dublin and Birmingham combined to produce Kevin Hayes and Frank Foley; both were Dublin-born and Birmingham-raised. Kevin was succeeding Tom Caluori as the London Organiser; Frank came later as our man in Birmingham. Later on, both of them, with me, assisted in the restart of the movement in Ireland. With Kevin or Frank at different times, I drove many hundreds of miles in Ireland and each of them used to sharpen up my Irish perceptions, though both of them remembered Ireland only as children. We used to have endless discussions about the British presence in Ireland, Kevin and Frank both being solid Republicans.

Jim Dearlove, another son of Middlesborough, was looking after Liverpool and the north-west as I arrived. He was tough and taciturn. Sometimes long-winded requests would receive a one-word answer – 'No!' He was an ardent supporter of Yorkshire cricket – nobody else's. Later, he succeeded Paul McGee as General Secretary. With Jim too I drove many miles, in his case throughout the north-west and later throughout the north-east and Scotland. Jim was amiably anti-clerical and I had to do my best to defend my fellow priests. After a run of negative responses from various priests whom we had called on, we both agreed that it had been a rough day but we gave thanks that neither of us would be neurotic about it. We consoled ourselves with fish and chips and sugared almonds.

A Durham miner's daughter was the North-East Organiser. This was Liz Jobson and she was a true working-class militant. She managed the YCW cause in the great centres of Middlesborough, Gateshead and Newcastle with splendid verve. She was surrounded by huge, hairy, motorbike-riding lads. It took me quite a while to tune in to the variations of the north-east accent. At first, I found the Newcastle lads almost incomprehensible. My first adventure with the north-east YCW was to attempt the Lyke Wake walk, a forty-mile bash across the North Yorkshire Moors from the ruins of Mount Grace Priory to Robin Hood's Bay on the coast.

Liz was the impresario of the walk. She met the walkers at every road crossing point in her battered old Volkswagen beetle loaded with 'sarneys' (sandwiches) and drinks. My Londoner's limbs were not trained for such an exertion. I got about two-thirds of the way and then my legs seized up completely. The next day – a Sunday – I could scarcely get out of bed to say Mass.

During my seven years as National Chaplain, all the organisers who were there at the beginning completed their contracts and other remarkable young people took their places. Mary Bligh came to headquarters from Birmingham where she had led a very successful section at Northfield in the shadow of the Longbridge Motor Works. She had also figured prominently in the West Midlands region. Mary took on the role of Assistant National Secretary in London. She left us after about two years to return to teaching, her previous job. Jo Cullen was another Irish-born product of the Birmingham YCW. She too had figured largely in both her local section and in the region. Jo succeeded Mary at headquarters but with the new title of Assistant General Secretary in the revised structure, and she also had the role of School-to-Work Organiser. Jo's time at school had yielded one O level; years later, she collected a first-class honours degree in Social Policy at Warwick University and went on to gain a PhD.

When Jim Dearlove succeeded Paul McGee as General Secretary at headquarters, Pat McGeever came on to look after Liverpool. Pat was a Leeds lass of Irish ancestry. We rescued her from a sociological course at Sheffield University. Eventually, she succeeded Jim Dearlove as General Secretary. Paul Edwards and Rob Hart came from the Norris Green district of Liverpool. Both were unmistakable Scousers and they used to do a marvellous double act in celebration of the Liverpool idiom. Paul became the organiser for the north-east and Rob worked Liverpool and the north-west after Pat McGeever.

Warrington contributed Christine Kerr to the national

team. She too came to London as an Assistant General Secretary but did a lot of effective fieldwork in her home region. Paul Spencer was another product of the north-west. He came from the Kirkby housing estate on the edge of Liverpool where he had led some excellent social efforts to help improve the quality of life on that bleak estate. Paul succeeded Frank Foley as the organiser for Birmingham. Another Birmingham recruit to the team was Paul Henson who later took over the region from Paul Spencer. Paul Henson was another skilled guitarist. He was also touchingly devoted to Aston Villa FC. The final recruit in my time was John Sheen from St Helen's. John was a product of the deeply rooted Catholicism of Lancashire. He too came to London as a member of the headquarters team.

Most of the above-mentioned married within the movement, and I had the great pleasure of conducting the weddings in a number of cases. Two marriages occurred within the team: Jim Dearlove and Jo Cullen married and so did John Sheen and Pat McGeever.

A precious figure at YCW headquarters, before, throughout and after my tenure of the national chaplaincy, was Frank Lane. Frank became an organiser in the national team shortly after leaving the navy at the end of the Second World War. In 1958, the new post of Administrator had been created for him and his continuing service to the YCW of England and Wales was a crucial part of the stability and authenticity of our movement for over three decades. Apart from his family (his too was a YCW marriage) the movement was Frank's life. His influence over a long succession of national teams was massive but he never usurped their responsibility for the YCW of their day. When he died in 1992, a vast concourse of YCW people gathered for his Funeral Requiem at the Catholic church at Thornton Heath in south London which had become home for him, his wife Phyllis and their family. But Frank was born a Bermondsey boy and in his heart remained one until the day he died.

Two others at headquarters must be mentioned. Christine Barnes was our secretary in the front office for several years. She was a YCW of Crayford in Kent. Christine was the first to welcome an Irish priest called Micheal Liston. 'Micheal' is the Irish form of Michael and sounds like 'Meehall' in English. The said Micheal became one of our great friends and subsequently led the restoration of the YCW in Ireland. Christine was succeeded in the front office by Margaret McSweeney whose husband Dan had been another very prominent Bermondsey YCW during and after the war. Margaret too was a thorough 'insider' of the movement and we all valued her presence and contribution enormously.

Events

Very soon after I joined the team, I embarked on a tour of our regions. To begin with there were four: Newcastle and the north-east, Liverpool and the north-west, Birmingham and the midlands, and London and the south. Mercifully, I enjoyed driving. During the next five years, I averaged around 20,000 miles a year. I always had one of the national team in the car with me and we got to know each other very well on these long journeys. In each region, I had to go around with our regional organiser, meet the regional team and the existing chaplains and try to excite other priests (and sometimes sisters) with the message of the YCW. There were always sections to visit and regional meetings to attend. I would also attempt to meet the local Catholic bishop and members of the regional management committee.

Each region would have a training weekend at least once a year. This was in addition to a programme of national events. YCW events followed a well-tried pattern. The boys and girls would muster on a Friday evening and there would be an introductory session heralding the business of the weekend, settling enquiry groups and allocating special responsibilities, including always a liturgy committee which shared with the chaplain (usually me) the task of preparing the weekend Masses and other prayers. The theme of a training weekend could be the 'See–Judge–Act' method of enquiry, the elements of leadership or a current national campaign like 'Apprentice training', 'The situation of shop-workers' or 'The family'. The YCW identified four dominating areas of concern in the lives of young working people – education and training, work, leisure, family and relationships. Any of these could provide the theme for a training weekend.

The regional team with their organiser would have planned the sessions carefully. Talks would be given by designated YCWs and enquiry groups would follow. Standing up and making a speech before an audience of between fifty and a hundred people was a formidable undertaking for our boys and girls, especially when they were doing it for the first time. But by stages some of them became very vigorous and cogent speakers. Organisers needed to be good speakers and it was splendid to see how they grew into the task and, when the opportunity offered, were able to hold the attention of groups of bishops, business men and trade unionists. There was a time when the words 'and that's about it' were a recurring conclusion for our tyro speakers, but such stereotypical phrases would be gently pointed out and corrections made.

For young people attending a YCW event for the first time, it was impressive to find ideas being put over and serious topics discussed by other youngsters such as themselves. Even hesitant talks were listened to with rapt attention and the boys and girls would become absorbed in a discussion. There is a place in YCW training for the contribution of well-informed and fluent adult speakers. But a special authenticity belongs to the thoughts of 'someone like me' highlighting a common experience.

Weekend programmes would be very full. The Masses would be fully participatory with a lot of guitar music and a nice blend of solemnity and informality. It was incumbent upon the chaplain to give a homily that was both relevant to the lives of the boys and girls and worthwhile in content. Always on the Saturday evening there would be homespun entertainment. Unlike students who always seemed to relax in jeans and floppy jumpers, our girls would always pretty themselves up for Saturday evening. Most often the entertainment began with some kind of drag show. Frank Foley was a particularly good entertainer. All YCWs of his time will remember his rendering of 'Scarlet Ribbons'. Various others had party pieces. I used to lead an all-join-in version of a German kindergarten piece which I called 'Das Orchestra'. The guitarists would take over at a certain stage and there would lusty renderings of traditional songs from the regions. The Geordies would always give us 'Blaydon Races' and 'Cushy Butterfield', the Scousers would render 'In My Liverpool Home', the Brummies 'Wild Rover' and the Cockneys 'My Old Man'. After these declarations of regional pride, there would be modern folk music and finally dancing.

Every year we would have a National Training Weekend which would generally launch a national YCW campaign. There would also be a Key Leaders Weekend which would advance the training of our regional leaders. The annual National Council was a very solemn proceeding. This brought together delegations from all the regions and decisions were made about the well-being of the movement, its internal affairs and finances and our relations with the international YCW.

In my time, we also resumed overseas summer schools, having become good friends with the German movement, the KAJ – Kristianische Arbeiten Jugend. On two successive years, Peter Bussy, our Training and Development Organiser working with our German friends, took us first to Bonn and then to Dusseldorf. By this time, our movement in Britain had ramified into Wales and the East Midlands, and the Irish YCW had restarted. Representatives of all these locations piled into the coach that set out from London to Germany. Our bases in Germany were church conference centres.

The objects of the two summer schools were to study the situation of young workers in Germany, to have a glimpse of German industry and to enjoy ourselves. We had lots of encounters with our friends of the KAJ. Factory visits were laid on and we were even received by representatives of the municipalities.

There was also a certain amount of internal business. One year in Germany, the girls got together to make a declaration of feminine principles. The lads were inclined to scoff but their grins disappeared when they realised how much in earnest the girls were. Our German friends found our youngsters a tremendously lively and entertaining lot. Steve Chambers from Newcastle, always known as 'Chankers', was a true clown. At every gathering he did a hilarious rendering of 'Old King Cole'. The German boys and girls scarcely understood a word of it but they all collapsed with laughter at his antics.

About halfway through my time as National Chaplain, our great friend and advocate, Monsignor Derek Worlock, Archbishop of Liverpool, released one of his priests, Fr Tom Delaney, as an Assistant National Chaplain. Fr Tom had been a most successful YCW section chaplain in every parish to which he had been posted. He made no claims to being a great speaker but he was a marvellous trainer of YCW leaders, which was the classic role for a priest in the movement. As a member of the national team, he did great work in spreading the YCW in the East Midlands. Eventually, he succeeded me as National Chaplain in 1980.

The YCW in Ireland

The Ardoyne parish in Belfast was the seed bed of the movement in Ireland. On a visit to Dublin in the mid-

1970s, I met the Irish founder, Fr Declan O'Sullivan of the Passionist Order which still runs the Ardoyne parish. At the time I met him, he was very elderly and was employed by his order as archivist and librarian at their Dublin headquarters. He was delighted to learn that I had come to talk to him about the YCW in Ireland. His face lit up and he hurried off to find his YCW treasures. He explained to me that the planting of the movement in Belfast had been greatly assisted by the fact that the Ardoyne parish belonged to a religious order which was able to take initiatives that the diocesan parishes might hesitate to take. Fr Declan had got the YCW message directly from Brussels and like the early Bristol group in England began by using the name JOC. Indeed, he showed me a press cutting which described the Belfast Movement as 'JOCism'. From the beginnings in the Ardoyne, the movement in Belfast spread widely throughout the city and elsewhere in Northern Ireland. He confirmed that he and Fr Gerard Rimmer in England had agreed at a Catholic Social Guild conference at Oxford in or about 1937 that the title of the movement in English should be 'the Young Christian Workers'.

During and after the Second World War, most of the Falls Road parishes had YCW sections. Former Belfast YCWs were strongly Republican in sympathy when the troubles broke out in the late-1960s, but most of them exercised a moderating influence in days when Republican feelings were very high in the Catholic community. A notable example was Sean Cooney who had been an ardent Belfast YCW in his youth but as a middle-aged man, caught up in the bitterness of sectarian conflict, laboured with might and main to restore a mixed community in an area that was being rebuilt after having been devastated in the early phase of the conflict. This, the Farringdon Gardens project, succeeded only partially, but the very fact that there was an attempt at encouraging Catholics and Protestants to live together again was a little light in the darkness of those days. Sean found time to help us restart the YCW in Belfast.

Kevin Hayes and I made the first visit to Ireland in 1975 where we made contact with members of a Dublin YCW group that had existed in the early 1970s. One of the Dublin girls was about to marry an English lad whom she had met on YCW events. It was a beautiful conclusion to one small YCW chapter in Ireland but, alas, it did not lead to the opening of another. During that visit, however, Kevin and I did manage to 'sell' the YCW to a group of priests in Dublin and, without knowing it, we enthused one of them, Fr Denis Laverty, who started a section in the Donnycarney parish. Denis later became the second national chaplain of the restored Irish YCW.

Frank Foley and I made further trips to Ireland and by this time we had the enthusiastic participation of Fr Micheal Liston as well as the solid commitment of Denis Laverty. We held promotional events in Dublin which proved quite successful and we embarked on a grand tour of Ireland taking in the North. Frank, Micheal and I spent many hours together in my car and had many merry moments and a few anxious ones. Negotiating the border on our way from Dublin to Belfast, we were stopped by a black British soldier with his hand up. The soldier questioned us about our destination and purpose politely enough. As we drove on, Frank exploded in the back of the car, 'Fancy, the presence of the British army in Ireland being represented by a black soldier!' I replied, 'Frank, I will have no racism in this car!' Sean Cooney was our guide throughout Belfast. We needed at all points to know where we were and what was the colour of the district – orange or green. We had a number of good encounters in Belfast and one of them produced a new section under the auspices of some sisters in the Crumlin Road.

Elsewhere in the North we had less positive responses. We did have a very friendly meeting with Bishop Daly of Derry and a sticky one at the presbytery in Enniskillen. While we were being given a meal there, the housekeeper couldn't believe that an Englishman like me could be a

Canon Charles meets Pope John Paul II at a private audience in November 1989.

The South London Caribbean community celebrates Canon Charles' Silver Jubilee in 1991.

Helen and Patrick baptised at St Vincent's, Clapham Common, in the late 1990s.

St Teresa's, Northiam - 'our little church in the middle of a field'.

genuine Catholic priest and she slapped a plate of food in front of me with evident hostility. Frank and Micheal could scarcely contain their mirth. I had the last laugh, though, because before we took leave the lady had a change of heart and pressed some money into my hand as a Mass offering. I let the other two know that sometimes grace could transcend nature!

Limerick diocese, where Micheal belonged, developed a very active YCW region. Micheal became the first National Chaplain of the new YCW in Ireland. At the time we are speaking of, there were flourishing YCW regions in Dublin and Limerick with isolated sections in Belfast, Wexford and Cork. These days produced some remarkable YCW leaders. Two of the Limerick boys became youth consultants of national importance. With others they produced a magazine called *Resource* which became very influential among people involved in the Irish youth service. Another Limerick YCW, Noel Kirwan, became a priest and served for a short time in Middlesborough where he restarted a section in a parish with a famous YCW history. The Dublin YCW opened Cardijn House and was able to fund two full-time organisers. I attended the tenth anniversary of the restart in Ireland. This was held in Dublin with the mayor and one of the bishops of the diocese present, and the fruit of the Irish movement even in this short time was marvellous to behold.

International problems

During the late 1970s, we in England became very perturbed about the ethos and policies of the international team based in Brussels. Josef Cardijn had died in 1967 and no notable priest had emerged to succeed him. Moreover, the JOC on the Continent became infatuated with the 'Principles of 1968'. This was the year of the great uprising in Paris by a combination of workers and students which nearly unseated Charles de Gaulle from the French presidency. The ideology behind the uprising was a kind of romantic Marxism which rippled among students throughout Europe and North America. In the international JOC, there was a powerful move towards detaching the movement from all sponsoring bodies, both of the Church and of government agencies. At the same time, the international team began to behave like the Commintern in Moscow. National movements were scrutinised for authenticity – they were expected to be organisations of radical working-class militants. There was an international assembly at Beirut in the early 1970s which gave the international movement a distinct Marxist twist and this was confirmed and extended at a further assembly at Linz in Austria four years later.

At Linz a 'Declaration of Principles' emasculated the Christian character of the movement, so much so that the Vatican began to consider withdrawing its recognition of the international JOC as a Catholic organisation. Together with the ideological revision that was going on, there was also an abandonment of honest democratic practice. Some of our national team liked the sound of the voice that was coming from the Continent but we had reason to dislike the way the international team was behaving. We had two well-briefed delegates at Linz but it was made impossible for them to get a hearing. They came back thoroughly fed up with the whole proceeding. The nearest approximation to the heavily ideological and secularised spirit of the international movement at this time was the Militant Tendency which blighted the British Labour movement in the 1980s.

It was true that the YCW could become a tame outfit, an amiable adjunct to parish life. The very large movements on the Continent were easily adulterated with sport and recreational preoccupations. In England we stood for Cardijn authenticity – a YCW movement that was both thoroughly working class in character and firmly Christian in its inspiration.

Matters came to a head with the expulsion of the German

movement by the international team. The KAJ was judged to be too closely allied to its adult movement, which had become right of centre. The Germans approached us for support. Three of their leading people came to see us in London. They explained the intricacies of the KAJ in Germany and how certain parts of it had become influenced by the ethos emanating from Brussels. We decided to set up an alignment to resist the outlook and activities of the international team in Brussels. The Flemish girls movement quickly joined us and a little later so did the French boys. Both the Flemish boys and the French girls veered strongly to the other side. (It should be explained that most national movements at this time had separate organisations for boys and girls and often their outlooks differed. The YCW in England and Wales became integrated in the 1960s and the German KAJ – a post-war movement – had never been anything other than mixed). Our alignment cherished the Christian character of the movement. We believed that the international should be an alliance of national movements rather than a centralised Commintern, and we felt that there was a great need to restore proper democratic process in international dealings.

This international split continued throughout the 1980s. The issues remained roughly the same but the alignments changed. By the early 1990s, the Germans had switched sides and the Maltese and Italians had joined the English and French boys in what might be called the orthodox camp. The Irish YCW, which had shared the English outlook at the beginning, also changed sides in the 1980s. By 1992, there were two international movements, one approved by the Vatican, the other going its own way. It is devoutly to be hoped that one day this breach can be healed.

Cardijn's JOC was always meant to be both a movement of the Church and a movement of the working class. While he was in full vigour, these twin characteristics were held firmly together. No one could doubt Cardijn's working-class commitment any more than his Church commitment.

In considering the secularising path taken by the international team from the Beirut Assembly onwards, we have to bear in mind the massive influence of the Communist Party in working-class society on the Continent. This influence began to wane only in the 1980s. The French JOC for its part was fishing in the same pond as the very large French Communist Party. It would be surprising if it did not on some occasions adopt the same tone of voice. In the summer of 1977, a coachload of us from England went across to Paris for the fiftieth anniversary of the French movement. There was a huge concourse of working youth in the public park of La Counerve in the working-class district of St Denis in Paris. It was worth the while of all the top politicians to turn up, and the Communist Party had a special display in the park and also a representative on the platform. There were a number of French bishops present, but these kept a very low profile. During the great Mass that took place in the afternoon a number of the youngsters signified their devotion by raising the clenched fist!

This experience of the French JOC gave me an immense respect for their movement. The politicising and secularising pressures were manifest and the official church presence was muted. But the French chaplains were thoroughly committed to a Christian movement and they carried the bulk of their boys, and to a lesser extent their girls, with them. One of the leading members of the boys' national team offered himself for the priesthood at that time. This would not have been remarkable twenty years earlier, but in the late 1970s it was an heroic act of faith.

A key factor in the spiritual health of the movement and its gospel effectiveness in secular society lies in the quality and commitment of its chaplains. Cardijn used to declare that the priest is both everything and nothing in the JOC/YCW. He was everything because without him there would be no awakening, no training and no perseverance in what is a very demanding apostolate. He is nothing in terms of the action taken by the boys and girls. Unless they are able to conceive and commit themselves to some action for Christ's sake, nothing of any value happens. When it does happen the chaplain has the secret delight of seeing young worker apostles in the making.

An important contributory cause of the Marxist and secularist tendency of the 1970s and 1980s was a failure on the part of a significant number of chaplains. In the post Vatican II days, the movement attracted some priests who had become unsure of their priesthood. I met one in particular during a consultation about immigrants in Holland who scarcely behaved as a Christian, let alone a Christian leader. Other chaplains married girl leaders and one declared his commitment to the working class by giving up his priesthood and going to work in a motor car factory! Perhaps as harmful to the movement as these defections was the neglect of many priests who had seen something of its value and yet had neglected to give it the commitment it merited.

Bright the vision

I was National Chaplain of the British YCW from 1973 to 1980. I look back on these seven years as a very rich chapter of my life. Our national headquarters at 106 Clapham Road was always humming with life. The YCW headquarters team was tremendously fertile with ideas and projects. Upstairs, Family and Social Action (FSA) had its national offices. This was the adult movement which grew out of the YCW. In 1991 it changed its name, and a good part of its orientation, to Movement of Christian Workers. During the greater part of my time with the YCW, Pat Keegan was still in charge of the FSA and came to 106 most working days. With him and Frank Lane under our roof we never lacked experienced brains to pick and mature judgements to invoke. As valuable a counsellor was Michael Foley, Pat

Keegan's assistant, who eventually succeeded him in charge of the FSA. Michael had been the leader of the YCW national team in the 1960s.

An important joint project of the YCW and FSA was our quarterly review *New Life*. This was sub-titled, 'A review of the social apostolate'. Frank Lane, Michael Foley and the current leader of the YCW national team were on the editorial committee and we drafted in a few outside sympathisers at various times. Fr Bob Bogan, who was National Chaplain of our parallel movement the Young Christian Students, was editor when I came to 106. I succeeded him after a couple of years. The *New Life* committee was an exciting ferment of ideas. At various times we did a lot of good thinking about marriage and the family, Christian education, industrial democracy, contemporary spirituality and a number of other topics. *New Life* merited a much larger circulation that it ever achieved. Certainly it was a very lively vehicle of ideas and some of the most forward thinkers in church and social affairs were willing to write for us.

Quarterly meetings at 106 were a luminous feature of life for members of the national team. These would be prime opportunities for sharing and planning. We would always have an educational session. Most often we would invite a distinguished person in church or society to come and share his or her thoughts with us. On one occasion Cardinal Hume came and spent the middle of the day with us. One whole day of a team meeting would be devoted to spiritual recollection. There also had to be an evening out when we would have a meal together and go to the theatre. It is worth mentioning that all these things were financed on a shoe string. Frank Lane, our Administrator and Controller of Finance, might give us some money for the evening out, but all other relaxations had to be paid for out of our vocational salaries.

The Church in Britain – as on the Continent and elsewhere in the world – has a marvellous treasure in the men and women who were formed by the YCW in their youth. In industrial areas of England, Wales and Scotland there are cohorts of former YCWs who are continuing to work as Christian apostles in the trade union movement, in teaching, in the social services and some in public life. And they are the backbone of many parishes. One of our number – Maurice Foley, a member of the national team in the 1950s – became an MP, a Labour minister and a deputy EEC commissioner. A considerable number of others became local councillors. Although the YCW is all about the lay apostolate, many of our members have entered the priesthood and the religious life.

On 10 June 1995, well over a thousand former YCWs gathered in Liverpool Cathedral for the dedication of a memorial sculpture to our deceased chaplains and members. Our good friend Archbishop Derek Worlock, who was very ill at that time and close to his own death, performed the ceremony in the cathedral chapel dedicated to St Joseph the Worker.

10
Caribbean chaplaincy

I already knew a number of Caribbean families and individuals from my days in the Brixton parish. As time went on I was able to renew some of these friendships but there were two significant new beginnings. Through the Little Sisters of Jesus at Fulham, I met Edith Bruney from the island of Dominica who introduced me to her brother George and his wife Rose, their sons Michael and David and their daughter Debbie. At that time they were living in south-west London at Southfields. Through George and Rose and their children, I soon became friends with a group of families – children and young people as well as adults – mainly from Dominica. The second beginning came about through John Bonaparte and Charles Gaillard in Peckham. John and Charles were already engaged in Christian education in St James' parish. Both were St Lucians and both had aspired to the priesthood as young men. They were also assisting Fr John Robson who had created the role of Caribbean Chaplain in Westminster diocese across the river. Fr Robson had discovered that his work in Westminster brought him into contact with families in south London and John and Charles were happy to help him develop these connections. Now that I had arrived on the scene, Fr Robson was content that they should assist me instead.

The South-West London Catholic Caribbean Council

There were four pioneer families in the south-west and with them I began to have Saturday evening home Masses. These were a great innovation at the time but all who took part discovered that Mass in the home could be both intimate and devout. We always sang, we always had spontaneous prayers and I always gave a little sermon. At Holy Communion time it was generally necessary to step over children on the floor to reach the Blessed Sacrament. After the Mass there would always be a substantial supper and we would talk and laugh, sometimes till after midnight.

We rotated these Masses from home to home until one evening we had a very serious discussion. The families loved the house Masses and the social evenings that followed, but they thought that it was time to take our association further. The upshot was that we floated the South-West London Catholic Caribbean Council (SWLCCC). We had a run of special meetings drawing up a constitution. Soon we had subscriptions and a bank account, headed note-paper and badges. At this stage other families and individuals came into the story. We began to keep the Feast of La Salette which is a cherished annual event in Dominica introduced by the French missionary priests who served the island. We also began a series of very well-attended dances to raise money. The first one took place in Fulham town hall and thereafter we hired hotel ballrooms. Rose Bruney led the catering effort for these occasions. She was a highly skilled professional caterer who later became the catering concessionaire at the Architectural Association in Bedford Square. The buffet alone at our dances justified the cost of the ticket. We often had the Blue Wonders as our band. These musicians were the Casimir family from Dominica and their friends, and they played with tremendous verve.

I was very keen to attract the boys into the YCW. The difficulty was that my frequent absences from London on national YCW business gave me too little chance to chaplain them properly. However, I did manage to persuade Michael and David Bruney, Peter Royer and Adrian Charles to come to a London YCW training weekend at Haywards Heath. At this time they were all between sixteen and nineteen. They were the only black young people among about forty or fifty white ones. On the first day all four were glued together, but by the Sunday of the weekend they had separated out and were beginning to relate to the others and take part in the discussions. The white boys and girls for their part did everything they could to make them welcome. My efforts, though, to form them into a section never succeeded. We were very good friends and I could discuss life issues with them confidently. But they needed a lot more nurture than I could give them if ever they were to become an effective group. It was also true that they had much more of a student mentality than a young workers' one and this too inhibited real progress. In later life all of them became young professionals.

On three occasions we had family events at Hengrave Hall in Suffolk; two of these were weekends and the other was a summer week. The community at Hengrave Hall – sisters and lay people – gave us a warm welcome. The weekends were a mixture of serious discussions for the adults with special features for the children and young people, plus social evenings – pretty much the pattern we had worked out for the Abbey Wood weekends. We used to have Mass and other prayers in the beautiful mediæval church in the grounds which had a Saxon round tower. The summer week was less successful because the weather was gruesome and it was difficult to keep the youngsters occupied. Nevertheless we formed a fine cricket team to take on some YCW boys camping in the grounds. Several of our young mums were accomplished batswomen – one had been a member of the Guyana national women's team – and with a little help from the males of our party we gained a handsome victory.

All went well with the South-West Council for about four years. We had built up a considerable number of supporters and were articulating the sense of Catholic community and of black identity. Most of the Council members were Dominicans but a lot of other West Indians came to our events. The next goal was to set up a centre – a place where I would live and where the Council would find its focus. We thought long and hard about the sort of centre that we wanted. Should it be club premises, a hall, a residence or a mixture of these? And where should it be? There was our parallel South-East organisation to consider – its people too had to be catered for. Indeed, we looked at a very likely place at Nunhead in south-east London. This had a hall attached to quite a large house. At this stage, however, we could not be sure of the necessary funds. And it was a long way off for our South-West people, who were then providing most of the impetus.

Meanwhile, I was a lodger at the West Hill, Wandsworth, presbytery and had lived apart from my books and other effects since I had left Abbey Wood. Now in my early fifties I dearly wanted somewhere to call home. At one point I negotiated for a flat in Wandsworth; at another I considered the offer of a row of shops in New Cross. In the summer of 1977, however, a house became available on the western side of Clapham Common – 135 Nightingale Lane in Balham. The Holy Family sisters had bought the house as a small novitiate and as a centre for social involvement in south London. Now they were planning to move this work to Milton Keynes and the house was for sale. Our South-West Council liked the house and the location. It was less good for our South-East people. Nevertheless, the South-East organisation agreed that 135 Nightingale Lane would do as our united headquarters. The diocese were ready to acquire the house from the sisters, who asked a very modest price because they wanted to encourage the work. The sisters also left a lot of furniture behind which was a huge boon because all I had was a bed, a table and a lot of books.

I moved into the house in early December 1977. It had been built in the 1930s, badly damaged by a land-mine during the war but very well restored. It had six bedrooms of various sizes and a garden front and back. Alas, the management of the house became the cause of a stubborn dispute between myself and my South-West friends. I took the view that if the house was to be my home, I would have to exercise ultimate control. The leading members of the SWLCCC wanted it to be their centre with me living in it. In retrospect, I am not sure if we ever understood each other properly or if a little more patience and forbearance on my part might have resolved the matter satisfactorily. The sad thing was that the dispute led to the break-up of the SWLCCC. In the years that followed most of my friendships with the constituent families were restored but I have to regard the loss of the SWLCCC as one of my failures.

The South-East London West Indian Catholic Organisation

With the help of the St Lucians John Bonaparte and Charles Gaillard who were active parishioners at St James' in Peckham, I now began to visit Caribbean families in south-east London. Most of the families were St Lucians and I gradually built up another circle of friends. As in the south-west, the next step was to initiate house Masses. Again, these struck a deep chord. We sang enthusiastically, prayed spontaneously and there was warmth and simplicity in the whole celebration. Our house Masses had some of the character of the charismatic movement. They were certainly a new experience of the Mass for most of our people.

The emerging black Catholic community of south-east London was a lot larger and geographically more concentrated than in the south-west. Shortly after the launch of the SWLCCC, we began to plan a similar organisation for the south-east. Felton and Floretta Joseph's house, 9 Crystal

Palace Road, became our first headquarters. We had Sunday afternoon meetings there discussing the shape and substance of our organisation. Eventually, the South-East London West Indian Catholic Organisation – SELWICO – was born. Its aims paralleled those of the South-West Council. These were to encourage the practice of the Faith among Caribbean Catholics, to draw them out of their isolation with social events and to help needy families and individuals. In addition, SWLCCC was keen to be a voice for West Indians in matters of justice; SELWICO resolved to allocate funds to help the folks back home, especially in education. In the years that followed, both Dominica and St Lucia suffered severely from hurricanes and both SWLCCC and SELWICO sent significant relief aid to their homelands. We did this too for Jamaica and the Antigua group of islands when these were devastated. In the case of Jamaica and Antigua, however, the Chaplaincy raised money by a general appeal in the Catholic diocese of Southwark.

SELWICO too went in for fund-raising dances. Our favourite location was the North Peckham Civic Centre in the Old Kent Road. This was a smart municipal venue and modestly priced, but was only available until 11.30 p.m. when our people were just about getting warmed up. Another snag was that we could never get control of the bar there and this was where the money was made.

Seaside outings were a speciality of SELWICO. These would take place on the Sundays of Bank Holiday weekends. I would always arrange for Mass at the Catholic church in the resort that we had chosen. After the outward journey this would be the first feature of the excursion and most people would come. It was important, however, that Mass did not take too long! With Mass accomplished, we would all make for the beach or promenade. The family parties would separate out for mammoth picnics after which the youngsters would disappear to the pier or fun fair until going-home time. Very few of our people, young or old, ever went into the sea for a bathe – it was too darn cold, they said! Our folk had strictly Caribbean standards for sea-bathing. We all did some drinking and there was great merriment which often spread to other people around us. The journey home was always very cheerful. There would be plenty of music, sometimes with dancing in the aisle of the coach and always a community-sing.

These were our secular outings. We also initiated two annual pilgrimages, one to Walsingham in June and the other to Aylesford in Kent in August. The Walsingham pilgrimage became a national West Indian event and people came to it from all over England. By the 1990s, we could expect well over a thousand participants. During the 1980s, the Aylesford pilgrimage became an all-London event and it too attracted towards a thousand participants. Both pilgrimages are built around a long and joyful Mass. The singing has been led by Caribbean choirs from various dioceses and sometimes we have steel band music. Once established as annual events, our pilgrimages began to draw a lot of other people who enjoyed the joyfulness and vitality of Caribbean worship. Our people also loved the afternoon rosary processions with the traditional Marian hymns.

John Bonaparte and Charles Gaillard were my key collaborators in south-east London. Both were young middle-aged and unmarried when I first knew them. Charles became the manager of Bridges, our choir and cultural group, and, shortly after it was formed, John took on the management of our steel band, Cariba Steel. When Special Ministers of the Eucharist began to be recruited, John and Charles were among the first to be trained and they assisted at the distribution of Holy Communion both in St James' parish and at all our Caribbean liturgical events. In the fullness of time John married, and he and his wife Lista have a son, Kerry. Greatly encouraged by the clergy of St James' parish, Charles began training for the permanent diaconate. He was duly ordained deacon in July 1986 and exercised his ministry in St James' parish, and at all our Chaplaincy events. John too entered the permanent diaconate in July 1991, with the steady support of his wife Lista as well as me. In September 1993, Charles achieved his life-long ambition of becoming a priest. Although permanent deacons are not expected to proceed to the priesthood even if they are unmarried, the Archbishop of Castries decided that he would like to have Charles back home in St Lucia as a priest. By then, Charles was in his early fifties. With others of his priest and deacon friends in south London, I was present at his ordination to the priesthood in Castries Cathedral – the fulfilment of the vocation he had first felt as a young man. John replaced Charles as the deacon for St James' parish in Peckham and he was also recognised as my Caribbean Chaplaincy assistant until he, Lista and Kerry also returned to St Lucia in 1996. Back home, John continues to exercise his diaconate in the parish of Soufriere.

Visits to the Caribbean

As soon as I had become the Caribbean Chaplain for Southwark diocese, I knew that I would need to educate myself by a visit to the Caribbean. Many thousands of Caribbean people had arrived in Britain in the post-war years – roughly 15 per cent of them Catholics – and very few of the native British, myself included, had any idea of their background. Our then archbishop, Monsignor Cyril Cowderoy, agreed to help finance the trip after I had been a year in the job.

Trinidad was my first stop. The Archbishop of Port of Spain, Monsignor Anthony Pantin, had arranged for me to stay at Arima in the centre-north of the island. Fr Hilary Clarke, the parish priest, a Trinidadian, gave me a splendid welcome and inducted me into the religious and cultural life of the island. At Arima it was clear that I was experiencing a vibrant Catholic culture and a great sense of missionary purpose. Fr Hilary was always looking to set up fresh Mass centres. I regularly accompanied him to Sunday morning Mass at Comuto Junction where the Catholic community gathered under a house on stilts with chickens clucking round the altar and the people arranging themselves on a fascinating variety of perches including boxes, bins and benches. When I returned to Arima in 1981, 'The Junction' had its own church.

The parish church of Santa Rosa in Arima was very large and was always thronged on Sundays for each of the three Masses beginning at 7 a.m. I was vastly impressed by the fact that every sick and housebound parishioner received Holy Communion each Sunday. At the end of Mass, troops of special ministers of the Eucharist came forward to collect the Blessed Sacrament to take to their individual charges. There was also a parish lunch scheme managed by Fr Hilary's Irish Dominican assistant, Fr Denis Power OP, and also a small home for destitute elderly people managed by the parish. I was happy to leave some money for this in memory of my mother, who had died shortly before I departed for the West Indies.

I learned that the vitality and care that characterised the Arima parish was true of parish life throughout the eastern Caribbean. Our Catholic West Indians in London had deep Catholic roots and had been very well looked after by their priests at home. I also discovered a marvellous liturgical idiom in the eastern Caribbean and especially in Trinidad. I brought back records of liturgical songs and we incorporated them into our worship in London. One of these, 'Wake Up My People', became the signature tune of our South-West Council. In Trinidad I also discovered the steel band. In the run up to Carnival, which reaches its climax on Shrove Tuesday, 'pan music' pervades the evening air throughout the island. One evening, driving back to Arima, Hilary stopped the car by a pan yard with the instrumentalists in full cry. I was exhilarated with the sound and fascinated by the instruments and the absorption of the players. There and then, I vowed that we must have a steel band in south London.

Carnival in Trinidad

My stay in Trinidad culminated in the Carnival. Hilary Clarke and some of his friends had already introduced me to the lore of the calypso. We went to most of the 'tents' in the run up to the Carnival. Originally, calypso music and the people who performed it – 'calypsonians' – were regarded as 'base, common and popular'. Most calypsonians were men but there were always some good women. Performances originally took place in rough old marquees on the outskirts of Port of Spain – the tents. In the fullness of time, the old tents were replaced by substantial auditoriums and each of them – I remember four – featured some of the most notable performers.

During my 1975 visit the two leading calypsonians were Lord Kitchener and Mighty Sparrow. Lord Kitchener was likely to produce the catchiest tune which would be acclaimed as that year's 'road march'. In 1975 the road march winner was Calypso Rose with 'Do Dem Back!' – a wildly popular number. Mighty Sparrow was awarded the accolade of 'calypso king' for the best songs of the year. Each Carnival brings forth a new crop of calypsos. They are songs that tell a story. Some make political comment, others are sermonettes, a good number are very vulgar. For many years, Chalkdust, an ex-schoolmaster, has been the arch-exponent of the political calypso. His audience waited breathlessly for the punch-line to each verse and there was always a howl of mirth and appreciation as he hit the spot. Singing Francine was one of the best sermonisers. Vignettes of life were the forte of Mighty Sparrow. Many of his calypsos – written as well as performed by him – were highly suggestive but they were always killingly funny. Sparrow eventually became so pre-eminent as a calypsonian that he ceased to go in for the competitions. He set up in a permanent auditorium of his own called 'Sparrow's Hideaway'.

The calypso fascinated me and I lapped up all the visits

we made to the tents – some of the performances were in distant locations when the tent teams went on tour. 'Dis Place Nice' performed by Lord Valentino became my favourite. The drift of the story was that Trinidadians are so busy 'feting' (going to parties) that they don't notice all the fearful political problems around them. The appeal for me was in the chorus with the heavily ironic line, 'Trinidad is nice; Trinidad is a paradise!' Hilary Clarke thought it 'a calypso for meditation'!

The great Carnival competitions – for best steel band, best costume band, Carnival king and queen, best calypso, confirmation of the road march winner – all take place during the weekend before Lent. On the Monday there is 'Ole Mas', which is a parade of comic turns, mostly performed by children and young people. 'Ole Mas' I think means 'Old Masquerade' but I never figured out the tradition behind it. The climax of Carnival comes on Shrove Tuesday with a huge parade of costume bands each depicting a theme and some of them mustering over a thousand participants. There are a number of very well-known Carnival impresarios who determine the theme for their particular band and allocate parts in it to all who apply. Participants pay for their costumes and help to make them up. During my second visit to Trinidad in 1981, one such band was called Food and Drink and the revellers were dressed up as wine glasses, chicken legs and bunches of grapes. The centrepiece costumes of the king and queen of the band were the most elaborate and artistic. I remember marvelling at the centrepiece of another band during the 1981 Carnival. This was 'The Mystical Pheasant' and it was a most remarkable and beautiful creation about the size of a mini-van. The costume was constructed around an aluminium frame, the head and plumage were a kaleidoscope of colour and shimmered in the sun as the dancer inside moved with the music. I took a number of photographs of the Pheasant and it remains for me one of the most evocative images of Carnival.

Steel bands and brass ensembles were also doing the

rounds throughout the day. Each costume band had to have at least one source of music. All along the route families and friends were having parties. The Trinidad Carnival has now become a huge international draw. People come from North America and Europe as well as the rest of the Caribbean and parts of South America. In terms of drawing power and artistic verve, it is probably second only to the carnival of Rio de Janeiro, but there would be aficionados in Trinidad who would not accept second place.

John Archer House

I moved into 135 Nightingale Lane in the south London borough of Balham in December 1977, and was immediately grateful that in transferring their work to Milton Keynes the Holy Family sisters had left all that furniture behind. Charles Gaillard moved in with me for the first six months and he was the first of a long run of lodgers. In the summer of 1978, Max and Rita Noriega from Trinidad came for a holiday, and while they were with me Rita prepared a supper party to which we invited Marjorie Redhead, whose sisters I had met in Princes Town in Trinidad during my 1975 visit. Marjorie had a flat very near to 135 and I had already been to see her there. The result of that evening was that Marjorie gave up her flat and came to live at 135 where she took charge of the domestic front and, as time went on, the garden as well. In these early days, she was still working as a nurse at the South London Hospital in Clapham.

This was the beginning of the burgeoning of the Chaplaincy. I was still with the YCW but travelling less and less. Very shortly, we established Bridges, our choir and dancing group, as a proper organisation. Ricky Mayers was our first master of music. At first 'the girls' – actually a number of mums and a lot of teenage girls with a foursome of young boys – met every summer Sunday at 135 and practised their singing in the main living room and their dancing on the lawn. Ricky signed up a lady skilled in Caribbean folk dance, and one of the dances she taught the girls became their opening number – the ever-to-be-remembered, 'Tambourier' (tambourine player). Modest fame came almost at once. The girls appeared on television in a programme celebrating the cultural diversity of London. They also did an extended programme at a Festival of London held at St Martin's-in-the-Fields. Another high spot was a performance at the Commonwealth Institute for the celebration of St Lucia's independence.

The name 'Bridges' was suggested by one of the younger girls because she saw the purpose of the group as building bridges between the races. The name caught on and the group was Bridges from then on. The girls chose a brown and beige ensemble as their uniform and looked very well in it. Thereafter, Bridges sang at all our Chaplaincy celebrations and pilgrimages and we also initiated a programme of parish visits. To begin with, I used to prompt an invitation to sing a Mass at one of our parish churches. Later, I had no need to prompt them. Bridges, together with Ricky and other musicians, delighted the predominantly white congregations with their Caribbean idiom and their joyful sense of worship. Nearly always they were applauded at the end of Mass.

Sometimes Bridges would be accompanied by the boys and girls of our steel band, Cariba Steel. The formation of Cariba Steel realised the ambition of my first visit to Trinidad. I borrowed £500 from a friend to buy our first pans. The band began as a male preserve but it soon recruited the four sisters of one of the original boys. Its launch became a practical proposition when we discovered Selwyn McSween who was researching in London for a doctorate in Caribbean economic history. Selwyn was a highly skilled panman, having played with the Desperados, one of the leading steel bands in Trinidad. For more than a year, Selwyn trained our boys and girls until they were able to do their own arranging. Soon they were able to take on engagements; they paid back the starting loan and invested in more pans, equipment and uniforms. John Bonaparte became their manager, as Charles Gaillard had become the manager of Bridges.

Caribbean Catholic

Shortly after the opening of 135 Nightingale Lane, we launched our much needed monthly newsletter, *Caribbean Catholic*. The original editorial team was myself and Mable Thompson, a St Lucian with strong Guyanese connections. As a young married woman Mable had worked as a journalist on two newspapers in Guyana. In England, with two sons to bring up, she entered the Civil Service and progressed from a typist to a senior grade. She became an expert in computers.

Caribbean Catholic featured news from the West Indies, matters of concern to the Caribbean community in Britain, requests for prayers and a Chaplain's Footnote. Another regular item was 'People, Places and Events' which comprised a diversity of news snippets – baptisms, weddings, exam successes, anniversaries and every conceivable sort of celebration. As main articles, we covered Brixton's troubles in detail, hurricanes in the West Indies, educational developments and a number of issues of justice affecting our people, including the immigration policies of the UK government.

The most notable achievement of *Caribbean Catholic* was to make known the plight of Anastasia Smith, a seven-year-old child from Guyana, South America, who was suffering from a serious heart condition. Anastasia's mother had brought the child to London in the hope of treatment at the Great Ormond Street Hospital. Because Guyana is an independent country, though a member of the Commonwealth, Anastasia had no claim on the National Health Service. The hospital was more than willing to treat her but it had to have some money. We made an appeal to the readers of *Caribbean Catholic* which was taken up by the national Catholic weeklies *The Universe* and *The Catholic Herald*. Money flowed in from all parts of the UK and Ireland. We were able to pay all the bills at Great Ormond Street, send Anastasia and her mother to Lourdes and find the return air fares to Guyana. Sadly, the doctors found they could not operate to cure Anastasia's condition, but they were able to prescribe expensive medicines to alleviate it. To our sorrow, Anastasia's condition worsened and two years later she had to be brought back to London, where she died. Fr Howard James, our first 'home-grown' black priest, had got to know Anastasia during her Lourdes pilgrimage. He and I officiated together at her funeral in London. Her body was taken back to Guyana for burial.

Our first issue of *Caribbean Catholic* in October 1979 circulated 400 copies. When sabbatical leave forced me to cease publication in December 1991, with issue no. 147, our circulation had remained steady at 1,200 monthly copies for some two years.

Another undertaking focussing on our Chaplaincy centre was the South London Catholic Caribbean Credit Union. I had been impressed by the practical value of the credit union movement and went to see a branch operating in the crypt of St Giles' Anglican Church in Camberwell. The leading member was a lady from Jamaica, and all during the evening of my visit there were comings and goings of people of different races and conditions. It was clear that a credit union branch could have great social value as well as financial benefit for its members. The Camberwell people helped us to get going at 135 Nightingale Lane. We were a little tentative to begin with but before long our pioneers got the hang of it and we were soon able to offer loans of up to £50. By 1992, both our membership and our corporate resources allowed us to offer loans of £1,000 to those who had established sufficient credit-worthiness.

I have always described credit unions as a very Christian

way with money – it is a means by which money can be made to do its proper job, which is to minister to human need. There is no interest that accumulates on individual members' deposits, no 'breed of barren metal', and the interest charges on loans are very low. Indeed, interest is charged only on the amount borrowers still owe. The effect of regular saving by our members was to create a pool of money which could be tapped into as they encountered extraordinary expenses. Nearly all of our people have to live up to the limit of their incomes and so have to look for extra money when larger than usual expenses occur. Our credit union has enabled members to go to the Caribbean for the funerals of relatives. We have helped to keep small businesses afloat and kitted out children for new schools. I have paid my car insurance with a credit union loan and part-paid for my trips to the West Indies.

Congress Group

In 1980, the Catholic community of England and Wales held an unprecedented National Pastoral Congress in Liverpool. Bishops, priests, sisters and brothers, and a large preponderance of laymen and women, took council together about the great issues confronting the Church and society. Each diocese recruited a representative delegation proportional to its total numbers of known Catholics. Around 2,000 delegates in all took part in the Congress, which lasted for a long Whitsun weekend.

Places in the diocesan delegations were precious but I pleaded that the Southwark one should include a sufficient number of 'ethnic' representatives. Our Chaplaincy was allotted eight places, including two for the youth delegation, and we included two Goan representatives within our number as well. We prepared carefully for the event, submitting a number of papers relating to the topic headings of the Congress. At the Congress itself, our representatives made a notable impression. We were mainly interested in issues of racial justice but some of our number engaged in family and educational topics. The Liverpool organisers agreed that Bridges and Cariba Steel together could present a Mass in Caribbean style in Liverpool cathedral on the Sunday afternoon. This was 'extra-curricular' to the Congress but nevertheless attracted an enthusiastic congregation.

The Liverpool Congress was a splendid experience of Church. At the final Mass in the cathedral, the full 2,000 delegates paraded in, truly 'an army with banners'. The Mass felt like the celebration of a missionary community. The Southwark banner was carried by one of our black young people, James McDonald, a member of Cariba Steel.

It was predictable, however, that the euphoria of the Congress would quickly dissipate. What was needed was the establishment of a national pastoral centre to develop all the themes of the Congress, to research them further and to set up training schemes for their implementation. Perhaps there should have been one such centre in the north of England and another in the south. This did not happen. In south London, though, our Chaplaincy was determined to carry on the Congress in terms of multi-racial and multi-cultural development. Our ethnic delegates at Liverpool, together with others we recruited, set up the Congress Continuation Group, and for the next ten years we pursued a programme of educational and social action.

As a group we held regular meetings to identify and pursue issues of justice affecting black and Asian people. Each year we organised a study weekend to present such issues and build up a corps of people who would actively pursue the vision of a multi-racial Church and society. Our first weekend focussed on Catholic parish life – how could we encourage the full participation of black and Asian Catholics in their parish communities? We moved on to issues of police and community relations, the apparent failure of the educational system for a lot of black youngsters, family life in the black community, small businesses, registration for citizenship, mental health among black young people, care of the elderly and relations with black Pentecostal congregations. We also had a number of 'issue days' at which we would invite specialist speakers to inform us on certain complex questions. One of these was the implications for black and Asian Britons of the Maastricht Treaty on the future of Europe. Sometimes we would take specific action from these studies. When the government restricted the right of Commonwealth passport holders to UK citizenship, we developed a campaign to encourage all such people to register for citizenship. In the case of the Maastricht study, we petitioned the Foreign Office to seek at least the same degree of protection for our black and Asian people in Europe that anti-discriminatory legislation gave them in Britain.

Marjorie Redhead

I have spoken of Marjorie Redhead's great act of faith in coming to live at 135 Nightingale Lane. From the autumn of 1978 until her death in 1987, Marjorie was at the heart of all that went on at the Chaplaincy. I sometimes thought that as many people came to the house for her sake as for mine. Even while she was still working as a full-time nurse, she coped with all the catering for a succession of meetings and receptions. She was also marvellously green-fingered in the garden, tomatoes and roses being her speciality. After the house had been open for five years, Archbishop Michael Bowen came for a fifth birthday celebration. We had a Mass in our small chapel (the converted garage) with the congregation overflowing into the hall and porchway and up the stairs. A massive tuck-in followed.

That night we named 135 'John Archer House' in honour of a former mayor of Battersea, the son of a Barbadian father and an Irish mother. John Archer had been elected mayor of the old borough of Battersea in 1913 and his election was national news. *The Times* solemnly reported that 'a man of colour' had become the leading citizen of a London borough. In his acceptance speech, John Archer declared to the voters of Battersea that what they had done would ring round the world – they had shown that they were more concerned about what a man had done for the people than about the colour of his skin. We chose to name the Chaplaincy John Archer House for four particular reasons. First, the house was located on the territory of John Archer's old borough. Second, he was a Catholic who maintained his Christian witness throughout his public life. Third, he was a great 'pan-Africanist' – he was devoted to the international movement for the liberation of black people and he took part in all its congresses. Finally, he was sure of the concept of 'a black Englishman'. One of our quests in the Chaplaincy had been to give content to the identity of 'black and British', especially for our young people. John Archer was our embodiment of this.

One of our young men, Felix Henry, had carved the name 'John Archer House' on an oak board. This was solemnly blessed by the Archbishop and then ceremonially hung in the porch.

Marjorie was our heart and stay at John Archer House until she suffered a sudden heart attack one Sunday morning and died within hours. Her death at the age of sixty-five was a devastating shock and a heart-rending grief. We held a Requiem Mass for her at the large church of St Anselm's, Tooting Bec. We filled St Anselm's for the occasion and the Mass, beautifully sung by Bridges, lasted nearly two hours. I had the privilege of leading the Mass and preaching. There were priest friends from Trinidad, Australia and Ireland and our south-west area bishop, Monsignor Howard Tripp, presided. Marjorie's family in Trinidad wanted her to be brought home for burial. I flew out with her coffin and she had an equally beautiful farewell in the Catholic church at Princes Town in the south of Trinidad. Marjorie was carried into the church by eight young nephews. She now lies beside her mother and father in the churchyard.

In the following September, we had a special memorial Mass for Marjorie in the garden of John Archer House. Claude Sandy, one of our stalwarts, had constructed a little memorial shrine at the bottom of the garden with a statue of Our Lady, some scallop shells that we found among Marjorie's things, and an inscription from me on a piece of marble. Andrew Redhead and Margaret Redhead, Marjorie's brother and sister, and Anita, Andrew's wife, had come from Trinidad especially for the occasion. The garden was full of people, including Monsignor Howard Tripp, who again presided over the proceedings.

11
Brixton again

In the late 1960s when I was a curate at Corpus Christi parish, we used to think that Brixton was good at race relations compared with trouble-torn Notting Hill north of the river. But even in those days of relative innocence, it was becoming apparent that major underlying problems were beginning to break the surface in south London. Among these were the low achievement in school and truancy of many black youngsters leading to rising levels of teenage delinquency. There was also an incipient drug market, mainly in cannabis, and plenty of signs of the fragility of family life.

When I returned to the Brixton scene as Caribbean Chaplain in the mid-1970s, there had been a considerable deterioration in community relations. By stages, the police had become trapped into anti-black attitudes. They often behaved as if any group of black youngsters on the streets was up to no good and they were frequently abusive and insulting. There was zealous use of the 'Sus' law to sweep up youngsters whom the police suspected of being up to something. The Council for Community Relations in Lambeth, the CCRL, sponsored several schemes to ameliorate the tension that was growing between police officers and black youth. There was a 'Help on Arrest' project which recruited a panel of suitable adults (clergymen, youth workers, etc.) to sit in on police questioning of young black suspects. This was needed because it was often difficult to involve parents.

A lot of the trouble the police were having was a product

of inadequate training and poor community understanding. They took a very long time to realise that the cardinal sin police officers commit in dealing with black people is to show them lack of respect. Moreover, the poor relationship between the police and the black community gradually became politicised. The Labour majority in the Lambeth Council became very 'Militant Tendency' in outlook. Vehement support for the black community was at the top of its agenda and this led the council into conflict with the police.

Tragedy at New Cross

By 1981, the Brixton stage was set for trouble. There were outside contributory events. The St Paul's district of Bristol had suffered several days of serious disturbances the previous year. The Bristol police were unprepared for the scale and violence of the trouble and did not handle it well. Similar trouble was brewing in Liverpool, Manchester and Birmingham in 1981. A significant aggravating factor in south London was the New Cross fire tragedy of January 1981. An all-night party had taken place in a house in New Cross with lots of black youngsters involved. Shortly after dawn, an explosion occurred on the ground floor and within minutes the house was engulfed in flames. One of our Congress Group members lived across the road from the house and saw it all happen. A policeman arrived within minutes and the fire brigade soon after, but they were powerless to save the lives of those still trapped inside. Sixteen young black people lost their lives in the fire and another died later.

The recriminations were immediate and passionate. There had been signs of National Front activity in the area before the fire, and many black people were convinced that a racist attack from outside the house had caused it. Almost as bad was the seeming indifference of the authorities. A similar disaster had occurred in Dublin at the same time and messages of sympathy had been sent by the Queen and Mrs Thatcher, the prime minister. But at New Cross it was a case of 'sixteen dead, nothing said!' This was the cry of thousands of black people and white sympathisers who took to the streets some days later. There was a brief street battle in the course of that march provoked by militant groups whose intervention was now a standard feature of any street demonstration.

The Christian churches deserve an accolade for the amelioration they brought to the situation. Great trouble was taken over the funeral services of the victims by the various denominations. St Paul's, the Anglican parish church of Deptford, figured prominently, and the Catholic archbishop led a special service for all the victims in the local Catholic church. I was in Jamaica on my second tour of the Caribbean when the tragedy occurred and I learned by telephone that one of our Bridges girls, Linda Henry, was among the victims. On my return, we had a deeply moving Memorial Mass for Linda with the church filled with our young people. Every January for the following ten years, the churches of the borough of Lewisham held an ecumenical memorial service for all the boys and girls who died. By these means, the black community were able to live through the tragedy and move from anger and frustration to sorrowful remembrance.

The Brixton eruption

On the Saturday of the Palm Sunday weekend of 1981, I was driving back from an ordination at Abbey Wood when it became clear from traffic diversions that there was an emergency in Brixton. A helicopter clattering overhead emphasised the ominousness of the situation. In addition to the general discontent surrounding the New Cross disaster, tension had been running high in Brixton for some days.

To combat the high levels of street crime, the Brixton police had initiated 'Operation Swamp', which entailed drafting in squads of young plain clothes officers who stopped and searched large numbers of black youths. There was trouble outside a mini-cab office in Atlantic Road on the Friday evening when two policemen tried to search a car for drugs. A large crowd gathered and a running battle began. Everyone in Brixton realised that the Friday night affray was an overture to further trouble the following day. No one, however, could have predicted the intensity and ferocity of the riot that ensued. Large numbers of black young people converged on Brixton in expectation of the trouble and there was evidence that other more sinister people, some of them white, had come to try and orchestrate it. The police were subsequently convinced that there had been a conspiracy to riot. In my judgement, the factors already described were sufficient to start the disturbances but it is likely that they were aggravated by certain hard men. There is some evidence that white strangers were busy making petrol bombs.

There is a certain progression to the kind of riot that Brixton experienced that April Saturday and the pattern was repeated at a further serious disorder in Brixton in September 1985. An underlying grievance is the basic predisposition to riot and tension such as that generated by Operation Swamp is a contributory factor. Almost any incident can then ignite the explosion. There are those who exploit the disorder, some motivated by extreme political opinions, others by criminal dispositions. Finally, there are the people who move in to loot and rob – even to rape – while the police are struggling to contain the rioters.

When the riot subsided in the early hours of the Sunday morning, over 150 police personnel and a similar number of rioters had been injured. The George IV pub in Railton Road and several shops had been burned out. There had been widespread looting in the central Brixton shopping area and well over a million pounds' worth of damage had been done. TV cameras had captured the whole scene and the lurid details were front-page news throughout Europe and North America. We were used to such mayhem in the streets of Belfast and Londonderry but nothing like it had been seen on the British mainland. There was sporadic trouble on the Sunday evening but for the most part the fury was spent on the Saturday afternoon and evening.

The Home Secretary, William Whitelaw, descended on Brixton the following Monday morning with London's senior policemen. Our archbishop also came and met the head of the Council for Community Relations. He toured the streets and visited the two Catholic parishes of Brixton. There was a general state of shock throughout south London. Very shortly, Lord Scarman was chosen to conduct a public inquiry into the events leading up to the disturbances and this brief was soon extended to include the underlying causes. He opened his enquiry at Church House in Westminster and afterwards held public sessions in Lambeth Town Hall. Organisations and individuals were invited to make submissions and Lord Scarman also went out and about meeting groups of people in the streets, visiting schools and youth clubs and consulting with community leaders and Brixton police officers.

The upheaval was of enormous concern to both the adults and young people of our Catholic Caribbean community. Our adult Congress Group discussed it at great length, and so did the boys and girls of our latest Young Christian Workers Group. Both made submissions to Lord Scarman's enquiry and we invited him to come and meet us. He readily agreed to come to John Archer House one evening with Lady Scarman and his Civil Service secretary. He spent an hour with our adults in one room and then nearly two with our youngsters – three boys and three girls in their late teens – in another. He had come to us towards the end of the fact-finding phase of his inquiry and one could tell when the points raised were already familiar to him and when he was hearing some new angle. The boys and girls especially impressed him. None of them had actually hurled bricks at the police during the riot but they all understood the mentality of those who had, and they were able to express what it felt like to be young, black and angry at that time. These discussions at John Archer House were worth over a page in the appendix of the famous report when it appeared in late November 1981.

The Lambeth Consultative Group

The report proved to be a watershed in the development of race relations in Britain. Lord Scarman had managed to reach a genuine understanding of the problems of black people. He had the imagination and compassion to appreciate their 'wounds in the soul'. His report too was marvellously balanced in judgement and surprisingly radical in its proposals. He had praise for the police who faced attacks of unprecedented ferocity and yet just about managed to hold the line. He had noted the breakdown of dialogue between the Brixton police and Lambeth Council and he was alarmed about the alienation of black young people. He was sure that these dysfunctions required urgent remedial action.

The report proposed that a consultative mechanism should be set up in Lambeth borough (and similarly in all municipal areas) so that there could be a continuous dialogue between senior policemen and representatives of the people in all matters to do with law and order. He envisaged these representatives to be both local councillors and other community leaders. In January 1982, the Home Secretary summoned a large assembly of Lambeth politicians, policemen and community representatives to the Home Office to consider the implementation of this part of Lord Scarman's report. We suspected that he wanted to get the consultative process under way before the first anniversary of the disturbances. It was an odd assembly. There were representatives of predictable bodies like the churches, chambers of commerce and trade unions. I was invited on the strength of Lord Scarman's visit to John Archer House. Among the less obvious invitees were the Brixton Rastas and the Chairman of the Brixton Domino Club. Most of those present were fumbling with the idea of this new consultative process and a group of us were deputed to get it into better focus for another meeting.

Eventually, the launch was made at Lambeth Town Hall with one of the ministers of state at the Home Office, Timothy Raison, in the chair. The first business of the meeting was to choose a chairperson. Two or three people were nominated and turned the job down. Then I was named and in no time was elected unanimously! Mr Raison retired and we got down to business immediately.

Present at this inaugural meeting were all four of Lambeth's members of parliament, a large number of councillors, the top policemen of the borough and the disparate collection of community representatives I have described. We were embarking on uncharted and very choppy waters. We learned afterwards that few people in central or local government or in the police rated our chances of success very high. But before we parted that evening at Lambeth Town Hall, we had made two crucially important decisions that went a long way to ensuring subsequent success. First, we agreed that community representatives must outnumber politicians and policemen in the group so that we could get as near as possible to the thoughts and feelings of the ordinary citizens of Lambeth in all their diversity. Second, the police commander, Brian Fairbairn, agreed that he would consult us about any major initiative that he wanted to undertake, including operational ones, except when in the nature of the case secrecy was essential. In the latter case, he would always account to us retrospectively. This commitment went way beyond any offer of co-operation that the police had ever made before and it was immensely confidence-inspiring. Brian Fairbairn deserves to be remembered in the annals of community/ police consultation for this remarkable concession. He went on to play a key part of the development of the group in its first pioneering year.

We had to have a name, and without any public debate the committee clerk allocated to us by Lambeth Council, Francis de Lima, named us the Community/Police Consultative Group for Lambeth. As soon as we had a name, Francis de Lima saw to it that we had notepaper and all other evidences of our identity.

We decided to meet fortnightly in public session at Lambeth Town Hall. For months we spent most of our time criticising the police, and this was a gruesome time for the senior officers who attended every meeting. We were a motley collection of people, some very vociferous. The Lambeth MPs were likely to attend along with a considerable number of local councillors, most of them Labour ones. From the beginning, we were also an open forum – anybody with a grievance could attend and with the chairman's permission (and sometimes without it) have his or her say. In the early days, we also had rapt media attention. Reporters from *The Times* and the *Guardian* were always present, and if there was the least sign of excitement the TV cameras would be clamouring to get into the meetings.

Brian Fairbairn and his colleagues bore up well under the strain and gradually began to think there might be some value in the frenetic process of consultation. After some months on the defensive, he presented us with a paper on the crime situation in Lambeth describing the law and order problems with which he had to cope. The Group gradually swung round to consider what its responsibility might be in helping the police to protect the community. There followed months of discussion about muggings, burglary, drug-related crime, street disorder, crimes involving cars and so on. Having been highly critical of the police, we were gradually becoming very pally with them. There came a point when we realised that there was a subtle peril in this cosy relationship. Mercifully, the Group was sufficiently well earthed to understand that if we drifted too far from sentiment on the streets we would be useless. At the same time we were learning to be a responsible body.

'The Front Line'

As a result of these discussions, we launched a Serious Crimes Committee as a permanent sub-committee of the Group. This comprised elected members of the Group along with the leading CID officers of the Lambeth police district. It was supposed to be chaired by the Vice-Chairman but in the event the job fell to me. We spent a lot of time talking about improved lighting on housing estates, strengthening doors and windows, targeting known criminals, and surveillance of the drug market in Railton Road. At this time, the police had very limited control of what was then known as 'the Front Line' – the area around Railton Road. At one of the Group's full sessions, Brian Fairbairn presented us with a straight question: 'What am I to do about the Front Line?' His problem was that a firm police operation to gain full control of the area would almost certainly provoke another riot.

The Railton Road area – sometimes just known as 'the Line' – was certainly a hotbed of crime. It was an open drug market, a muggers' sanctuary and a haven for unrestricted drinking. At the same time, for a certain section of the West Indian – particularly the Jamaican – community, it was their home territory, a little transplant of down-town Kingston in London. And as such it had a certain social value. Together with the community relations officer of the Brixton police, Chief Inspector Alex McPherson, whom the Front Liners trusted more than most policemen, and Mr Courtney Laws, a Jamaican who ran the Brixton Neighbourhood Association, I managed to set up a meeting with some of the Front Liners. They all agreed that things had got a little out of hand. They were even prepared to consider the relocation of some of the drinking dives and their coming within the bounds of the law. However, it was a very fragile accord, and the problem was not resolved without another confrontation.

This came in November of 1982. The Lambeth Council, again briefly under Conservative control, ordered the demolition of numbers 50, 52 and 54 Railton Road (all owned by the council) which were the most notorious drinking dives. Notice had been given to the occupiers and the demolition gang got to work early one morning with police protection. The police presence was unobtrusive to begin with and the work proceeded without hindrance. By the middle of the day, however, Railton Road was thronged with Front Liners and the crowd was seething with indignation. Their citadels were coming down before their eyes! There was a march on the town hall, and on the way a group of hard men attacked Lloyd Leon, the Jamaican manager of the Atlantic pub. Lloyd Leon, who was a Lambeth councillor and a prominent member of the Consultative Group, had the courage and the uprightness to oppose black sentiment on some issues of law and order.

When dusk fell disorder broke out. There were fires and a brief street battle, but this time the police were better equipped and better trained and quickly gained control. The sequel occurred the following Tuesday evening at the town hall when the Consultative Group had one of its regular meetings. The Front Liners arrived in force, many of them with their faces swathed in scarves. And with them, there was a full turn-out of anarchists, hard-line feminists (one group was called Spare-rib!) and a number of unattached but very strident individuals. The media had got wind that we were in for a lively evening and at least four television crews, a battery of other photographers and tape-recording reporters all turned up. It was mayhem from the start and quite intimidating. One of the tape-recording specialists stuck his microphone in front of the face of everyone who hurled abuse and I had to threaten to have him thrown out. I can't remember how I thought we could make good the threat. Amazingly, some semblance of order was gradually restored and all the protestations of the Front Liners were coherently recorded.

We all felt very limp at the end of that evening but quietly convinced that it had been remarkable vindication of the Group. With a big grievance to complain about, it had been worth the while of the hard men and women to come and give vent at a Consultative Group meeting. And it was far better to have a verbal punch-up at the town hall than to have more trouble on the streets. Many of our members declared afterwards that this evening established the Group as an essential part of the Brixton scene. We had 'come of age'. Fraught as that evening was, there was an even tougher one to come in the time of my successor in the chair, Astel Parkinson, who was a local youth worker of Jamaican origin. This followed the second big Brixton eruption in September 1985, triggered by the accidental shooting of Mrs Cherry Grose by a policeman who was attempting to arrest her son. There was a huge invasion at the Group meeting the following Tuesday, so much so that we had to shift the proceedings to the main assembly room at the town hall. There were even some black militants dressed up like IRA-type paramilitaries. That evening, a distinct threat hung over the meeting that people could have got hurt. Again there was chaos to begin with, but by stages the platform was able to set up a routine that all those who wanted to lambast the police should queue up before the microphone to do so. We had a new police commander by this time, Alex Marnoch, who managed the protest admirably. No attempt was made to minimise the mistake, every sympathy was expressed to Mrs Grose and a full enquiry was promised.

Following this second outbreak of disorder in Brixton and the consequential turmoil at our ensuing meeting, the

Group held a 'members only' session at the West Indian Ex-Servicemen's Club at Clapham. Some of the members were inclined to say that the Group had failed. The very thing that we existed to prevent had happened again – what was the use of carrying on? It was greatly to the credit of the Group that this opinion did not prevail. It was said with deep feeling, 'What hope is there for Lambeth without us?' The resolve of that evening to continue was the second high moment for the Group.

Study and influence

Not all our meetings were as lurid as these. We spent many hours in full session going through the Police and Criminal Evidence Bill (known as PACE) which became law in 1985 and 1986. We did this almost line by line under the guidance of a diminutive Quaker lady, Greta Brooks, who was one of the keenest minds in the Group. Greta Brooks steered us through the most contentious parts of the bill and we were able to make some very effective representations to the Home Office. One of our successful modifications was a requirement that the police must get the permission of a magistrate to hold a suspect for more than forty-eight hours. Douglas Hurd, then a minister of state at the Home Office, happened to be visiting the Group when we debated this issue and there was reason to think he accepted the point on the spot.

Greta Brooks subsequently became a very successful chairperson of the Group. A further achievement of hers was the creation of the Lambeth Panel of Lay Visitors to police stations, another of Lord Scarman's recommendations. Dark things had been said about the treatment of suspects in police stations and the Home Office agreed to the principle of random visits to police stations by approved ordinary citizens who were given the right to interview anybody in custody who was willing to see them. The

Lambeth panel members – twenty of them – were recruited and trained under the auspices of the Consultative Group and its secretariat became responsible for the Panel's administration. This too proved to be a most effective Lambeth initiative and has been copied by many other London boroughs.

Another notable study we undertook concerned the race relations component in the training of recruits at the Police College at Hendon. Maurice Smith, a founder member and later a vice-chairman of the Group, led this effort. The Hendon course was well meaning, but there was scarcely any involvement of black or Asian people in it. When our original study was presented to the commandant of Hendon of that time, he was disinclined to accept our findings. Some years later, when the Group's critique was brought up to date and re-presented to Scotland Yard officers responsible for training, it was accepted in toto.

The Serious Crimes Committee was renamed the Crime Prevention Committee in deference to the sensitivities of some of the Lambeth councillors. With its new label, the Committee got a little more co-operation from the council and we were able to conduct a very comprehensive law and order survey on a central Brixton housing estate. This survey revealed grisly facts about life on the estate. The fear of crime was such that nearly all the tenants barricaded themselves into their homes with multiple locks and in many cases with fierce dogs. The estate was in fact very pleasantly laid out and the housing standard was high, but with fear of crime so dominant all the communal areas were a wilderness and the domain of disorderly youngsters. The survey led to a very doughty effort to bring together all the various professionals who worked on the estate. There was a very long list of these: health visitors, probation officers, housing welfare people, social workers caring for the elderly, permanent beat police officers and many others. The hope was that all this expertise could be mobilised in support of the existing fragile tenants' association to enable the people to take control of their estate and gradually to improve its quality of life. An honest attempt was made to bring this about, but it has to be said that the results were meagre. Morale on the estate was very low and nearly all the most capable tenants were bent on moving away.

Some years later, the Crime Prevention Committee commissioned a study of street crime in the borough. A professional sociologist, Elizabeth Burney, produced a report which was widely noticed and admired. She was able to put the problem of street crime into its social context and indicate the kind of remedial measures that had some chance of success. In particular she deplored automatic custodial sentences for young muggers and applauded efforts that were being made in several probation districts to show youngsters an alternative to delinquency in special training schemes.

The Lambeth Consultative Group achieved its tenth anniversary in March 1992. It has been the model for similar groups that became mandatory in all London boroughs under the PACE Act. I think of it as a very significant development in local democracy. Over the years, the Lambeth police had tacitly made themselves accountable to us. We provided a social framework within which they could operate confidently, and we also embodied the responsibility of the whole community for law and order in the borough. Now nearing the end of its second decade, the Group's regular meetings are still very faithfully attended and there is no doubt that it is the recognised forum for any major discontents involving law and order throughout the borough.

The quest for multi-racial Britain

Disturbances at Brixton and other racially mixed neighbourhoods represented the dark side of the moon in British race relations. In and after 1968, American cities had their big upheavals which cost many lives and vast damage. It is greatly to the credit of President Lyndon Johnson that he drew a positive conclusion from the dismaying excesses of that time. For him and his leading associates, the conflagrations in American cities were a spur to the building of multi-racial America. A deliberate effort was made to advance black and Hispanic Americans in the government service, in education, in the police and armed services, in the professions and in the social services. There was also a great increase in the numbers of ethnic minority Americans taking part in politics at all levels. Within little more than a decade, black Americans were representing the United States abroad, many cities had black or Hispanic mayors and police chiefs, and in the late 1980s America's top soldier was Colin Powell, the son of Jamaican immigrants into the United States.

I began to think that Britain had more to learn about multi-racial development from North America than from the Caribbean. In 1984, I had the opportunity of spending a month in Canada and the eastern United States. For the Canadian part of the tour, I joined an inter-denominational party of clergy and laity from Britain interested in Christian social concerns. I spent a weekend in Montreal in a French-speaking parish and the rest of the time in Toronto and Ontario. I was enormously impressed with the liberality of Canadian life. Canada has developed as a nation of two identities, French and British, but she also accommodates a large number of other ethnic, religious and cultural minorities. All are allowed to maintain their language, customs and values within a broad umbrella of Canadian nationhood. Our party visited Brantford, the home of the Indian Mohawk Confederacy, and Elmira, where the Old Order Mennonites, descendants of the sixteenth-century European Anabaptists, remain undisturbed.

In the United States my address was c/o the Greyhound Bus Company. I had bought one of its cheap touring tickets in London and I certainly had my money's worth. I travelled only in the north-eastern states and had friends to visit in each of my stages. In Buffalo, I attended a gathering of black Catholics which proclaimed the message that in the United States black people did not have to be Baptists! The service included a video featuring black Catholics in Christian history – all the way from St Augustine of Hippo to St Martin de Porres in South America and the Uganda Martyrs.

A former fellow student at the Beda College in Rome welcomed me to his parish in Louisville, Kentucky, a former stronghold of immigrant German Catholics which had become mainly black. He had celebrated this dual inheritance by setting up an Afro-German restaurant in the parish!

In Washington, I stayed with a former police chief of New York City. Pat Burke had been a remarkable success in the toughest police job in the United States. He and his family were also very devout Catholics. I had met Pat and his wife on police/community conferences in Britain.

Moving on to New York City, my host was the parish priest of Holy Family Church in Harlem. He was a fellow member of the international Jesus Caritas Priests' Fraternity. The vast majority of his people were either black or Hispanic. The priests had to speak both English and Spanish. At the time of my visit, the parish was preparing to open its crypt to provide winter shelter for some of New York's huge army of homeless.

My final port of call was Boston where I was entertained by Episcopalian friends whom I had met during my Cambridge University days. One lunchtime, however, I met up with Claudia Bramwell, a black girl of Jamaican ancestry who had belonged to us at Corpus Christi in Brixton. Claudia had moved to America as a teenager. She had become a lawyer and the mother of two children and was having a flirtation with the Black Muslims of Boston. I gently reminded her that she already had a good religion.

Canada came across to me as a racial and cultural mosaic compared with the melting pot of the United States. In Canada, each little piece of the picture retains its separate colour. The United States processes its human beings and makes them into Americans. They may be Irish-Americans, Polish-Americans or African-Americans, but the identity that really matters is the American. Both these multi-racial and multi-cultural forms of North America are great achievements. Canadian citizenship is cherished by all its diverse peoples. No citizen of the United States doubts his or her status as an American whatever their ethnic background.

Integral progress

In Britain, we still have some way to go in giving substance to the identity of 'black and British', especially for our young people. By the 1990s we could claim to have made some progress, but not enough. The 1992 general election returned five 'ethnic' Labour MPs. In Cheltenham, normally a Conservative stronghold, the electorate rejected a black Conservative candidate in favour of a Liberal Democrat. Bill Murray from Jamaica heads the largest of our trade unions and Patricia Scotland, whose parents came to Britain from Dominica, is our first black woman QC. She has since been made a peeress and a government minister. Of course, black men and women figure very prominently in British sport and entertainment, but all these are modest achievements compared with the progress that has been made in the United States. We can take some comfort in the fact that the multi-racial progress that we have made in Britain is integral: that is, it represents a general advance in understanding and appreciation by the population at large. By virtue of the anti-discriminatory legislation that we have, Britain has declared a righteous will in multi-racial matters. But the general population needs a clearer vision of the cultural richness of contemporary Britain.

Signs of this modest but integral progress are evident in the south London Catholic community. In 1985, the Catholic diocese of Southwark opened its first sixth form college at Clapham, dedicated to the great apostle of Asia, St Francis Xavier. From the very beginning, St Francis Xavier (SFX) declared its multi-racial character. At the inaugural Mass, prayers were said in the languages of many parental belongings. The student body, fed by eight Catholic secondary schools but attracting other youngsters too, is a true reflection of the young life of south-west London in all its ethnic and cultural diversity. There is still some way to go before the staff has the same diversity, but to be a student at SFX is to receive an education in multi-racial Britain.

Another positive sign of integral progress is the number of black people who are becoming Catholics through the ordinary life of our parishes. We have the RCIA (Rite of Christian Initiation for Adults) programme operating in most south London parishes. This is a course of Christian education involving numbers of parishioners as well as priests and sisters. Towards three hundred men and women join the Church throughout the diocese each year through RCIA parish groups. At least a third of these will be black people, mainly of Afro-Caribbean ancestry.

A great affirmation of integral development was made at the first National Congress of Black Catholics which was held at Roehampton in south London in July 1990. For the purpose of the Congress, 'black' was interpreted not as an ethnic category but as a socio-political reality, encompassing people of Indian, Chinese, Mauritian and Vietnamese origin as well as Afro-Caribbeans. Only Catholics who were black in this sense took part as delegates but very many friendly white people were invited as observers. The Congress roundly condemned all manifestations of racism, including those which sometimes appear in the Catholic community. It affirmed, with equal vehemence, that there could be only one Catholic Church in Britain and that black people claimed a full part within it – in the priesthood and the religious life and in all kinds of lay responsibility.

12

Clapham and Rye

Silver jubilee

I celebrated my twenty-fifth anniversary as a Catholic priest
on Saturday, 27 April 1991. It would be more true to say
that it was celebrated for me because our Caribbean Catholic
community were hosts for the occasion and had made most
of the arrangements. The parish priest of St Anselm's,
Tooting Bec, made his large church available to us as he
had done for Marjorie Redhead's funeral and we filled it to
overflowing. Claude Sandy led the musicians and his niece
Susan Lewis conducted the choir – a considerably augmented Bridges – in a memorable Mass. Most of those
present belonged to our Caribbean community but there
were also a large number of personal friends from various
phases of my life, including my Anglican days. Bishop
Hugh Montefiore, retired Anglican Bishop of Birmingham
and an old comrade from Cambridge days, paid me the
compliment of coming in full canonicals and saying friendly
words about me at the end of the Mass. Also present was a
former student of Peterhouse who was an Anglican priest
working in south London. By this time my own family had
shrunk to three, myself and my sisters Nellie and Betty.
Nellie escorted by her son Michael came to the lunch party
we had at John Archer House the following day while
Betty sat in the place of honour at St Anselm's. The sermon
was given by my friend Canon Edmund Arbuthnott,
with whom I shared an enthusiasm for both the Young
Christian Workers and the Jesus Caritas Association.

Edmund had survived the destruction of the Dockhead Presbytery in Bermondsey by a V2 in 1945, and in the post-war years he was the subject of one of Eamonn Andrews' *This is Your Life* TV programmes.

We held the reception at the Balham Polish Club, a few hundred yards down the road. Our original intention was to descend to St Anselm's basement hall but I realised with just a fortnight to spare that it would have been far too small. Mercifully, the management of the Polish Club was able to make its ballroom available. This was one of the largest halls in south-west London and proved only just big enough.

Sabbatical leave

It was suggested to me that a Silver Jubilee ought be followed by a sabbatical. Our archbishop readily agreed to my being away for the first six months of 1992. My close collaborator John Bonaparte had been ordained a deacon in July of 1991 and was ready to cover Caribbean Chaplaincy events for me. I signed up two priests to be available if required. One of them, Fr Tony Charlton, was already in residence at John Archer House and he agreed to manage the establishment in my absence with the help of Therese Felix, my part-time secretary.

I began my sabbatical half-year on 6 January 1992 with a three-month stay at Massingham St Mary in Norfolk. This was a retreat centre run by the Daughters of Jesus, who were very good friends of mine from many visits. I had planned to do some writing during my six months' leave and I started hesitantly to word-process my thoughts on race relations in south London and the work of our Caribbean Chaplaincy. To my surprise I got the hang of direct input to a word-processor quite quickly and the story seemed almost to write itself. It was subsequently published as *Some of Us are Black* (Family Publications, 1993). At

Massingham I also had the enchantment of seeing winter unfold into spring in the Norfolk countryside.

For a long time I had cherished the idea of revisiting Italy with a car. A week before Easter that year I set out to drive to Rome for a ten-week stay at Palazzola, the villa belonging to the English College in the Alban Hills. The journey was quite an adventure because I would be alone for three or four days in foreign parts driving on the right-hand side of the road. It turned out to be an exhilarating experience. I have a feeling for Romanesque architecture and sculpture and I took in marvellous examples of it in Burgundy, Provence and Pisa. I was also able to visit Cita at her home near Florence. From Palazzola I made many trips in central Italy, revisiting places I already knew from my Beda College days and discovering many others. I also rose to a little more literary activity. I roughed out an account of the Young Christian Workers movement in Britain which eventually appeared under the title of *Worker Apostles* (Catholic Truth Society, 1994).

I returned to London in June 1992. The following year I made my fourth trip to the Caribbean for the ordination to the priesthood of Charles Gaillard, one of our south London St Lucia-born deacons. Charles' priestly ordination was the centrepiece of a grand tour of the Caribbean, taking in Trinidad, Jamaica and Antigua as well as St Lucia, where the ordination took place.

Charles' ordination had a heart-breaking sequel. In January 2002, he had just finished celebrating the early Sunday morning Mass at Castries Cathedral when two drugged-up young men stormed into the cathedral and began to torch members of the congregation. Charles in his vestments was badly burned and Sr Teresa Egan from Ireland, who had spent forty years in St Lucia, was stabbed to death. Charles died a month later of a heart attack while recovering from his burns in the neighbouring island of Martinique. The whole island of St Lucia cried out in anguish at his and Sr Teresa's death and at the violence done to other members of the congregation. I made the journey to Castries for his funeral, representing the Archbishop of Southwark and our south London Caribbean community.

St Vincent's, Clapham Common

In August 1994, Archbishop Bowen asked me if I would be willing to become parish priest of St Vincent de Paul, Altenburg Gardens, on the other side of Clapham Common.

I went to see the Archbishop and explained the complexities of my role as Caribbean Chaplain and listed all the additional commitments I had acquired in the course of it. These included my chairmanship of St Vincent's Community Centre in Brixton, my board-membership of Cathedral Employment Enterprises, my governorship of the St Francis Xavier Sixth Form College and my participation in the Community/Police Consultative Group in Lambeth. More recently, the Archbishop had made me Chairman of the Justice and Peace Commission in the diocese and this had proved a delicate and time-consuming task. Nevertheless, I said dutifully that I would do as he directed.

As this negotiation with the Archbishop began, I was engaged in leading a Jesus Caritas 'Month of Nazareth' at Massingham St Mary in Norfolk. As is our custom in the Jesus Caritas movement, I talked over all the elements of my situation with the small group of priests who were there for the 'Month'. Taking into account my age – I was in my seventieth year – and the value of the jobs in which I was already engaged, they urged me to avoid taking the parish if I could. If the Archbishop was insistent, we all agreed that I should accept St Vincent's and trim down as many of my existing commitments as possible.

So it proved: the Archbishop did not change his mind. He agreed that he would have to replace me as Chairman of the Justice and Peace Commission. He was in no position to appoint another priest to look after the Caribbean community so we agreed that I would continue to be Caribbean Chaplain with the help of our remaining deacon, John Bonaparte, who had now succeeded Charles Gaillard at St James', Peckham. I tried to lose the chairmanship of St Vincent's Community Centre in Brixton, but I had to handle some very teasing problems there before I was able finally to hand over to my deputy, Colin Douglas, in 1996.

I kept on the Sixth Form College and I stayed with Cathedral Employment Enterprises which, after a big upheaval in 1994, was transformed into Myrrh Training.

Having thus shed a number of tasks, I arrived at St Vincent's for the Feast of Christ the King on the last Sunday of November 1994. Bishop Howard Tripp, our area bishop, came to induct me the following Sunday in the presence of the mayor of Wandsworth and the then MP for Battersea, Mr John Bowis, and his wife. I was not the only innovation that Advent Sunday evening – we had four girls serving Mass for the first time. This was no credit to me; the girls had been chosen and prepared before I came.

Job training for the most disadvantaged

This is a convenient place to tell the story of Cathedral Employment Enterprises and its successor company, Myrrh Training. Cathedral, as it was known, had ramified from a small local community employment project to become one of the largest voluntary training agencies in Britain. By the beginning of 1994, we had 1,500 trainees, many of them black young people, and nearly all of them with minimal prospects on the labour market. We had a full-time staff of 170 helping our trainees to gain National Vocational Qualifications (NVQs) and actual jobs in a wide variety of skills. These were: care of children and care of the elderly, hairdressing, horticulture, catering, printing, computing and office skills, motor engineering, painting and decorating, carpentry and construction. The annual budget was over

£3 million, nearly all of it paid for by the government's industrial and commercial training programme. The presiding genius of the whole operation was Fr Hugh Bridge, a priest of the Southwark diocese. He was assisted by a devoted team of senior managers and others for whom Cathedral was not only a job but a cause. The Board too was highly committed to the work and, in spite of all the tribulations the company was to suffer in 1994, stayed together in support of Fr Hugh and the management team.

The company was always seriously under-capitalised and there were recurring cash-flow problems. This problem was aggravated when the government agencies decided to pay us retrospectively: that is, we were to be paid by results, often long delayed. Cathedral had to expend large sums of money in setting up training programmes and paying salaries before we could expect our fees from the agencies working for the Department of Employment. From the summer of 1993 to mid-1994, we tottered from crisis to crisis. Our cash-flow problem was aggravated further during this period when the government agencies halved the rate at which we were to be paid. A recurring monthly problem was to pay the wages of our staff. At one point, the Southwark diocese came to our rescue with a bank guarantee of £75,000. Sadly, the diocese eventually lost all this money.

Our bank finally called a halt and required us to submit to scrutiny by a high-powered accountancy firm. A strange series of meetings ensued between the accountant's staff and members of our Board, some of them convened at less than six hours' notice. A meeting was called on 15 June 1994, at which those members of the Board who were able to attend were told that Cathedral had to stop trading *at once* – there was no prospect of our being able to meet our commitments. With such an emphatic declaration by representatives of such a prestigious firm, there was nothing the Board members could do but agree that Cathedral had to go into voluntary liquidation. This was a bitter moment. Retrospectively, we were not sure we had received the best advice. At this time, Cathedral was owed a great deal of money by the government's agencies. As the crisis mounted, we had sought the help of the Department of Employment. We had good reason to think that the Department wanted to keep us in business – no other training agency was catering for the same levels of disadvantage as we were – but it seemed unable to hasten the process by which we were paid for our services. Following our liquidation, the firm dealing with our insolvency garnered in hundreds of thousands of pounds of delayed payments earned by Cathedral.

The consequences of our liquidation were grievous. Our trainees had to be found alternative courses; a year later places had not been found for many of them. All but the senior staff were declared redundant and could only be paid back wages by the realisation of our capital assets, which all went under the hammer. Remarkably, the key team of Fr Hugh Bridge, Harry Spanswick, Susanne Ekrem and Eugene Mgbemere stayed together, some of them without pay for months on end.

Ironically, just days after the decision to liquidate was taken, we found a benefactor who could have saved us. He remains anonymous by his express desire; his benefaction of £250,000 made it possible for us to replace Cathedral Employment Enterprises with Myrrh Training. Myrrh was a dormant company formerly owned by Cathedral which the liquidator allowed us to re-animate. Gold, frankincense and myrrh were the gifts of the Wise Men from the East who came to worship the infant Jesus at Bethlehem. Myrrh in biblical symbolism signifies a burial and we had had one of those, but with the frankincense of many prayers and the gold of our benefactor, we were all confident that our new company would rise like a phoenix from the ashes of Cathedral. In the years that followed, the new company was painstakingly put together and was able to resume some of its former courses, though with fewer staff and trainees. There were further crises to come, but at the millennium Myrrh Training was still on its feet and delivering training to its special clientele.

The work of a parish

Throughout 1995, I was re-learning parish life. I had left Abbey Wood parish in 1973 and although I had done a number of parish locums in the meantime, I had been spared the relentless demands of parish life for over twenty years. I had worked hard at my non-parochial jobs, but I was used to a much more flexible schedule than a parish could give me. At the same time, I was getting a little old and creaky. On the plus side, I had an excellent young curate to begin with, Fr Michael Galea from Malta, and the people of the parish were marvellously welcoming and supportive.

St Vincent de Paul parish occupies the Clapham Junction area of south-west London. It has a large segment of Clapham Common with some handsome eighteenth-century houses surviving on the west and north sides. There are a lot of substantial late Victorian and Edwardian streets all around the Common and a populous area called the Shaftesbury Estate which was a planned housing scheme begun in 1872 to accommodate 'artisans'. It was this development which compelled the creation of a new Catholic Mission. In 1903, a large house – 36 Altenburg Gardens – was acquired with an orchard by its side suitable for future development. The ground floor of the house became the first place of worship; a fine classical church was completed on the orchard site in 1907. The church is curiously unassertive – people do not notice it until they get within fifty yards – yet it is quite large.

At one time, the St Vincent's community was predominantly south Battersea upper working class, with some well-to-do families from around the Common. Nearly all Catholic parishes in Britain have a core of people of Irish ancestry; St Vincent's is blessed with many such parishioners and they are among its most active people. There is also a splendid Charismatic prayer group whose members cannot do enough for the parish. Nowadays, the parish is ethnically and culturally very mixed – at least thirty countries of origin are represented in the congregation, with a large number of Afro-Caribbean people. The St Vincent's community also encompasses a considerable section of the London social spectrum, all the way from low-income families and individuals to many professional and managerial families. The Clapham area is known to abound in young families. In 1995, we set up nearly thirty marriages (most took place elsewhere) and we had fifty-two baptisms. The 11 a.m. Mass on Sundays has become notable for our Children's Liturgy, organised by a splendid corps of young parents. The church is swimming with children and once a month there has to be a Folk Mass with a child-friendly sermon.

Parish life is a continuum of high moments, problems, sadnesses and challenges. One of our best-loved and most devoted parishioners, Patrick Ryan, received the papal award of the Beni Merenti Medal at our patronal festival in September 1995, and Kathleen Seglias, for many years our parish accountant, received the same award from the archbishop when he came for a Confirmation in July 1997. All the time we lose cherished elderly parishioners, and some young ones. In the late 1990s two centenarians died, one Caribbean and one white. As a community, we support a number of good causes like care of the young homeless; we help to right wrongs like the practice of abortion and unjust imprisonment, and we have campaigned against the ghastly legacy of landmines in Africa and South-East Asia. In ecumenical matters, we developed a close relationship with a nearby high-church Anglican parish which includes a joint Guild of the Blessed Sacrament.

St Vincent's has the great good fortune to have the Daughters of Divine Love working in the parish. These are sisters from the eastern region of Nigeria, and quite apart from what they do their very presence is a source of joy and confidence for the whole parish – a rich return for the great European missionary effort of former years. Jon Dal Din, a married man and father of seven grown-up children who has led the St Vincent's catechetical programme for a number of years, was ordained to the permanent diaconate in the year 2000. It is my successor's good fortune to have the benefit of his help.

The millennium at St Vincent's

At the beginning of 1998 all was going well at St Vincent's and we were busy with our plans to celebrate the millennium. By then, an American priest, Fr David Clark from the diocese of Portland, had been with us for a year. Fr Dave, as he liked to be called, was a very friendly and unstuffy person; he was also highly competent in various aspects of ministry and he soon became very popular in the parish. He had come to England to study for a PhD in archaeology at the University of London. His arrival was not only a great help in the weekend life of the parish, but he would also look after all the essentials when I wanted to be away. No one could mistake the fact that we had a Yank abroad at St Vincent's but by stages he became acculturated to England, even to the extent of becoming fascinated with cricket. My parting gift to him – at his request – was a cricket ball!

We had committed ourselves to three major projects for the millennium. In the first place, we aspired to raise £25,000 for Third World causes under the auspices of the Catholic Fund for Overseas Development. This was in response to the Pope's call to make the millennium a year of Jubilee – a year of 'putting things to rights', which included help for the poor. By Christmas 1999, the parish had raised the full sum. Second, we had fixed 15–23 May 1999 for a parish mission to be led by priests of the Catholic Missionary Society. The Parish Council was very keen that the centrepiece of our millennium preparations should be a spiritual event. This duly took place and was very well supported in the parish. The third project was mainly my idea. I thought we should have some kind of monument in the church. We eventually agreed that this should take the form of three statues in some vacant niches over the church entrance. In the centre was to be a figure of Christ on the cross and on either side the two great martyrs of the English Reformation, St John Fisher and St Thomas More. Mother Concordia of the Benedictine Sisters at Minster in Kent undertook to sculpt them for us. She had trained as a sculptress before she became a nun and she was able to accept a certain number of commissions while still in charge of her community. Her work was very much sought after. The statues were duly delivered and erected and were solemnly blessed on 1 October 1999. The parish was delighted with them.

Illness strikes

In January 1998, I began to be aware of the symptoms which led to the diagnosis of prostate cancer. The diagnosis was made at St George's Hospital at Tooting and confirmed during Holy Week of that year. Further tests indicated that the problem was very treatable. The radiologist at St George's who put me under the X-ray machine was a parishioner and was full of optimism as he took a first look at the pictures – 'no sign of spreading', he assured me. And so it proved. Alfredo (he was Spanish) was a messenger from God. Sadly, less than a year later Cardinal Hume had the same test with a grievous result. His cancer had spread and was inoperable.

The treatment I was advised to have was radiotherapy at the Royal Marsden Hospital at Fulham. This would begin in October and would mean a daily visit to the hospital for ten weeks. I was warned that while the treatment was not dangerous, it was debilitating and it was unlikely that I would be able to work during the sessions.

At the same time I had to give thought to the situation of my younger surviving sister, Betty. She was a widow of eighty-two and lived on her own in a little house at Rye in Sussex. It had become clear that she could no longer manage on her own, even with a good deal of Social Services support. In July of 1998, I arranged for her to go into residential care in Rye. The Department of Social Services requires that elderly people's capital assets be realised to contribute to the costs of their care. This meant that my sister's house would have to be sold. She had always wanted me to have it and had made her will accordingly, but if it had to be sold at that time to secure her maintenance, it would be gone for ever.

Retirement

I thought furiously about these matters and eventually decided that the best resolution of the problems was for me to retire. I was seventy-four in June 1998. I had wanted to stay at St Vincent's until the millennium at least. By that time I would have passed the customary retirement age of seventy-five and it would be reasonable to bow out sometime during the year 2000. I decided to ask the Archbishop to accept my resignation and I further asked that the diocese should buy my sister's house and let me live in it until further notice. The purchase price of the house would finance my sister's care and the diocese would retain the capital asset. There was another reason for me to seek retirement. A friend of mine, Fr David Standley, had been on sabbatical leave and was now hoping for a parish in south London. In my judgement, David, ten years younger than me, would do very well at St Vincent's. I made the suggestion to the Archbishop and he agreed. I was very pleased both for David and St Vincent's. It is not often in the Catholic Church that one can nominate one's successor!

In July of 1998, I let it be known at St Vincent's that I would be leaving before the end of the year. At the annual pilgrimage of our Caribbean community to Aylesford at the beginning of August, I announced my departure to my Caribbean friends. I told them that I would never cease to be their friend until the day I died but my retirement from London meant that I could no longer be their chaplain. I said these words on 2 August; on 30 August I was summoned to Our Lady of Sorrows at Peckham and found that the church was thronged with Caribbean people and other friends from all over south London. Immediately after my Aylesford announcement, an informal committee had been formed, notices had been made in a large number of churches, a choir had been got together to sing a beautiful Mass and there were vast amounts of food and drink for a reception afterwards.

At the end of January 1999, I was back at St Vincent's for an equally moving parish farewell. Among the many gifts I received was an album of St Vincent's with a large number of photographs and messages from family and other groups. There was room in the album for some photographs of the Peckham farewell, so it is now a valuable record of both celebrations.

Arrival at Rye

I left St Vincent's in mid-December before the renovation of my sister's house at Rye was complete. I had many offers of accommodation but I was glad to accept the hospitality of my friend Fr Ulick Loring at Holy Redeemer parish at Hollington, St Leonard's-on-Sea. I could make myself useful at Hollington over Christmas and it was an easy trip to Rye to see how the house improvements were going.

When he agreed to make it possible for me to take over my sister's house, Archbishop Bowen saw that there was a gap in the pastoral provision of the diocese that I could fill. The parish of Tenterden in the south-western margin of Kent belonged in the diocese of Southwark but there was a curious anomaly left over from the time when a new diocese of Arundel and Brighton was created in 1965. The new diocese comprised the counties of Surrey and Sussex. Tenterden parish now found that part of its territory was in the new diocese. The villages south of the River Rother, of which the largest was Northiam, were in East Sussex. Moreover, Northiam had a small Catholic church of its own which had been served from Tenterden since its inauguration in 1935. Tenterden prayed for 'Michael our Bishop' while Northiam's invocation was for 'Cormac our Bishop', Cormac Murphy O'Connor being the Bishop of Arundel and Brighton at that time. He later succeeded Basil Hume as Archbishop of Westminster.

Though the link between Tenterden and Northiam had been maintained since 1965, it was a considerable strain on the parish priest of Tenterden to provide a Sunday morning Mass at Northiam. Towards the end of 1998, a new parish priest of Tenterden declared that the Northiam Mass would have to be on Saturday evening. This was the situation when I came on the scene. Having no Tenterden or other weekend commitments, I was able to restore the Sunday morning Mass at Northiam, which is just nine miles from Rye. When this was announced I was bound to be popular.

St Teresa's, Northiam

St Teresa's has had a short but very interesting history. In the early part of the last century, Sheila Kaye-Smith, the daughter of a well-known St Leonard's doctor, was gaining a considerable reputation as a Sussex authoress. Her books were romances for the most part, with a great deal of well-researched Sussex and Kent history and background. At this time she seems not to have any strong religious convictions, but in going to live in London to further her literary career she began to attend St Alban's, Holborn, which was a notable Anglo-Catholic centre. She became an ardent Anglo-Catholic and at some stage wrote a book about it. She returned to St Leonard's and resumed her Anglo-Catholicism at Christ Church where she met the Revd Penrose Fry who was a curate in the parish. They fell in love and were married.

Towards the end of the 1920s, however, they both became disenchanted with the Church of England. One of the factors was the refusal of the House of Commons to endorse what came to be called the 1928 Prayer Book. The bishops of the Church of England wanted this further revision of the Book of Common Prayer, but the approval of Parliament was legally necessary. Certain additions and alterations in the new text could be seen as 'high church' or 'Catholic' and the evangelical or 'low church' element in the Church of England successfully campaigned against it. For those who thought like the Penrose Frys, the parliamentary vote was pure Erastianism – the secular authority frustrating the Church in a matter that was purely spiritual. This was a powerful reason driving the Penrose Frys towards Roman Catholicism. What was also important was the devotion they had both discovered to St Teresa of Lisieux.

In October 1929, they were received into the Roman Catholic Church by Fr Martindale SJ at Farm Street in London. By this time they had made their home at Little Doucegrove at Horns Cross on the outskirts of the village of Northiam. The nearest Catholic church was at Rye, nine miles away, so they petitioned the then Bishop of Southwark for permission to set up a Mass centre at Little Doucegrove. The Bishop agreed as long as they could find priests who could come and celebrate the Mass. In the next five years a small Catholic community developed, centring on an upper room in the coach house of Little Doucegrove. The zeal of the Penrose Frys and the co-operation of priests from all around ensured that Mass was said there every Sunday.

Eventually, the community outgrew the coach house. The Penrose Frys decided to buy a nearby field and build a church there. St Teresa's, Horns Cross, Northiam, was opened on 8 December 1935, with a seating capacity of just fifty people. Sheila and Penrose Fry survived until 1956 and 1971 respectively and are buried side by side in the little cemetery beside the church.

We are now well into the new millennium and I am moving towards my seventy-eighth birthday. I still miss the excitement and the kaleidoscope of life in London but I have caught the beauty and fascination of Rye and the enchantment of the surrounding countryside. St Teresa's and its people are a constant delight to me. I never thought that I would end up a country parson in my old age!